UNCERTAINTIES IN PEASANT FARMING

LONDON SCHOOL OF ECONOMICS MONOGRAPHS ON SOCIAL ANTHROPOLOGY

The Monographs on Social Anthropology were established in 1940 and aim to publish results of modern anthropological research of primary interest to specialists.

The continuation of the series was made possible by a grant in aid from the Wenner-Gren Foundation for Anthropological Research, and more recently by a further grant from the Governors of the London School of Economics and Political Science. Income from sales is returned to a revolving fund to assist further publications.

The Monographs are under the direction of an Editorial Board associated with the Department of Anthropology of the London School of Economics and Political Science.

UNCERTAINTIES IN PEASANT FARMING

A COLOMBIAN CASE

SUTTI REISSIG ORTIZ

LONDON SCHOOL OF ECONOMICS MONOGRAPHS ON SOCIAL ANTHROPOLOGY

Volume 46

Routledge
Taylor & Francis Group
LONDON AND NEW YORK

First published 2004 by Berg Publishers

Published 2020 by Routledge
2 Park Square, Milton Park, Abingdon, Oxon OX14 4RN
605 Third Avenue, New York, NY 10017

First issued in paperback 2021

Routledge is an imprint of the Taylor & Francis Group, an informa business

Publisher's Note
The publisher has gone to great lengths to ensure the quality of this reprint but points out that some imperfections in the original copies may be apparent.

ISBN 13: 978-0-367-71721-6 (pbk)
ISBN 13: 978-1-85973-839-9 (hbk)

ACKNOWLEDGEMENTS

The field work on which this study is based was made possible by a grant from the Organization of American States; the subsequent research was carried out under the auspices of the Consejo Nacional de Investigaciones Científicas y Técnicas, Buenos Aires. The opinions expressed in this book are those of the writer and not necessarily of the sponsoring institutions.

I am greatly indebted to Dr Duquez Gomez and the staff of the Ins i u o Colombiano de Antropología for their help and co-operation during the field research; to Bernal Villa and Hernandez de Alba for relevant information about Tierradentro, gained through their personal experiences; to the people of San Andrés and their parish priest for their hospitality and trust as well as for their patience with my persistent interrogation.

The critical remarks made by Professor Firth, Dr Barić and J. I. Jones have helped me clarify some of the ambiguity in the original text, written as a thesis for the doctoral degree. The book shows the imprint of many discussions, arguments and helpful questioning by my colleagues and students at the London School of Economics; their comments have served to urge me to develop the argument further than I had originally intended. Perhaps most of all I should thank the peasants of San Andrés who, with their down-to-earth comments, have preven ed me from indulging in too many woolly explanations.

S. R. O.

CONTENTS

MAPS

FIGURES

TABLES

Introduction

The term peasant evokes either a distant world of romantic struggles, or of idyllic freedom, or of serfdom and drudgery, depending on the author and the period. It is difficult for even the most learned of scholars to shed the emotive connotation of the term and to describe the world of the peasant as real and not totally unfamiliar. The peasant's goals and aspirations are not altogether different from our own; his behaviour can be explained without having to resort to a different logical framework; his uncertainties are phrased differently, perhaps, but his response to them is similar to ours. Peasants are not endowed with a different soul or a different perception of the world from ours. If they behave differently, if they shy away from recommended policies it is because they are either less informed about certain events, or perhaps better informed about the realities of their physical, social and economic world than we are.

In this book I hope to explain the economic behaviour of Páez peasant farmers in Colombia. I consider their production strategies (what they plant and how much they plant) as rational reactions to a particular socio-economic environment. This environment is not peculiar to Páez Indians; it is in many ways similar to the socio-economic environment of other peasants. The Páez Indians, for example, are like other Colombian peasants in that they plant coffee for sale, like to ride horses and would like to have enough money to travel to the cities and send their children to school. They are different from other peasants in that they represent a very poor sector of the population of Colombia, they live far from urban centres and some of them speak a different language from their compatriots. The special characteristics of their environment will become apparent later. It is the more general and theoretical points that I wish to emphasize here.

In the field of economic relations the population of peasant producers is characterized by its heterogeneity, the small population, the relative independence of each producer, and the limited output of each farmer. It is heterogeneous in the sense that not all producers share the same aspirations, the same knowledge, or the same responsibilities or hold the same amount of capital assets; each unit of production is different from the next. The productive units consist of only one family, their technological knowledge is limited and the amount of land they control can yield only a small surplus for sale. Furthermore, although they participate in the national economy they form a specific sector within it, which, owing to its geographical isolation has only limited contact with market economy. The peasant sector consists at the same time of a number of geographically distant and socio-politically semi-autonomous communities amongst which there is little or no communication. Hence we can say that the peasant sector is subdivided into a number of very small subsectors which are linked not to one another but to the national economy through the export of coffee and the import of hard goods and certain staples. Each of these subsectors consists of about 300 to 400 producing units.

Peasant economies have been discussed as a special case of primitive economies (Nash 1966), as sectors of national economies beset by fluctuating prices and capital shortage (Wolf 1966) and as societies where the market principle prevails, 'but does not determine the acquisition of subsistence or the allocation of land and labour resources' (Bohannan and Dalton 1962, p. 3). Such approaches have helped to elucidate particular problems of marketing, social sanctions that affect the allocation of factors of production, and incentives for trade as well as for saving and investment. But they have too often led to an over-emphasis on the mechanism developed to cope with particular problems, as if they reflected a basic principle of organization of peasant economies.

SOME APPROACHES TO THE STUDY OF ECONOMIC ANTHROPOLOGY

A relevant example of such undue emphasis is the concept of spheres of exchange, which was suggested by Bohannan in his careful analysis of Tiv distributive systems. He noted that the flow of goods is not random but that it follows certain channels and that certain goods are exchanged only for certain other goods; for example, it is morally wrong for a Tiv to exchange food for brass rods. Nevertheless, Bohannan tells us that these ideally unacceptable exchanges do happen, and that in fact Tiv hope to gain prestige by exchanging goods of a lower value with others of a higher value, that is to convert goods from one sphere to another. The moral indictment which sanctions certain types of transaction does not seem to operate consistently and one wonders whether the statement that 'it is bad (*vihi kwagh*) to trade brass rods for food', and 'very bad to trade your marriage ward for cows or brass rods' (Bohannan 1955, p. 64) while referring to a basic moral value, might not also refer to the advisability of exchanging one scarce factor of production for another readily available factor.

The concept of spheres of exchange may be a useful descriptive device but it has been used by Bohannan to imply a basic principle of organization in certain economic systems. The moral statement serves to guide decisions about transactions, but it is not necessarily the reason why food is not exchanged for a slave. A statement to the contrary is devoid of meaning, since a good or bad transaction is no more than a restatement on an ideological plane of transactions that the Tiv try to avoid; hence it explains nothing at all and further confuses the issue. It could only serve as an explanation if one could say that the moral statement is a logical extension of the Tiv conception of the universal order. Bohannan clearly explains why women are exchanged for women and not for slaves, but he does not explain why slaves are not exchanged for food. The concept of spheres only states graphically that certain exchanges take place while others do not. Furthermore, as L. Joy (1967) has indicated, it obscures the fact that exchanges across spheres do take place, and therefore gives the reader a wrong impression of the flow of goods within the society.

This over-emphasis of certain characteristics of distributive mechanisms indicates a failure to understand the basic elements of peasant economies when contrasted in particular with market economies. An analysis of exchanges and rates of exchange in a market economy is important because they guide production. The activities of the firm depend on the knowledge that the factors required to produce the goods can be purchased, that the output of the firm will find buyers, and that prices do not fluctuate randomly but in response to certain principles. Shackle (1965) has stressed that the concept of equilibrium is central to economic theories of decision-making because it gives order and meaning to economic actions; knowledge of availability of resources is possible if we assume that equilibrium operates. Furthermore, in market economies there are a number of specialized institutions such as banks, entrepreneurs, stock markets, etc. whose operations ensure that capital is made available for production rather than hoarded, as well as ensuring that a certain level of production of a variety of goods is maintained. It is important to recognize that, in purely economic terms, where there is a market mechanism, it is of greater importance to the functioning of the market economy than exchange systems are to the functioning of a non-market economy, i.e. of a primitive economy. This is so because market mechanisms have both integrative and distributive functions, whi e an exchange system – at least from an economic point of view – has a purely distributive function. The existence of a demand sector may induce a peasant farmer to produce for sale or barter but this knowledge or lack of knowledge will not entirely affect his plans of production. He probably already controls the land he needs, the seeds will have been saved from his last harvest, and the labour and tools he controls himself. In this sense a peasant farmer does not depend very much on the goods produced by others in order to continue his own production and as a large proportion of his harvest is consumed by himself and his family a knowledge of the principles of distribution is not imperative to a rational decision. A rational decision requires a bounded universe of known possible actions and possible outcomes of such actions. Peasant or primitive farmers possess that knowledge because they mostly produce directly for their own consumption. This rather obvious but important tautological statement has been neglected. Studies have concentrated on detailed analysis of rates of exchanges instead of concentrating on the process of decision-making, which is really what determines amounts and types of production. Knowledge of distribution systems is not, of course, irrelevant, but knowledge of distributive factors is not the core of the information necessary to make a productive decision as it is in a market system. In peasant and primitive societies the fundamentals of economic organization can only be elucidated if we analyse the decision-making process. Salisbury (1962) had to consider individual goals and the means of achieving them in order to understand the meaning of the valuation differences in Siane. He concluded by saying that '. . . the presence of discrete scales of value, each depending on a different standard of valuation, is not an unfortunate accident. It is a simple mechanism ensuring that subsistence goods are used to maintain a basic standard of life below which no person falls; that free-floating power is allocated peacefully, with a minimum of exploitation (or disturbance of the individual's right to subsistence) and in accordance with accepted standards; that the means of ensuring flexibility in the society do not disrupt the formal allocation of statuses in the society or the means of gaining power' (p. 212). A similar but less elaborate mechanism is discussed here with reference to the Páez farmer.

FORMATION OF COALITIONS IN RESPONSE TO MARKET CONDITIONS

Subsistence goods are seldom sold for money and never exchanged for coffee; an Indian is criticized if he is seen too frequently selling food in the market place; he is expected to consume it or to lend or trade it with other neighbours and friends who are in need of food. Coffee, on the other hand, is not consumed, because to a Páez coffee stands for cash and hence is a scarce and necessary resource. In fact, these two spheres of activities are kept more or less distinct; the meaning of this separation can be understood when productive decisions are analysed. As to the Siane, food to a Páez is a necessity for survival and a sufficient supply must be preserved. Sanctions are expressed in moral terms when an Indian is known to sell his food for profit instead of saving it for friends and neighbours in need. The barter of food or its sale at a 'traditional' and very low price is the mechanism which protects a member of the community from the risk of starvation. Unlike the Siane, this insurance mechanism cannot be described as a traditional valuation of food, but as a response to present conditions. Hence, a simple mechanism to ensure that subsistence goods are used to maintain a basic standard of life is to be found not only in primitive societies, but also in peasant societies.

Páez and Siane examples indicate how under certain competitive conditions of the market a farmer can insure himself by withdrawing certain exchanges from market arrangements. In the region of Colombia discussed here the cash crop market is so organized that it affects the price of hard goods thus: the lower the national coffee price the lower the total cash income of the Páez Indian and the lower the profit made by the middlemen who are local residents; these middlemen, who are at the same time the local traders, then have less capital to stock their stores, their sales decrease and as a result they raise the price of certain hard goods (for example, tools) in order to make ends meet. Thus it is not a case where supply and demand curves are symmetrical. The balance is here affected by the middleman, who protects himself by controlling the supplies of hard goods brought into the area. Furthermore, as will be explained in detail later, the price of coffee does not depend on local supply. The market is imperfect and the marketer copes with market resistance by very fine price discrimination, charging one sector of buyers more than another sector. This is not an unusual solution; the difference is that the sector which pays the higher price for hard goods is the poorer Indian rather than the wealthier consumer.

Distance and poor communications add numerous constraints to the markets for cash crops and manufactured goods. The number of traders who import goods and export coffee is small and expansion by any one of them within a short period of time can seriously affect the activities of all other traders. Trading relations develop and continue to be maintained through personal contact. A farmer prefers to trade with someone whom he can trust; he knows that his knowledge is limited and while learning about the commercial cash world it is easier to buy from a co-parent, a boss or a friend. Even after he has gained some confidence in his own commercial ability the farmer may try to develop personal trading relations with a trader in the hope of receiving important fringe benefits, such as credit. Not all traders are in the same position to offer fringe services to any farmer, hence some are in a better competitive position than others. The market is therefore highly imperfect and a subsistence farmer who decides to produce for sale has to operate within it, just as traders must, but the peasant farmer lacks the knowledge, capital or the contacts available to traders, middlemen and wealthy farmers.

The imperfections of the market also result from the small scale of the marketing activities, the complex nature of trading relations and the heterogeneous nature of the population – some farmers are more sophisticated and have easier access to capital than others. Hence, the behaviour of any one farmer or trader is heavily affected by the behaviour of every other farmer and trader, as long as they gear their production to sale in the market and depend totally on market transactions. In an imperfect market the producer must pay attention not only to the price index but also to the behaviour of other producers and entrepreneurs. The result of competition is that some fail, others succeed, while still others opt out in search of other opportunities. Industrial firms cope with the consequences of competition either by producing a specialized product, or marketing so as to add to the usefulness of the product (at least for a special sector of the market), or by forming coalitions with other firms whereby prices and outputs are maintained. Farmers cannot often produce a specialized product, or control distribution and output to cater for particular needs. To control production when technology is limited is very difficult. But farmers can quite easily form coalitions, which is what Páez peasants have done. The socio-political framework of Páez society makes the formation of a coalition easy and restricts the number of individuals who may join the coalition. Restrictions on the sale of food in the market place should be seen not as a sign of traditionalism but as the action of a coalition, designed to maintain a low price of food. The consequence of this reaction is that while reducing uncertainty it also limits opportunities for the accumulation of capital. The feasibility of coalitions is contingent on two conditions which are met by the Páez community discussed here: Firstly, that the cash crop is not a basic staple and, secondly, that the community is of the type known as a closed corporate community (Wolf 1955) so that the members of the coalition are defined and co-operative relations can be easily established. There are many peasant communities elsewhere in Latin America, which do not meet these requirements. Panajachel (Tax 1953) for example, is a very different example and it would be interesting to compare the economic system of this community with that of a Páez community. But even in Panajachel there seem to exist 'traditional prices', and therefore the valuation of goods does not always correspond to dynamic market factors. No coalitions occur in the coffee producing sector of the Páez economy in spite of the very uncertain return of this crop. As producers contribute only an infinitesimal amount to the total national coffee production, coalitions would be ineffective. The reaction of the farmer to the uncertainties of coffee prices is to lower costs and perhaps limit capital investment.

DECISIONS, PRODUCTION AND EXCHANGES

I have briefly explained that traditional types of exchanges should be examined as responses to market conditions. Theories about spheres of exchange, about the effects of a marginal linkage, with market economy, etc. help us to gain a better understanding of the consequences of these coalitions for the economic system of the particular society. But a study of the process and outcome of decision-making helps to explain the formation of coalitions and to integrate findings about types of exchanges with other facts about the allocation of resources. In this book I shall pursue this approach.

It must be remembered that, after all, the patterns of production, consumption and distribution which make up an economic system are the result of the aggregate of decisions made by firms and by individuals to produce, to buy, to sell and to consume. These decisions are rational insofar as a producer or a consumer makes choices, from the possibilities he foresees, which will with a minimum of uncertainty increase the utility of his assets. The fact that I postulate that a great number of key economic decisions are rational does not imply that habit does not play a role in economic behaviour. In fact, habit is a consequence of rationality; it implies that when an individual meets a situation similar to one he has met before he will respond in the same rational fashion. Habitual behaviour also allows the farmer to focus his attention on new developments. An individual can only perceive and evaluate a limited number of stimuli and factors. The fact that he can act habitually, or according to tradition, makes it possible for him to act rationally at key decision-making points.

It is obvious from a consideration of our own actions that we do not always plan ahead and that we are not continually collecting information and evaluating alternatives. We often answer inquiries about our future with 'how can I tell what I am going to be doing so far ahead?'. Sometimes we compare prices in different grocery shops, but once we find a place which satisfies our needs, we consider, quite correctly, that further search would be a sheer waste of time and energy. Many of us shop at a particular grocer's simply because his shop is on the way from the office to the train and we do not trouble to turn the corner to find out whether there is a cheaper or better supplied shop; by so doing we have not only failed to discover the opportunities available but we have also failed to pose the problem of where one should shop. Furthermore, the hypothetical shopper of the example, unless she is rudely treated by her grocer, will probably continue to buy at the same place even when a new shop opens a few doors away, though a new supermarket may perhaps attract her attention if its prices are sufficiently lower and widely advertised on the front. If we want to convince ourselves that she is a thoroughly rational shopper, always alert to changes in her environment, we can excuse her behaviour by suggesting that her grocer gives her better service and that what she loses in price she gains in quality. Though this can often be the case, it is not a foregone conclusion; we ought to recognize that although opportunities are often available and obvious, we do not always confront ourselves with them. We sometimes act out of habit or tradition, and only certain changes in the socio-economic environment will make us stop and plan either for the immediate or the distant future. It does not follow, however, that we act irrationally most of the time, but that planning decisions are, after a point, time-consuming, costly and exhausting. There are personality types which are more prone than others to evaluate and to pose an action as a problem requiring a decision; obsessives are a case in point. But there are also conditions relating to the socio-economic environment which prompt the individual to stop, evaluate and decide.

Consumer behaviour has been analysed with a view to determining when individuals plan their purchases ahead of time and when they do not. Katona (1963) discusses the external and psychological conditions which define decision points of consumers and producers: 'Genuine decisions are made occasionally. They require the perception of a new situation and the solution of the problem raised by it; they lead to responding to a situation in a new way. In contrast habitual behaviour is rather common. We do what we did before in similar situations. Routine behaviour, or using rules of thumb, are suitable terms to describe the second form of behaviour' (p. 49). Price-setting as well as regular budgetary expenditure are prime examples of habitual behaviour which is neither more nor less than the repetition of a previously made decision. Simon (1958) calls these two types: programmed and non-programmed decisions. These labels are confusing because they describe how decisions are expressed rather than how they are reached. More relevant to our case is his suggestion that, when faced with a complex situation, individuals hesitate and deliberate for a considerable period of time so that the action overlaps with the decision.

The case of the Páez farmers argues a third type of decision, which in Katona's classification is included in the type 'habitual behaviour', and is more fully implied in Simon's brief description of non-programmed decisions. When my Indian informant answered impatiently that he planted neither more nor less than he needed he was telling the truth. But what he had planted that year was not exactly the same as he had planted the previous year; I would refer the reader to Table 29, in which the figures can be compared for two consecutive years amongst those families who had already commenced or finished planting. What the Indian plants is not entirely dependent on habit, as Katona would have us believe and though he certainly makes use of 'the rule of thumb' method, the amount he plants is the result of his evaluation of what he thinks he will need given his expectations and the availability of factors of production. Nor is it simply the partial overlap of decision and action. These decisions are *not* intended to be made shortly before planting, but in the course of production; it is understandable that any attempt to obtain information as to what the Indian intends to plant always irritates him somewhat. In our society too certain decisions are made in the course of action; for example, price-fixing as well as budget expenditures are often not the result of habitual behaviour, as Katona supposes. If price-fixing, and for that matter daily household purchases, were habitual, then prices would only be affected by the principle of supply and demand, and household purchases would not break the weekly budget. It is because individuals and firms act rationally that there is a certain order and predictability in the aggregate result of their actions, and, therefore, that there is an economic system. The order is complex, however, and predictions are not always easy. One of the inherent complications is that the action of one individual affects the actions of others with the result that some of them will withdraw from competition while others will form coalitions, just as in a game where each player has to outwit a number of opponents. In the Páez case the complication of one action affecting another is reduced for two reasons: that part-subsistence production makes for relative independence of one unit of production from other units; and that subsistence implies that decisions are geared to satisfy the needs of the producing unit.

Before summarizing the relevant theories on expectations and decisions it is best to keep in mind the nature of the population of producing units in the Páez case discussed here. I have already mentioned that they are relatively though not totally independent of one another. Furthermore, the units are not homologous as each household is at a different stage of the domestic cycle, and hence has different consumption needs, and some individuals have greater managerial ability, or greater experience with the outside world which affects the level and type of their aspirations. Páez producing units are similar to each other in one respect: the degree of information they possess about outputs and prices. The information available to the farmer is minimal and creates uncertainty thus making it nearly impossible for him to formulate a number of expectations. The Páez farmer knows that coffee prices fluctuate, but he also knows that he is incapable of predicting the changes. The number of component units is also very small, about 300 producing units. Both these factors, the limited number of producing units and the heterogeneity of the units, would make for a very imperfect market if they were competing with each other. While this internal imperfection is cancelled out by the maintenance of at least the part-subsistence character of their productive endeavours, they have to operate within the national market which is equally imperfect.

All decision models drawn by economists start from the assumption that choice is rational – an assumption that I shall confirm in this book for the Páez case. By using the term *rational behaviour* I assume that an actor is faced with a number of choices of courses of action and that he will select one course of action because that particular choice will bring him greater satisfaction. In other words, the actor will rank the courses of action open to him, and will select one. To discuss choice in terms of satisfaction is in many ways just as objectionable as to talk of choice in terms of outcomes but it eliminates one problem – the implication that maximization of quantities is the main object of a decision. The term 'utility' would be more appropriate as it does not bear the emotive implication of the term 'satisfaction', but utility has been used in many specialized ways, for example, by von Neumann and Morgenstern (1967) in their application of game theory to the analysis of decisions.

A course of action may bring satisfaction not necessarily because it will yield an increase in cash, or because it will yield greater amounts of any good, but because it will satisfy a particular want.

Social scientists are well aware that wants are socially defined and that they may vary from culture to culture; for this reason it is important to describe first the social background to economic action. But as Simon (1955) has pointed out, even within a given culture wants are not clearly defined absolutes; they change as the aspiration level of the actor rises. The aspiration level is in turn intrinsically related to the information available to the actor as well as to his evaluation of the expected outcome of the whole set of actions and not just the one which is his concern at the moment. For example, when one of the Páez farmers decides not to celebrate a community *fiesta* he must consider how this might affect his status in the community against his chances of moving into the world of the Whites.[1] If he is a wealthy Indian peasant he may save some of his resources and forgo a community *fiesta* because he foresees the possibility of being accepted by the higher social class of White peasants; but if he is a poor Indian he will not have such an aspiration. It is for this reason that Simon (1956) has criticized the concept that people are maximizers; he suggests instead that they are satisfiers. Accepting his criticism that there is no maximum which is equally perceived by all actors in the same culture and even of the same ideology, it is difficult to use the principle of rationality without assuming that every individual in choosing a course of action is attempting to maximize something, even if that something is satisfaction. The principle of rationality also assumes that wants are unlimited even if the immediate aspirations are not.

Economists, in certain circumstances, express all wants in terms of cash incomes as when dealing with producers whose assets are liquid and whose wants can be purchased. This simplification is not warranted when discussing decisions made by consumers or by peasant farmers. For example, in order to be accepted by a White peasant an Indian farmer must have a fine horse with a good saddle, and to acquire these two items he will require cash. On the other hand, if he wants to raise his status within the Indian community he will have to celebrate a *fiesta*, for which he has to plant more than sufficient food and acquire a calf (by purchase or by breeding it). In subsistence or part-subsistence economies, farmers work directly to achieve a particular goal; wants are not easily transferable, nor, of course, are assets. Land is a given factor and

[1] The term 'White' is used locally to refer to non-Indians. For a fuller explanation of the category of people to whom it refers, see footnote 18, ch. 1.

further expansion can seldom be contemplated. Preference for a particular course of ac on must take these limitations into account. A peasant must maximize each of his various wants and he must consider that in some cases the satisfaction of one will conflict with the satisfaction of another. A course of action must be selected which will not result in conflict between wants which rank equal in preference. Here it is important to remember that not only may wants vary as aspiration level rises, but that all wants are ranked in order of preference by each actor.

Decisions are not made on the basis of a simple means-ends relation at any par cular point but as part of a sequence of social actions (Smelser 1963, pp. 20–34). When a Páez Indian decides to plant more coffee he has to take into account that he may be able to do so only by asking for exchange labour and that in order to attract his neighbours and kinsmen he must have maintained friendly relations with them. This in turn implies planting sugar cane to produce beer and to have reunions to which he will invite kinsmen and neighbours. On the other hand, if an Indian has money available he may decide to hire labourers and in this way avoid social obligations. Furthermore, when an individual chooses a par cular course of action it is because he believes that by it a particular want will be more intensively satisfied than if he had taken any other course of action. For example, a farmer may delay the planting of subsistence crops, not necessarily because he ranks another want higher than that of feeding himself and his family, but because he believes that if he delays planting, weather conditions will favour a higher yield than if he plants immediately. Simon's conceptualization of economic man as a satisfier is therefore not adequate unless he assumes that without attempting to reach a maximum, economic man attempts to increase satisfaction.

In some cases a farmer can predict with reasonable certainty the outcome of his actions, and he will choose accordingly. However, in most cases a farmer will not know with certainty what will or may happen; all that he can say is that he has certain expectations as to the outcome. Thus he is making a decision without sure knowledge of prospects, or, stated differently, he is making a decision under uncertainty. Not only do weather conditions vary to an extent that makes it impossible to determine the chances of crop failure, but farmers lack the technical knowledge to enable them to evaluate the chances with sufficient accuracy. As Shackle

(1955, p. 4) has pointed out, for decisions to be made with certainty four conditions must be met: 1, that frequency ratios must be obtained from numerous and uniform sets of performance; 2, that performances can be repeated; 3, that the experiments from which the frequency ratios are derived do not destroy the circumstances in which they were performed, hence that it does not become a unique act, and that the system remains stable; 4, that we consider only the total result of a large number of trials and not each trial separately. A Páez farmer cannot determine frequency ratios. His economic environment is changing; his assets are so limited that he can invest them in a venture once and never again if that venture fails; his technological knowledge of production limits the number of possible decisions – for example, coffee is planted once in a lifetime when he is young and an inexperienced farmer. We can thus only conclude that the decisions of Páez farmers are made under uncertainty.

We owe to Shackle the recognition that most decisions are made under uncertainty; both creative decisions and decisions on agricultural activities fall into this category. When an actor makes a decision under uncertainty he cannot be expected to consider all the probabilities of an event; his decision must be based on expectations as to the probability of any one particular outcome. Shackle's contribution to the theory of decision-making is to substitute for probabilities of actual occurrences subjective evaluations of probabilities, that is, expectations. There are a number of possible outcomes to any action, some of which will be regarded by the decision-maker as likely, others as unlikely. The desirability or otherwise of an outcome will then be evaluated by the decision-maker against the degree of potential surprise which he assigns to each one of the outcomes.

Choice can only be made by an individual when he is confronted by a number of possible courses of action and can formulate an expected result for each particular course. Decisions are possible because every individual has only a limited knowledge of his environment. In fact, complete knowledge of the environment and of opportunities available would complicate the evaluation of outcome to such an extent that a decision could only be arrived at with the help of a computer. Although uncertainty limits the number of expectations an individual is able to formulate, the possible courses of action are still too large for him to be able to assume that all of them are considered when making a decision. A model which attempts to analyse the process of decision-making should determine the number as well as the type of expectations which are likely to be considered by an individual. Shackle does not really resolve this initial problem; he simply assumes that an individual is capable only of deciding between alternatives: the hypothetical outcome which will bring the decision-maker the greatest enjoyment and the hypothetical outcome which will bring him greatest distress or misfortune. Both will be evaluated to the degree of enjoyment or distress and the degree of potential surprise attached to each. Shackle labels this set of alternatives *focus gain* and *focus loss*. If the focus gain outweighs the focus loss the decision-maker will be stimulated to act, but if the contrary is the case, he will reject the venture. Of course, a hypothetical outcome considered by the actor as extremely enjoyable will also probably surprise him and he might therefore disregard it as highly unlikely. Other outcomes regarded by the actor as more likely to occur will probably also be disregarded, in this case because no great enjoyment is expected.

The model suggested by Shackle is interesting both because it attempts to portray how decisions are arrived at and because of its simplicity and clarity. However, several criticisms have been levelled against him for over-simplification. These criticisms do not entirely destroy the usefulness of the model, but modify it and suggest limitations to its applicability. It is, for example, difficult to explain how an individual can consider only alternative outcomes when he seldom treats a decision as a unique act but as a step in a series of past and future decisions. In an attempt to resolve this difficulty, Shackle (1961, p. 182) suggests that after evaluating the focus gain and focus loss of each opportunity, the decision-maker will envisage the number of different and mutual exclusive circumstances which will ensure the focus gain and focus loss of each one.

Egerton (1960, p. 70) points out another limitation in the use of Shackle's model. He asserts that an investor cannot take into account solely the focus outcomes, but must consider the whole shape of the potential surprise curve. The two focus outcomes do not give an indication of the riskiness of the project.

O'Connor (1957, p. 16) has pointed out that the model substitutes surprise as a measure of certainty for frequency ratios, as a measure of credibility of a hypothesis, forgetting that frequency ratios are important to the decision-maker to help him formulate his own beliefs as to the credibility of an event.

Carter (1957, p. 52) wonders whether it is correct to expect a decision-maker to focus on only two outcomes at any one time: a focus gain and a focus loss. He suggests that 'a strong favourable stimulus might occupy the mind to the exclusion of all the chances of loss. It is possible to devise experiments in which it is clear that attention is focused on more than two outcomes; but these are admittedly artificial, and I was first led to take the matter seriously by the occurrence of a complicated Stock Exchange situation in which it seemed clear that three outcomes were simultaneously present in the minds of investors.' The problem of simplification of possible outcomes is resolved by Carter as follows: 'Attention wil at once be concentrated on *typical outcomes* in imagined future situations; the first rule of simplification being that all variables must be reduced to few discrete values. The number of outcomes depends partly on the liveliness of the imagination in conjuring up alternative future situations, and in part on the distance of the image-date (i.e. on the time available for the disturbing elements to enter in). . . . The formation of the set of typical outcomes is a process of broad judgement very difficult to analyse. The mind seems to be under some pressure to reach definite decisions; the sensation of "not knowing what one thinks" is unpleasant, and therefore one tends to give undue weight to any scrap of firm information, and to brush aside disturbing factors because they are too vague to be assessed.' According to Carter all factors to which weights can be assigned are considered in selecting one strategy; these include: other strategies, the pay-off of each strategy, and their degree of potential surprise. Carter's model is more attractive than Shackle's in that it seems closer to a description of the actual process of decision-making. Ożga, however, criticizes it (1965, p. 290) because it does not attempt more than to predict within the limits imposed by our own ability to perceive, and does not explain why it is that at certain steps one strategy is preferred to another, while at a later step the preference may be reversed.

A more serious criticism which can be levelled against Carter's model is that though it postulates rationality of choice it suggests that in some cases this is impossible and that some decisions are therefore irrational. According to him, when all of the foreseeable outcomes are uniformly good or uniformly risky, the actor will be overcome by doubts and decisions will either be irrational or impossible. It is, of course, true that certain individuals may in such circumstances make irrational decisions. But the argument suggested by Carter encompasses more than circumstantial cases; he implies that under uncertainty rational decisions and rational behaviour (to distinguish from objective rationality) are impossible. Carter compares this situation to those where doubt will prompt the actor to look more carefully into the matter and by so doing increase the number of opportunities he can perceive; under uncertainty, then, the decision model will become so complex that evaluation of possibilities will be intellectually impossible. According to this theory, we must conclude that an individual faced with opportunities which he cannot rank, will look for another course of action, or hedge between undecided possibilities, or trust to chance. Another possibility, not considered by Carter, is that the individual may lower his aspiration level and thus be able to rank and evaluate possibilities. These assumptions are necessary because Carter starts from the proposition that opportunities confront the individual whereas the reverse is true: it is the individual who confronts himself with opportunities by recognizing their existence. Some realities are difficult to avoid, bankruptcy for example; but on the whole it is safe to assume that individuals do not face decisions unless they intuitively feel that a decision is possible. Until then a producer continues to act 'according to tradition' and planning ahead will occur only when a planning decision is feasible, given the information available to the producer. Thus we do not have to conclude, as Carter does, that a producer arbitrarily selects the opportunities and strategies which he will evaluate in order to avoid situations of doubt (though this may be so in individual cases), nor must we accept as an inescapable conclusion, that where uncertainty is too great, order is impossible. If we reject the underlying assumption in Carter's argument we can again rescue the existence of an economic *system*.

The above criticisms of Carter's hypothesis are supported by experimental results which indicate that the time required to make a decision relates to the degree of preference for the object (Audley 1960) and to utility. Mosteller and Nogee (1967) state that as the utility curve moves from positive to negative, the average time taken by the actor to play increases. Hayes (Shepard 1967) relates decision time to the number of variable attributes to be considered. This point will be discussed in the concluding chapter.

The difficulty in developing a model of decision-making which can be used to predict behaviour is in defining how the number of factors taken into account are determined. If there is no definite pattern in the selection then no model is possible; if it rests purely on psychological factors then it is neither for the economist nor for the anthropologist to construct such a model. Shackle's model can be used to predict but it is probably not accurate; Carter's model is probably closer to the empirical process, but it is difficult to apply.

Both these models take into account only the factors obtaining at the moment of choice and not the factors that define the point of decision-making. The dilemma which Carter pointed out, but did not resolve himself, can be overcome if we first see how the decision-making points are defined. Once we arrive at a model which defines decision-making points it will be possible to determine what factors are likely to be taken into account when choices are made. The hypothesis is that the opportunities considered are defined by the timing of the decision in the process of production. The actor will always consider the opportunities which are more immediate and relevant, that is, his perception is affected by the situation. The timing of a decision is not haphazard, nor are decisions always made in anticipation as some of the models discussed assume. Producers continue the same course of action as before. They choose *traditional* means until the structure of the situation changes so as to motivate a reconsideration of the original decision. It will be seen from a discussion of Páez peasant farming that not all decision-making points are similar in character and that changes in the structure of the situation will affect the decision-making points. For example, decisions regarding coffee production are made once in a lifetime. When the trees are first planted, the factors taken into account are expectations about stability of prices and price level. Decisions regarding subsistence agriculture are made during the course of planting, seldom beforehand, as the factors considered have to do with the immediate situation. The strategies selected therefore depend on what is perceived when a decision is made and this depends on whether the decision is made beforehand or not. I do not think that the fact that a change in a decision-making point affects the opportunities selected for evaluation questions the rationality of any of the decisions. Each of these decisions has a rationale of its own; they are made after evaluation of various strategies. The fact that the strategies are limited in number does not preclude the rationality of the final choice. A decision can be considered rational, though knowledge is limited and outcomes are uncertain.

To approach economic organization from an analysis of decision-making will help us to elucidate for a peasant economy, where productive units are relatively independent of each other, the factors which are taken into account when a decision is made and hence those which ultimately affect the economic organization of the peasant sector. It follows from this hypothesis that the same factors are not taken into account in each of the various economic activities; land, labour and price may affect some but not all of the economic activities. The solutions or choices can be understood in the context of the factors selected. The choice to sell or not to sell food on the market square can now be better understood, and the accuracy of the model of spheres of activity can now be questioned.

In the conclusion I shall itemize the factors that regulate production and indicate when (or in what activities) these factors are relevant, but first of all I shall describe the historical and social context of the peasant community. Land is discussed as a separate problem because its availability is determined and fixed early in life, the tensions and manœuvres are made rather in the context of family relations than of economic opportunities, when the son is not yet an independent producer. Following a brief discussion of resources and techniques of production I shall discuss the various decision-making processes and the strategies which are selected by farmers, as well as the factors which determine the strategies. I shall consider savings and investment as part of the decision-making process since a separate chapter would confuse the reader and within the framework of this book it would involve an arbitrary and unnecessary separation of decisions into types. It is after all almost impossible to discuss savings as distinct from investment in a peasant economy, as has already been pointed out by Firth and Yamey (1967).

Though this book discusses almost exclusively those decisions which can easily be classified as economic decisions, I am convinced that much can be gained from the application of this model to other aspects of social anthropology. It is an approach full of limitations; nevertheless, it can shed some light on certain processes which other techniques may obscure through over-simplification. In the same way that it allows us to understand better the concept of traditional behaviour and to reduce the rigidities of the concept of spheres of exchange, it may also help us to cope with specific problems of competition in politics and specific problems of social change. I shall make this point again, but rather briefly, in my concluding remarks when the decision-making model will be clearer in the minds of the reader.

PART I

THE LIFE AND HISTORICAL BACKGROUND OF PÁEZ PEASANTS

I

Tierradentro in the Past and Present

THE SETTING

In the western part of the department of Cauca, the southern Colombian Andes form a dense knot of criss-crossing mountains, none of them very high, ranging from 6,000 to 12,000 feet. This region is called Tierradentro (hinterland), a name that appropriately describes its isolation.

La Plata, a town of 2,416 inhabitants, with a row of small shops on its main street, is the transfer point for all passengers travelling to Tierradentro. Trucks converted for passenger use leave the town and cross the wide green valley which ends abruptly in a sharply rising wall of mountains. Steep slopes pressed compactly against each other apparently leave no room for valleys and passage through them seems impossible. But the bus continues north on the single unpaved road that enters Tierradentro; on the one side is a steep slope; on the other a sharp drop to the stony bed of the Páez river. At intervals there are small hamlets built on the small space at each side of the road, where the bus makes a quick stop and then continues climbing slowly around mountain after mountain. Valencia, a relatively important but small market town, lies at the half-way point. The next town is Guadalejo, now a desolate group of houses, but which once, when the motor road connection to Inzá ended there, was an active trading centre and held well-attended markets. In 1960 a new branch road to the main La Plata–Belalcázar road was finished and now once a week the bus turns in the direction of Inzá. Five hours after leaving La Plata it stops where the path that leads to San Andrés meets the road, only four kilometres from the settlement. The bus continues for a short distance until it reaches the bank of the Ullucus river where passengers descend to load their merchandise on to horses for the last lap of their journey to Inzá; the wooden bridge over the river

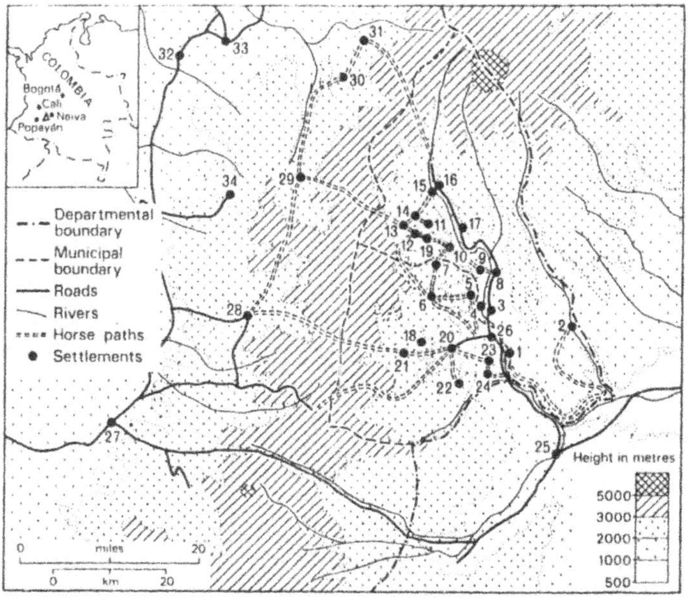

Map 1. Tierradentro Territory

The important commercial centres that link Tierradentro with the rest of Colombia are indicated in the insert; the small triangle represents the area covered by the map. The numbered circles indicate cities, small towns or Indian settlements. The Indian Settlements are:

1. Ricaurte
2. Araujo
3. Cohetando
4. Togoima
5. Santa Rosa
6. San Andrés
7. Calderas
8. Belalcázar
9. Avirama
10. Chinas
11. Vitoncó
12. Lame
13. Mosoco
14. San José
15. Huila
16. Tóez
17. Tálaga
18. Yaquivá
19. Suin

The following are White settlements and towns:

20. Inzá
21. Guanacas
22. Turminá
23. Pedregal
24. Topa
25. La Plata
26. Guadalejo
27. Popayán
28. Silvia
29. Jambaló
30. Toribío
31. Tacueyó
32. Santander
33. Caloto
34. Caldono

is too flimsy to take the vehicle, and furthermore the road beyond the river is often impassable during the rainy season. Five days later, early on a Sunday morning, the bus leaves again for La Plata scheduled to return the following Tuesday, providing outside traders attending the Saturday market at Inzá with the only sure means of return transport. Sometimes, with luck, it is possible to travel on the trucks that carry coffee or provisions, but more frequently, after waiting for many hours at the roadside, residents resign themselves to walking the 20 km to Guadalejo where the possibility of transport on the road that connects Belalcázar with La Plata is greater.

Belalcázar, though approximately the same size as Inzá (514 inhabitants), is more important since it is the seat of the regional church authority, and has the only secondary school in the region. More important still is its favourable geographical location on the border of the fertile gentler slopes and the small plains that stretch along the Páez river. This is the area that has caused Tierradentro to be known erroneously as a rich cattle country. It was one of the earliest areas to be settled after long battles with the Indians for control of the territory and the salt pans. It was also the first area of Tierradentro to be connected with the outside world by a direct motor road to La Plata, as a result of a national campaign for road building in the late 1950s. Thus, better communication and richer lands for agriculture and cattle raising has made Belalcázar more important and commercially more active than Inzá.

Before 1954 Tierradentro could only be approached on the west from the towns of Silvia or Tacueyó by crossing the high cold plateau on foot or on horseback. In the south an easier horse trail connected Inzá and Belalcázar with La Plata. The length of the journey, the discomfort of crossing the cold and windy mountain paths and the waves of banditry and civil war that had recently particularly affected this region of Colombia, discouraged ambulant traders from venturing in with much frequency. Thus Tierradentro has remained an isolated spot within a department of Colombia known for its poverty and backwardness.

Steeply sloped and eroded mountains that only rarely allow a narrow valley or a soft plain make up the topography of the region. Only at the higher altitudes, around 9,000 feet, do the mountains slope more gently and are still covered by virgin forests. At lower altitudes the ridges are rocky and steep, and the soil has been leached by constant cultivation and heavy rainfall. Only the flatter lowland areas around Guadalejo and Belalcázar, now owned almost exclusively by White settlers, open into wider, flat, temperate plains more suitable for agriculture.

The climate varies with the altitude, and while in the area of

San Andrés (5,000 to 6,000 feet) the mean temperature was never below 62° Fahrenheit, in the higher mountains around Mosoco (9,000 feet) it was about 53° Fahrenheit. There are no exact precipitation figures for the region and the estimate of 1,200 mm annual minimum given by government statistical surveys is based on that of the surrounding regions.[1]

At one time small gold mines were exploited in the mountains west of Inzá and some of the older Indians still remember travelling to Guadalejo to obtain salt from the salt pans. During the Colonial and early Republican period negro slaves were brought to work the salt mines in the neighbourhood of Belalcázar. At present, however, the wealth of the region depends on Indian agricultural development and on the larger cattle ranches and coffee plantations of the White settlers.

Narrow trails, dangerous and often impassable during the rainy season and reverently named *caminos reales* (royal roads), cross Tierradentro in several directions connecting the various settlements with San Andrés, Belalcázar, Inzá or Silvia; the settlements are as much as five to ten hours' ride on horseback apart, which accounts for the limited contact between the inhabitants of the different areas.

Except for the area surrounding Inzá and Belalcázar and the territory south of these towns, the greater part of Tierradentro is inhabitated by Indians living in reservations; out of a total population of 25,495, according to the 1951 census,[2] 20,000 are Indians,[3] most of them Páez-speaking. The Ullucus river serves as a boundary between the Páez and the Topa, and Guanaca Indians who live to the south and east. There are twenty reservations, of which eighteen are Páez.[4] Tóez, Huila, Páez, Tálaga, Avirama, Ricaurte, Togoima, and Cohetando are Páez reservations located in the

[1] División Técnica de Seguridad, Campesina, *Cauca*, Ministerio de Trabajo, Bogotá, 1957, p. 8.

[2] Departamento Administrativo Nacional de Estadística, *Censo de Población de 1951: Cauca*, Bogotá, 1954.

[3] Páez language belongs to the Chibcha linguistic family but its exact classificatory relationship to other languages of the same family is not certain. See Hernandez de Alba 1946, p. 922; Mason 1946, pp. 57–318.

[4] There are also three more Páez reservations in the municipality of Toribío, on the other side of the mountains. There is very little contact between these two groups at present, partly because of the difficulty of communication, but also because the Toribío Páez are closer to other commercial centres than to those used by the Tierradentro Páez.

temperate zone that extends from south to north along the main road to Belalcázar. White peasants and Indians have long lived in close contact here. In the higher colder regions the Mosoco reservation has been connected with Silvia and Belalcázar by a bridle path well travelled by traders who began long ago to visit Tierradentro to purchase potatoes and sell their city wares. Here White settlers have built their houses together with Indians around the church and school. Most of them left, however, after the settlement was attacked by bandits in 1956 and are only now slowly returning. San José, Lame, Vitoncó, Suin and Chinas reservations at higher altitudes, and Calderas in the temperate zone, are the more isolated and traditional of Páez reservations. Along with Mosoco, San Andrés, Santa Rosa and Yaquivá have had a high degree of contact with White settlers. In Santa Rosa missionaries have succeeded in establishing a well attended school and in influencing local events. Though there are no settled Whites or traders it is a prosperous little hamlet famous for its *fiestas* and hospitality. As a result of its proximity to Inzá, its site on the main line of communication with other reservations, and the immigration of White peasants in search of land, San Andrés has become a point of close but tense contact between Whites and Indians.

Climate and topography along with White immigration and varying degrees of contact with commercial centres are responsible for regional agricultural differences. Belalcázar, Inzá and San Andrés are the only temperate zones suitable for coffee; they are, also, areas which initially attracted White coffee-growers. The total volume of coffee produced is not very large compared with other regions of Colombia but the quality, though not registered as a brand type, is very good. Calderas and Santa Rosa are only slightly colder and the Indians cultivate similar crops to those grown in San Andrés, except for coffee; mountain maize gives a higher yield and for this reason larger areas are planted with this crop than is usual in San Andrés. The high altitude and cold winds blowing from the Huila mountain make the northern zone of the reservations of Mosoco, Lame, Vitoncó and San José too cold and wet for manioc, arracacha or coffee. The cash crop of this region is potatoes and the staples *ullucus*,[5] maize, broad beans, and beans; peaches, garlic and wheat are also cultivated where the climate is

[5] *Ullucus tuberosus*, a small tuber with a slight beet-like flavour, a staple product among those Andean Indians who live at higher altitudes.

suitable. But there are considerable differences in crops in each reservation; in San Andrés itself, for example, there are areas where no coffee is grown and wheat is the cash crop, or where potatoes and *ullucus* are used instead of plantain in stews.

HISTORY OF THE CONQUEST AND COLONIZATION OF TIERRADENTRO

At the time of the Spanish Conquest the Páez Indians, together with their neighbours the Pijao Guanacas, Guambianos and Paniquitá, occupied about the same area that the Páez occupy today. It was an area strategically located on a direct route between the Colonial centres of Quito and Santa Fé (now Bogotá), and the Spaniards were anxious to penetrate and pacify this territory which was also known to contain numerous silver and gold mines; but the difficult terrain and the warlike nature of the tribes made the task almost impossible.

The Páez, aided by the rugged terrain of the region, were the most successful in their fight to maintain independence. The Guambianos and the Guanacas, on the western side of these mountains, were more exposed to Spanish infiltration and only the Guambianos succeeded, to a certain extent, in retaining their individuality as a separate ethnic group. The Pijaos, who occupied the eastern slopes bordering the Neiva valley, fought savagely against the Spaniards and were eventually exterminated. According to Hernandez de Alba (1946, p. 915) the Andaquis migrated to the lowland jungles when they realized the battle against the Spaniards was lost. It is difficult to determine the exact location of each tribe at the time of the Spanish Conquest because of the confusion of names that appear in the manuscripts of the period. The Páez are sometimes mentioned as having attacked Popayán during the early period of settlement, and as having crossed the high mountains to settle in what was then Guambiano territory (Cuervo y Marquez 1920, p. 146). All the tribes were bitter enemies and as the result of inter-tribal fighting and temporary alliances territorial occupation must have changed considerably even before the Spaniards attempted to penetrate the area.[6]

[6] It is difficult to establish the boundaries or locations of the various tribes that seem to have inhabited the area; the languages spoken in the area were many and the Spanish chroniclers did not always list the same tribal names. See Hernandez de Alba 1946, p. 945.

In 1538 Belalcázar left Quito and attempted to cross the Cordillera Central, south of Tierradentro territory. Timaná was founded at this time and together with Popayán, founded in 1536, became the outpost for future penetration into Indian territory. In 1541 an unsuccessful attempt to pass through Tierradentro, this time from the north, was made by Belalcázar, but he was defeated by the Páez in Tálaga and had to withdraw. In the following twenty years Spanish soldiers who settled around the Páez and Pijao territory were barely able to retain their positions; attacks made by the Indians were frequent and savage. Another incursion from the north into western Páez territory by Domingo Lozano had a short-lived success. The Páez recovered their lost territory and destroyed many Spanish outposts including the silver mines at Plata Vieja. In about 1600 a new Spanish campaign of pacification succeeded in bringing the Guanacas tribe under control, and in completely exterminating the Pijaos. With Pijao, Guanacas and Timaná territory under control the route to Bogotá was finally secured and as the Páez withdrew further into this mountainous territory Spanish soldiers had little interest in further expeditions into the area. The Indians were left relatively undisturbed and in the period that followed, through slow and patient attempts by missionaries and priests, the ground was prepared for its eventual settlement by White farmers.

Missionary campaigns began in Northern Páez territory. A small Franciscan mission was established in Tálaga during the early 1700s; visits to the surrounding settlements of Vitoncó, Suin, Huila, Lame and Tóez were made on occasion. The priest José Fernandez Belalcázar entered Southern Páez territory from Guanacas in 1736, but no missions were established nor were regular pastoral visits made to this area.[7] Throughout this early period the intervening territory of Calderas and Chinas, isolated by two mountain chains, remained free of intrusions by soldiers and missionaries.

With the pacification of the area the *encomienda* system began to operate. Spanish *encomenderos* gained the privilege of exploiting the labour of those Indians assigned to them, and also of benefiting from the head tax paid by the Indian; in exchange, the *encomendero* was responsible for Christianizing and providing generally for the

[7] Uricoechica mentions that there were earlier short-lived attempts by missionaries in the 1600s; see his introduction to Castillo i Orozco, Paris, 1878, p. IX.

Indian population. Indians, referred to as chiefs by the *encomenderos* in their reports to the Crown, served as the liaison between master *encomendero* and subject Indians. The chiefs had to provide Indians for the mines or farms outside their territory where they worked for the *encomenderos*. Often these Indians never returned to their homes.[8]

San Andrés figures for the first time as an Indian settlement[9] in a census taken in 1719, for the purpose of tribute collection. These censuses were taken every two years, according to Otero. At that time San Andrés was divided into three *encomiendas* and one of them was also given the territory of Calderas and Avirama. The Tierradentro *encomiendas* were the last to be granted by the Crown, and thus the last to disappear as the original grantees died, or the period for which the grant was made lapsed.[10]

Those Indians who did not live within the territory of an *encomienda* were considered to be royal wards with crown officers as their tutors. These officers collected tribute for the Crown and served as mediators between the Indians and private individuals or government officials seeking their labour on farms, in mines or for public projects. Permission to draw on one-fifth of the adult male population of an Indian settlement for personal and public labour could be granted by the crown officer once an appropriate wage and maintenance provision had been agreed upon. The Indians

[8] As the Tierradentro *encomiendas* were granted very late they did not correspond with the earlier system of *encomienda* established in Mexico or Northern Colombia. The Tierradentro *encomendero* had no absolute right to permanent use of Indian labour, the amount and collection of tribute was supervised by the Crown and the *encomendero* did not have the right to live near his Indians or to sit in judgement over them. Further, an *encomienda* did not include a land grant and the *encomendero* could not make use of the territory where the Indians lived. For a detailed account of the *encomienda* system in the department of Cauca, see Arboleda Llorente 1948 and Fals Borda 1957a, pp. 131–53. For comparative material in Mexico, see Wolf 1962, ch. 9; and on Perú, see Kubler 1946, vol. 2, pp. 364–75.

[9] Pittiers de Fabrega 1907, p. 312, lists 34 Páez settlements, but the name of San Andrés does not appear in it; the list was compiled from missionary accounts of 1684.

[10] Otero 1952, p. 49. These tribute lists are of very little use because of their fragmentary nature and the incompleteness of their information. It is impossible to tell whether they represented a complete census, or merely referred to Indians working for *encomenderos* away from San Andrés. *Encomienda* boundaries seemed to change and original *encomiendas* to be subdivided if the population increased; or they might disappear entirely and not be granted again. The last document I discovered in the Archives of the University of Popayán listing an *encomienda* for San Andrés was 1733 (Document 3491 – Col c, 1–17t).

were supposed to be returned to their settlement, were not to be taken further away than 10 leagues and not to be away more than 3/4 weeks a year. Arboleda Llorente contrasts this with the Mexican *cuatequil* system and cites a document dated 1733 in which it is mentioned that Páez Indians often travelled more than 10 leagues[11] to work as *mita* labourers.[12]

Tribute lists have been found for San Andrés up to 1756, but no specific information as to *mita* service by the Páez has been discovered, apart from the reference cited. It is also difficult to determine when the colonial government succeeded, against the opposition of the autonomous *encomenderos* and new settlers, in establishing the legality of the Indian territorial occupation, and in drawing up the boundaries of the reservation. In some areas of Colombia this occurred as early as the 1600s, but there are few documents for this region of Cauca in the Archives or in government agencies, except for the incomplete tribute lists mentioned above.

At the beginning of the nineteenth century Inzá became a parish and missionary work in the area began. In 1807 the San Andrés church as it stands today was built by Joaquin Nuñez and he mentions that at that time the area was settled by 50 families, 9 of which were mestizos and 6 slaves.

With Colombian independence the reservation system came into effect and the paying of tribute was abolished. There is no reason to believe that the Indians of Tierradentro would not also have benefited from events that took place in the rest of Colombia though we have no specific information to that effect.[13]

Inzá became a settlement in 1876 and the municipality was founded in 1886. Páez Indians did not react favourably to the

[11] Arboleda Llorente 1948, p. 136, and for a particular description of rulings referring to the paying of tribute and *mita* system, see pp. 119–45, as taken from documents found in the Central Archives of Cauca.

[12] *Mita* refers to the compulsory labour system during Spanish colonial times as described in this paragraph.

[13] Simon Bolivar, in his famous decree of 5 July 1820, stipulated that reservations were to be returned to the Indians and later to be subdivided among the member families. In this same decree full citizenship rights were extended to the Indians. Furthermore, tributes were abolished by the law of 11 October 1821. While this legislation upheld the reservation system it a so recommended the eventual subdivision of the reservation land among the constituent Indian families. For a discussion of the confusion brought about by the law of 1820, see Cabrera y Moreno 1942, pp. 29–33. Many reservations were terminated between 1934 and 1950, but in Tierradentro all but two have remained.

increasing immigration of Whites. Quintín Lame in 1916 organized the Indians of Lame, Mosoco, and Vitoncó, and rebelled against the local settlers, marching South in the direction of Inzá where he was finally defeated. The rebellions continued with Quintín Lame and Pío Collo, both Indians from the North, as the main leaders. In 1932 and 1950 Belalcázar was attacked, but both attempts failed.[14] Resistance to White intrusion has since been restricted to local settlement, as in the case of Calderas reservation where not a single Colombian has been allowed to reside permanently, or as in San Andrés where only a few years ago Indians stoned houses to frighten their inhabitants.

Immigration was encouraged when the government decided to open up areas of settlement inside reser ation territory. These lands passed under the direct control of the municipalities in which the reservations were located; Indians who were living within these areas were allowed to remain as long as rent was paid annually, and the remainder of the land was parcelled out and sold to individual settlers. However, settlements did not develop in all the reservations; only San Andrés, Mosoco, Togoima and those reservations crossed by the road to Belalcázar have non-Indian settlers.

In Santa Rosa and alderas missionaries have established schools, but their influence and activities have not spread to other reservations. The remainder of the settlements are visited by the priests from the parish centres of Inzá and Belalcázar. At most once a month the priest comes to San Andrés, hears confessions, and the following morning, after saying Mass, departs again without having had much contact with anyone except the few White settlers. The extent of the territory the priest has to cover and the difficulty inherent in any catechizing attempts in this area, have resulted in only sporadic contact with Church authority and little participation in Church ritual except for the annual Indian *fiestas*. The direct influence of the Church in Indian affairs is felt mainly in the election of *capitanes* and in the approval of *fiestas* where celebration requires officiation by a priest. Páez are, however, considered to be Catholic, and so regard themselves.

Colombian settlement, and the economic development of the

[14] Gonzalez 1923; *Informe que el Secretario de Gobierno Rinde al Señor Gobernador*, 1923. (Unpublished; Archivo Departamental del Cauca, Popayán.)

area would have continued peacefully had it not been for the civil war and the banditry that, in recent times (most pronounced during the years 1948–58), have destroyed settlements and frightened away the population. The civil war reached Tierradentro in the early fifties. A large percentage of the male population of Belalcázar died in a local battle, and later persecution and bloodshed was common; this was the worst area of political convulsion in Tierradentro. Mosoco was attacked and burned about 1955 and the settlers escaped to San Andrés. The Municipio of Inzá suffered much less and San Andrés remained as a peaceful liberal pocket in a surrounding sea of conservative and liberal fighting, and the indiscriminate attacks of bandits. In 1959 peace was established, a general amnesty was declared and the well armed bandits of Tierradentro withdrew to their own conquered territory to the east of Belalcázar. They remained at peace until about 1965 when they again began incursions and attacks around Inzá. These political upheavals in Tierradentro resulted in internal migration of White settlers, and disruption of productive and trading activities. Cattle and crops were ravaged, houses attacked and inhabitants killed. Thus not until 1959 did settlers venture to increase their herds, or traders to travel alone into remote settlements or cross the northern areas where bandits had previously been entrenched. Even travel to La Plata had been dangerous, so that Tierradentro remained altogether stagnant throughout the fifties. The road-building programme initiated by the central government was intended to develop these isolated areas by bringing them into closer contact with surrounding economies thus rendering them more susceptible to military supervision.

As can be seen, not all Páez territory suffered equally throughout the *encomienda* period nor was it all subject to such intensive missionary campaigns. It was mainly the Northern territory which was affected during the earlier periods of contact. Towards the end of the nineteenth century the focus of White influence was strongest in the south in the growing centres of Inzá and Belalcázar.[15] These centres provided the manpower necessary to influence the surrounding Indian territory while the Northern reservations were

[15] Cuervo y Marquez, *op. cit.* Travelled through the Northern part of Tierradentro including the reservations of Mosoco, Huila, Tálaga, etc. in 1887 and he does not mention having encountered White settlers in the area.

at this point left alone.[16] The construction in the 1950s of the road linking Belalcázar and Inzá with Southern towns gave a great impetus to the south of Tierradentro, and isolated the reservations of Calderas, Lame, Mosoco, Vitoncó, Suin, Chinas and San José from intensive trading contacts. With the continuation of the road northwards more reservations came under the commercial influence of Belalcázar, while the intervening reservations are still serviced only by small local traders willing to travel over difficult terrain.

HISTORY OF THE SAN ANDRÉS AREA

At the beginning of this century the old church and four Indian houses, used only during *fiestas*, dominated the small plateau of San Andrés. Mountains flank this plateau on three sides, and the façade of the church faces the long narrow valley which drops abruptly and follows the winding course of the San Andrés creek. The Indians live and have their fields on the surrounding mountains.

It was not until Inzá was permanently settled in 1898 that the Indians of San Andrés began to feel the effects of Colombian colonization. During the period 1920–30 the sons of the Inzá settlers began to look for lands suitable for starting their own small coffee plantations. Some settled along the narrow valley of the San Andrés creek, forming a small nucleus of six peasant families. Soon afterwards others appeared, one of whom bought one hectare of land belonging to the reservation; the others remained just outside the reservation boundaries.

In 1926 the reservation of San Andrés lost to the municipal authorities the control of the land surrounding the church and the valley bordering the San Andrés creek (about 100 to 150 acres). This land was then declared an area of settlement and parcelled out in small lots to be rented or bought by any Indian or White who wished to build a house. The hostile reaction of the Indians to these newcomers delayed the development of a settlement around the

[16] From 1938 to 1954 the Inzá municipio increased its population by 30·4 per cent, mainly immigrant population, and Belalcázar by 10 to 20 per cent. The number of farms in Inzá municipio, outside the reservation area, multiplied by six times and in Belalcázar municipio farms doubled in number. (División Técnica de Seguridad, Campesina, *Cauca*, Ministerio de Trabajo, Bogotá 1957, pp. 12 and 19.)

church until 1940.[17] Boundary squabbles were frequent and the Indians expressed their resentment against the intruders by stoning their houses and restricting the use of the cemetery and the church. The newcomers found allies in about half a dozen mestizo families descended from reservation Indians who remained on the newly acquired municipal land instead of retreating, as other Indians did, to the surrounding mountain slopes. At present the land owned and cultivated by these mestizo families and their descendants falls outside the present reservation boundaries, though prior to 1926 it must have been reservation land.

The descendants of the mestizos and the new settlers intermarried and together with more recent immigrants, constitute the White[18] population of San Andrés.

In 1940 the first store in the hamlet was established by a mestizo; there was another store, which had probably been opened earlier, 4 km from the settlement on the path that led from San Andrés to Inzá. About 1956, when 23 families had settled around San Andrés, a second store was opened in the hamlet by one of the newer immigrants.

As the available land was taken over and political unrest restricted trading opportunities the growth of the White settlement levelled out. Fear of bandits spread through rural Colombia and some of the wealthier families of San Andrés sold their land and moved to the safety of the towns. Other families entered San Andrés from the more exposed surrounding areas, leaving again after 1959 when peace was re-established. At present the number of White families is 37, eight of whom maintain stores, though only two have a varied supply of stock throughout the year; the

[17] In 1936 there were only two buildings around the church when Perez de Barrada visited San Andrés. (Arqueología y Antropología Precolombinas de Tierradentro, Bogotá, 1937.)

[18] The term 'White' is locally used for the non-Indian population. The term mestizo is used only to indicate that the White has some Indian blood. Though a biological distinction is implied it is rather meant to differentiate the cultural and social backgrounds of Whites from those of Indians. It is equivalent to the term Ladino in Central America which is supposed to include both the White population and the mestizos (see Tax 1942, p. 45). The term Ladino is not used in Colombia and those descendants of Indians who have become assimilated are still referred to as Whites. If they live within a reservation, though in outward appearance they might be indistinguishable from Whites, they are called, and call themselves, Indians (see Sayres 1957, pp. 457–65). In Northern Colombia the term mestizo replaces the term 'White' (see Reichel-Dolmatoff 1961, p. 135).

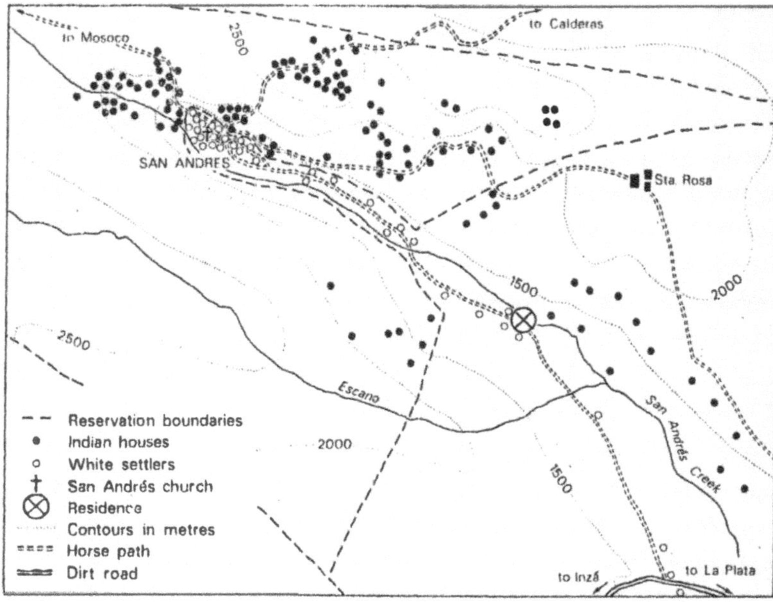

Map 2. Distribution of houses in area studied.

remaining stores are very small and suffer severely from the seasonal fluctuations of purchasing power.

POLITICAL ORGANIZATION OF TIERRADENTRO

Municipal government. The department of Cauca, like the other departments of Colombia, is divided into smaller administrative units called municipalities. These units have very little independence; the municipal mayors are appointed by the governor of the department; major decisions on matters of local importance are initiated and approved in Popayán, the capital of the department, and major criminal cases are tried far away from the district. Municipal authorities, however, have the right to levy land and market taxes which are their main independent sources of revenue. The extent of the Indian reservations whose land is not taxable, and the low rates paid by the other residents, reduces the importance of this source of income, so that it barely covers administrative expenses and leaves little scope for initiating local projects. The total annual municipal budget, which includes national government contributions to education, was in 1960 $55.182

Colombian pesos (approx. £2,200) for Inzá and $72,718 Colombian pesos (£2,800) for Belalcázar.[19]

Tierradentro lies within the boundaries of the municipalities of Inzá and Belalcázar and the area I studied is controlled by Inzá. All municipalities are divided into smaller units. In the case of Inzá and Belalcázar these smaller administrative units are of two types: on the one hand there are 20 Indian reservations and on the other there are the *veredas* or neighbourhoods. I shall not attempt to analyse the concept of *vereda* and its political organization as it is an involved subject with which this study is not directly concerned. I merely wish to point out that not all *veredas* represent the same kind of political unit or have the same degrees of corporateness.[20]

Not all documents dealing with Tierradentro list the same number of *veredas* or locate them on a map. The municipality of Inzá has three *veredas* that have been made into *corregimientos* with a *corregidor* whose authority is derived from the municipal mayor. The *corregidor* has administrative, judicial and police duties that often extend far beyond the boundaries of the *vereda*. This officer also serves as a liaison between the municipal mayors and the Indian reservation authorities. San Andrés is one of these *corregimientos*, but only during the last six months of my stay did it have an appointed authority. The amount of time needed for *corregidor* duties, and the amount of responsibility that they entail is disproportionate to the remuneration received. The *corregidor* in San Andrés was an outsider who had lost the land he had once had in another area and had settled in San Andrés. He was not eager to hold office and was planning to resign and move to another area where there were better prospects of establishing himself as a trader. Thus, San Andrés was again threatened with the loss of its privileged political position and it was unlikely that it would

[19] Departamento Administrativo Nacional de Estadística, *Boletín Mensual de Estadística*, año IX, no. 117, Bogotá, 1960.

[20] Originally a *vereda* meant a path or a narrow road or the route travelled by preachers. In Colombia the territorial origins of *veredas* may be traced to Indian communities, reservations and farm territories. Often they have little importance from the administrative point of view unless they are promoted to the level of *corregimiento*. They are commonly used to refer to ecological groups which do not always coincide with the political boundaries. This concept is of particular sociological importance in other parts of Colombia, where the non-Indian population is scattered over the rural areas more than it is in Tierradentro. For a more detailed discussion of *vereda*, see Fals Borda 1955, pp. 39–44.

quickly find a successor to fill the office. A secretary, in this case an Indian, was appointed to help the *corregidor* in his duties but he received no remuneration.

Reservation. The reservations are Indian corporate communities with their own local authority, occupying an assigned territory and governed in matters of land by laws that do not apply to other Colombian citizens. Members of these reservations otherwise have full citizenship rights.

Each reservation has its own elected and appointed authorities, referred to collectively as the *cabildo* or council. They meet regularly in open assemblies to discuss the affairs of the reservation and put resolutions to the vote, if necessary. All heads of households are entitled to participate. The council is elected once a year; re-election of any of the officers is proscribed[21] and customary law indicates that a period of five years must lapse before an individual can again hold office.

The outgoing officers suggest a list of candidates but further nominations can be made by the assembled members of the community. The permanent secretary, usually a White who can read and write, as well as draw up legal documents and petitions, reads out the names of the proposed candidates and an open vote is taken. There is very little, if any, interest in, or competition for, office. Usually only one list is presented, often not without much previous pleading with the individual candidates not to withdraw their names from nomination. The candidates are often threatened with fines by the municipal mayor if they persist in refusing to hold office. The elected officers have to be confirmed by the municipal mayor and receive from him the staff of office. The elected reservation council consists of five officers and their respective substitutes.[22] The *gobernador* is the most important officer; he must remain in weekly contact with the mayor so as to receive orders and report incidents. In the month when San Andrés had a

[21] Decree 162 of 28 April 1920, article no. 1, Colombia.

[22] The information gathered by me differs from the list of *cabildo* officers given by Hernandez de Alba, *op. cit.*, p. 945, and by Otero 1952, p. 32, who does not appear to agree with the previous author. This is not surprising as often the Indians did not remember the titles of each of the acting officers. It is possible that the names registered were those suggested by the mayor in office at the time, an outsider not familiar with the terminology of the region. The number and titles of the *cabildo* officers is established by custom and not by law.

corregidor trips to Inzá were avoided and messages from the mayor were received through this intermediary; complaints between the White and Indian communities had to go through this official channel. Orders to repair roads or public buildings are always passed from the mayor to the Indians through the *gobernador*. This officer otherwise has no authority. He is assisted by one *comisario*, two *alguaciles* and one *fiscal*. Whatever the original functions of each of these officials when the system of reservations was established during colonial times there is at present little difference between them. When the *gobernador* brings an order from the mayor the minor officers help him spread the news from house to house. This is no easy task and requires several days' walking up different mountain paths. The *alguaciles* have the specific function of delivering summonses and of taking all criminals to the Inzá jail. There are also two lifelong officers whom Hernandez de Alba (1946, p. 945) has referred to as representing traditional Páez authority. They are called *capitán mayor* and *capitán menor* (major and minor captain) and are confirmed in office by the parish priest after being elected by the Indian community. Their nomination is a compromise between the priest and the White community on the one hand, and the Indian community on the other. I was told that the essential requirement is that they be older members of the reservation, living relatively close to the settlement so as to be available for consultation. One of them, the *capitán menor* is elected from the more tradition-bound members of the reservation while the *capitán mayor* is someone able to sympathize with the outlook of the White community and the interests of the priest. But as their position is essentially advisory this difference does not result in any competition.

The older traditional *capitán* came to all the San Andrés markets, lived very close to the settlement and was often consulted by the *gobernador* on matters pertaining to the *cabildo*, and approached by Indians seeking advice on official matters. When the discussion began about repairing the old San Andrés church it was the advice of this *capitán* which threatened the cooperation of the Indian community. However, his influence was not always so successful, nor was his position respected. Where opinions differed, his own might not be given much weight, and some Indians volunteered to suggest that the *gobernador* should have greater prestige and authority. On the other hand the opinion of the traditional *capitán* was usually sought before any matter was brought up for discussion.

The *capitán mayor* was a 'progressive'[23] Indian of considerable wealth who was on good terms with the White community, though his relations with the priest were at the time strained. He seldom attended council meetings or came to the market place, and it was apparent that he was liked primarily because he did not interfere in reservation affairs, and for his general bonhomie and good humour. Both *capitánes* complained that the Indians showed little respect for their office and that people considered their advisory functions insignificant. On the whole, they interfered little unless they were asked to do so and served ittle apparent purpose; the *gobernador* was by far the more active figure.

For each of the elected officers a substitute is also elected; in July 1960, six months after their election, the work load had become so heavy that the officers, with the approval of the municipal mayor, resigned and their substitutes took office. None are paid or receive special privileges; on the contrary their farms suffer as a result of their time-consuming duties.

Until 1959 a treasurer was also elected for life and confirmed in office by the municipal mayor.[24] His functions were to collect money for land leased by the community and to administer the sale of the communal harvest used for community and church expenses. In San Andrés there was no free land which could be leased and the only communal property was the revenue of an old harvest and a few animals. The priest considered this to be church property, but the community gave the matter a wider and different interpretation. Cattle had been sold to pay for a lawsuit against a White neighbour and the priest insisted that this represented mishandling of funds; on his own authority he elected a White settler to the position of treasurer. As there are no more cattle and communal harvests are no longer carried out, the burden of collecting funds and administering them falls on the few White settlers. This new nomination is therefore more in accordance with changing conditions.

A sacristan is also appointed for life by the priest. Recently a

[23] These terms refer to differences in economic orientation among Indians of the reservation. See Chapter 8 for a fuller explanation.

[24] According to regulations set out in Decree 700, 26 November 1936, Department of Cauca, Colombia.

school officer has been nominated, whose duties are to ensure that each Indian family sends at least one child to school.

One of the main functions of the reservation council is to ensure that orders from the municipal mayor are carried out. These mostly concern repairs to the main paths connecting San Andrés with other settlements, and the maintenance and repair of the church and school. Its other important function is to deal with matters concerned with the allocation of land, as will be discussed in chapter 3. The *cabildo* also arbitrates when feuds within the family or between neighbours are brought before it. If a minor has run away from home a council officer is asked to bring him back; if two brothers or neighbours fight over damage caused by intruding animals, the council is asked to intervene, and it is hoped that it can also put an end to malicious gossip. But the *cabildo* has no power or authority to punish offenders and can really only rule on matters of land distribution. At one time, however, the reservation officers had power and authority to punish; Calderas reservation was the last, in 1955, to give up the stocks to which offenders were tied for punishment. Nowadays, if the council cannot bring about agreement between the two complaining parties one of them has to raise the matter with the municipal mayor or judge. When San Andrés had a *corregidor* a number of small complaints were discussed with him instead of with the council. However, he, like all other White authorities, had little interest in Indian affairs and felt that the matter was a waste of his time; 'Go and straighten it out yourself or I'll fine both of you,' would probably be his only response.

The lack of interest in Indian affairs on the part of the municipal authorities, and of the White population in general, the distrust shown by the Indians of White intrusion into the affairs of the reservation, and the ineffectiveness of the council, are all responsible for the general apathy in community affairs, and the feeling that individual matters are best handled by the parties concerned. The reservation council has the reputation of being unwilling to act except in more extreme cases, and only when the dispute has reached a violent stage do the parties approach the council or the *corregidor*.

The secretary of the *cabildo* is responsible for keeping all documents concerning land allocation, and for registering births and deaths. None of these duties were carried out carefully. The only census attempted remained unfinished.

All Indian adult members of the reservation are required to devote one day's labour a week, when communal projects require it. Monday is the traditional day for this type of work and, in 1960, a small group of Indians gathered at the sound of a bull's horn and worked through the day thatching and whitewashing the church, clearing the road and fencing the school yard or building a bridge. Not all participate on every occasion and, in spite of the threat of a fine by the municipal *alcalde*, the Indian *gobernador* seldom succeeded in gathering together more than 15 Indians. Some degree of participation is necessary to retain membership of the community, to confer the right to voice opinions in the council meetings and to receive land. Detailed conditions of membership will be reviewed in chapter 4.

THE SAN ANDRÉS RESERVATION

The territory of the San Andrés Páez reservation, 130 square kilometres in area,[25] stretches over mountain tops at times reaching an altitude of 9,000 feet, though most of it lies in the temperate middle altitudes. Scattered throughout this area are the houses belonging to approximately 300 Indian families, the population of the reservation.

The style of house construction, the dress of the Indians, their physical appearance and language, immediately distinguish them as a group. Some are bilingual, others can speak only Páez. They always speak of themselves as a community separate from the neighbouring White community, not merely in terms of membership of the reservation, or in connection with a different tradition, but because they feel they share a basic difference in attitude towards life, of interests, motivation, sense of propriety and even leisure. They are aware that they are not well thought of by the Whites; some accept this attitude without complaining, while others object aggressively. Mistrustful of outsiders, they hide behind a noncommittal polite behaviour which remains until intimate friendship is established; even then, though generous and helpful, they remain quiet and withdrawn even when surrounded by Indian friends. They strive physically and morally to remain as

[25] Gonzalez 1923; *Informe que el Secretario de Gobierno del Cauca rinde al Sr. Gobernador*, Popayán, 1916, chapter XVIII. There is no indication how the size of the area was estimated and the figures may be not more than a very rough calculation by a local administrator, as Tierradentro had not been properly mapped in 1961.

removed as possible from outsiders. I remember a father, when discussing the affairs of his married son, saying that no good would come of his living close to the Whites instead of in a remote site in the mountains. Not until I was well known in the area could I expect to find anyone at home if I approached a house uninvited; if the husband was away, the women and children would run to hide in the surrounding coffee grove at the first sound of my arrival. Bare legs and a glimpse of a trailing skirt would be seen disappearing through the foliage and I would be left waiting, surrounded by a harmless but noisy pack of underfed, puny, barking dogs.

Though the Páez Indians of San Andrés are nominally Catholics under the jurisdiction of the Inzá parish, they form a separate religious congregation from the Whites. Only in celebration of the town's patron saint's day do the two communities cooperate, but even then each one prepares its own separate *fiesta* which is offered on consecutive days. The system of *confraternities* does not exist in San Andrés; instead, a number of voluntary officers assume responsibility for making the necessary arrangements and bearing the cost. Not everyone feels obliged to offer *fiestas* frequently, but there always appeared to be a sufficient number of volunteers. The parish priests did not seem to concern themselves with the Indian *fiestas*, and usually no more than four took place annually.

Although t e Indian economy and the White peasant economy differ markedly in that the former has a strong subsistence orientation while the latter is primarily cash oriented, there is a symbiotic economic relation between the two communities. The Indians provide the labour for the plantations of the Whites, who consider this work degrading, and they offer a market for the trading activities of the settlers. The Whites, on the other hand, serve as intermediaries between the Indians and the Colombian marketing economy. It is this symbiotic economic relationship that has prevented the small White community, in spite of its original low capital level and persistent primitive techniques, from becoming a 'typical' poor Colombian peasant community.

The distinctiveness of the Indian community from the White peasant community does not imply cultural homogeneity for the Indian community. Some Indians differ from others in their outlook, aspirations and experience. For example, some are bilingual, others can speak only Páez, while some young people have not learned their parents' language; at the same time there are Whites who are also bilingual. Within the Indian community there are also more basic differentiations in economic orientation (see chapter 8).

Two sectors of the Indian community of San Andrés require special mention: the mestizos who about 1930 chose to break away from the reservation when an administrative opportunity permitted, and the wealthy 'progressive' Indians. Culturally these two groups are not very different and if similar administrative changes were to recur the 'progressive' Indian might repeat the decision of the mestizos. However, though the economic aspirations of the 'progressive' Indians differ from those of their Indian neighbours they still consider themselves, and are considered, as full members of the reservation. Instead of breaking completely away from the community they chose to rise within it, and by means of acquired wealth have gained a special position of influence and prestige within the Indian community as well as respect from the White community. According to the terminology derived from the analysis of Meso American and Peruvian communities it could be said that the 'progressive' Indians are becoming Ladinos or Whites. In one sense this statement would be correct; the 'progressives' have incorporated the economic aspirations of the Whites and have striven for a position of prestige recognized outside the Indian reservations. I believe, however, that by reducing this change in economic orientation to a simple desire to become a White, one overlooks the economic factors at play and the social context of economic action.

Some of the 'progressive' Indians have economic interests which not only differ from those of the rest of the community but which run counter to them; they are as a result both respected and feared. It is generally thought by the 'traditional' Indians that their wealthy 'progressive' neighbours will, from personal interest, try to bring about the dissolution of the reservation system, and hence they prefer not to see 'progressives' elected as *cabildo* officers. Furthermore, though considered to be Indians they are also referred to, somewhat pejoratively, as semi-Whites. It is not cultural 'passing' which is implied in the word semi-White but the suspected desire of the 'progressive' Indians to seek, together with the Whites, the subdivision of the reservation. This evaluation is correct; Whites would like to see the old system of Indian protection disappear so as to facilitate the purchase of land; the 'progressive' Indians would also like to be able to increase their holdings, and, more important still, to have freehold titles to permit the mortgaging of their land. Here 'passing' refers to a specific change in economic interest. Among the 'traditional' Indians there may be equally ambitious individuals, but they have contained their expanded economic activities within the reservation system, and are considered enlightened members of the Indian comm nity.

If the Indian comm nity is not homogeneous, neither is the White community. Its smallness and newness has tempered wealth and class distinctions which will probably become greater as time passes.

If I may venture to speculate I would suggest that when the reservation system disappears the present Indian community will be integrated into the White community at different levels. The process will be based on the choices open for individual action and the degree of acceptance or rejection by other Indians and Whites. The weakness of the *cabildo* and the absence of any religious organizations such as the *confraternities* of Meso-America will contribute to the rapid disintegration of the Indian community as a semi-autonomous social unit. This point will become clearer after the discussion of land tenure, land inheritance and distribution of food. In dealing with these points I shall discuss the economic and political mechanisms which function to keep the Indian community together as a distinct socio-economic entity.

AREA OF STUDY

The original purpose of this study was to observe and analyse whether commercial contact had affected traditional relations and patterns of exchange. Tierradentro was selected because of the existence of independent Indian communities not yet completely drawn into a market economy, thus providing a relatively simple situation which would permit the investigator to concentrate on the analysis of a few economic relations. The area was also known to contain a number of very different communities that would allow the selection of a community of particular interest to the study. The selection of San Andrés was partly fortuitous and partly intentional. I was offered a place of residence by the Institute of Anthropology, Bogotá, only 2 km from the San Andrés settlement. I was given a room in a small building where a nurse, a caretaker and a workman also lived. I lived there for 13 months during 1960–1. Difficulties in finding other lodgings and the special characteristics of the San Andrés settlement – recent White immigration and still more recent road connections with the outside world – decided its final selection for the study.

The San Andrés reservation is too large and too difficult to cover. Thus the study had to concern itself with only a section of the reservation. Selection was based on local economic differentiation which is due to agricultural specializations that respond to climatic conditions and to distances to the various market or trading centres. The area studied was that inhabited by Indians and Whites who used the San Andrés market and the San Andrés traders as the outlet for their coffee harvest and as the main purchasing centre. I have therefore taken an economic area, rather than a political area *per se*. In this book I shall discuss only the activities of the Indians, most of whom are reservation Indians, but 17 Indian tenant farmers living just outside the reservation boundaries are included as they are closely associated with the San Andrés Reservation and with the San Andrés market and in many cases are descendants of San Andrés Indians. On map 1 the area studied stretches from the motor road along the path that leads to San Andrés, and comprises also the mountains that surround the settlement to the north and east.

2

The Domestic Unit

THE KINSHIP SYSTEM

The nuclear family is the only effective kin unit in San Andrés. Corporate groups beyond the nuclear family are confined to the localized land-controlling bodies, the reservations. An individual belongs to a reservation because he or she was born in it, which means, in fact, that he or she belongs to the reservation of the mother or the father depending on the residence of the parent.[1] But a kinship tie in itself gives the individual no definite position in the life of the Páez community.

Though kinship is neither the only nor the most important factor which affects the economic activities of an Indian, it is certainly one of them. For this reason I shall here briefly summarize the terminological distinctions of the system and existing kinship obligations; in the last section of this chapter I shall attempt to evaluate the relative significance of kin and other social ties.

Terminologically the Páez kinship system does not distinguish between father and mother's kin. It is also generational, that is, all father's siblings or mother's siblings share the same term and no distinction is made between, for example, brother and parent's sibling's children. A sex distinction is made, however, up to two generations below Ego. I found a great deal of confusion among informants as to the terms to be used and noticed that a terminological distinction between nuclear family members and other kin was maintained by adopting the Spanish terms *hermanos* (brothers), *primos* (cousins) while if a cousin was very young he might be called *sobrino* (nephew).

Kin terms are not used as terms of address and respect is indicated

[1] For a detailed discussion of the prerequisites for reservation membership, see chapter 3.

by politeness or restraint and by extending a formal greeting. But formality and respect are not important aspects of Páez kin contacts; if an Indian sees one of his senior relatives very frequently he will greet him or her only casually and with a passing joke.

Surnames introduced by the Spanish missionaries[a] are passed down from father to children. There is a vague feeling of kinship amongst all individuals who share the same patronymic. 'We are cousins', they will say, using the Spanish term to denote no more than a vague relation. The rule of exogamy applies to each patronymic group; this has suggested to Bernal Villa (1955, pp. 165–88), I believe without foundation, that these groups represent survivals of the previously existing clan. Patronymic groups hold no property nor do they assume social, religious or political responsibilities.

Obligations amongst kin outside the nuclear family are vague and phrased only in terms of general assistance in case of emergencies which is clearly not obligatory. This undefined pool of relatives, who may or may not share the same patronym, nevertheless constitutes a possible source of assistance. In a crisis, however, the claim of an existing friendly contact counts more than the genealogical distance that separates the two individuals concerned.

RESIDENTIAL UNITS

The household, consisting most frequently of a nuclear family, is the most important social and economic unit in Páez society. Husband, wife and children work together in the same fields and share a very simple lonely dwelling perched on top of a mountain or on one of its steep slopes. The house, which the family shares with chickens, and guinea pigs, surrounded by flower bushes and small vegetable garden, and shaded by fruit trees, constitutes the small world within which the cycle of the Páez family is essentially lived. Separated from neighbouring houses by a coffee plantation, large maize and manioc fields, steep rock and mountain

[a] Spanish Christian names combined with Indian names already appeared in the documents of 1719, see Sig. 2892 (Col. c, 1–17t), Archives of the University of Popayán. In the last tribute document encountered, the combined names were still used as first names and the children were not given any of the names of either parent, see Sig. 3825 (Col. c, 1–17t), 1740, Archives of the University of Popayán, Popay . Only later was the Indian name used as a patronymic. This is substantiated by Castillo i Orozco 1877.

crevices, the Páez family has little incentive to visit even its closest neighbours.

The house itself is a simple, more or less temporary dwelling of mud, cane and thatch. The variation in style is, however, great and does not coincide strictly with differences in wealth. Some of the buildings are of simple and careless construction. A thatched roof is supported by a cane frame-work and the walls are made of uneven vertical canes tied together with reeds. The floor of packed earth is strewn with corn cobs, bunches of bananas and plantains, manioc and arracacha, the food supply for a few days. Drinking calabashes and aluminium pots are strewn about in seeming disorder.[3] Everything else hangs from pegs or gaps in the walls. Sewing needles are embedded in the canes; a bottle of kerosene and perhaps another of fer ented sugar cane hangs from any available hook along with several *jigras* – bags of looped fibre, full of clothing, food, and miscellaneous articles. One or more machetes are safely stored between the canes. A platform along one or more walls at a height of approximately 24 inches, made of split pindo canes,[4] serves as an extra storage area which is sometimes even used for sleeping. Otherwise hides are stretched close to the three stones that surround the fire in order to keep the family warm at night. Always present are a store-purchased hand mill for grinding maize and coffee, a block of salt, and a grinding stone. In a different room, if the house is partitioned, is placed a long hollowed trunk where the cane juice is fermented. Small blocks of wood that serve as chairs and head rests are often the only furniture, though sometimes, to my surprise, I was brought a locally manufactured chair to sit on while visiting some of the poorest households. In some of the bigger and better-made houses a table and a bench are kept in a corner and reserved almost solely for visitors. In the house of one of the wealthiest Indians a wooden bed is

[3] The average stock of utensils is: 2 or 3 metal spoons, a few home-made spoons, 1 or 2 kitchen knives, 4 enamelled bowls of different sizes, 2 or 3 enamelled plates, home-made wooden troughs, 3 or 4 aluminium cooking pots of different sizes, 1 or 2 clay pots. Families 1, 21 and 23 (see Table 31) had china cups and plates; family 1 used them to serve cooked food to customers on market days. Only family 1 did not own a purchased hand mill, used for grinding maize and coffee. Family 23 had a bread oven, seldom used because bread is expensive to make. The average investment in household goods was about $170 (Colombian pesos).

[4] Pindo (*cocos romanzoffiana*) are thin canes used for construction, while the tender shoots are eaten.

conspicuously placed in the main room.[5] In most cases, however, the small wooden blocks are the only comfort. Meat is stored exposed to the smoke on a *barbacoa* hanging above the fire. Near the house there is almost always a horse-driven wooden sugar press, built by local Indian craftsmen. The ground slopes all around the house and in some hidden corner a small cane menstrual hut may be found, though nowadays not all women use it.

Not all the houses are simple, one-room constructions with cane walls. Others are more sturdily built with mud, and white-washed walls are sometimes seen shining on the mountain slopes. Roofs of locally made tiles are at present considered desirable and, although only one Indian has so far built one, several aspire to save enough money to invest in a 'proper' roof.

Standing on one of the higher ridges one can see the roof tops scattered over slopes, ridges and mountain crevices like little hidden specks. They are connected only by a network of narrow paths often impassable except on foot, and dangerously slippery after rain. The Indians try to build their houses, if possible, close to the *caminos reales*, horse paths connecting the San Andrés community with others, and often no wider and not much safer than the smaller trails. However, the main consideration in house location is closeness to the family's coffee grove in order to discourage theft, and proximity to a source of water. The distance between neighbours varies; when a *camino real* traverses a flat surface near a stream of water sufficiently large to supply several families, two or more houses are built relatively close to each other. More often, the road rises sharply over a rocky promontory or other inhospitable terrain and half an hour's walk may be necessary to reach the next dwelling.

MEMBERSHIP OF RESIDENTIAL UNITS

The nuclear family is also a corporate landholding group and should ideally act as one economic unit. Family of procreation and

[5] Among the families studied, families 5, 21, 24 and 27 owned either a chair or a table. Families 21 and 23 were the proud owners of a small radio, sold to them by the priest who encouraged Indians to listen to the Catholic Radio station programmes. Families 23 and 27 had bought shelves for ornaments and the like and had framed family portraits hanging on the mud wall. In general, the Indians who wish to be respected by Whites spend more money on furnishings; others consider it unnecessary to do so.

household are here coterminous, until the sons and daughters set up their own household upon marriage.

This ideal pattern is not always followed and residential units consisting of more than one domestic unit or of more than one nuclear family do exist. Since the composition of residential units affects the operation of the economic unit it is best, in this case, first to discuss the nuclear family in the slightly wider physical context of the residential unit.

I have exact information on 119 residential units out of the total of 133 in the area studied. Father, mother and unmarried children are the only members of 91 households. In the remaining 28 other individuals share the house with the nuclear family. The following table lists the comp sition of these 28 households:

Table 1. Residence pattern

Members listed are those found in addition to nuclear family

Spouses of children with/without children of their own	15
Husband's mother	1
Single or married sister of head of household	4
Sisters sharing dead father's house	1
Illegitimate children of daughter	3
Wife's children from previous marriage	2
Other relatives	2
Total	28

When drawing up a table where only the kin tie with the household head is taken into consideration, we see that most of the cases are of married children with their offspring. This is the result rather of special circumstances than an attempt to prolong the life-span of the household by the retention of married chil ren. If we analyse the 15 cases where arried children with or without offspring share the same roof with their parents we can see the reasons that account for it. In three cases the son had recently married, had no children and intended to move as soon as his own house was built. Two sons and one daughter who had lost their spouses, and who were left with small children to care for, returned to the paternal home and would remain there until they remarried. In these cases a daughter had married a landless Indian who had moved in with her parents and helped his father-in-law, hoping to acquire land of his own, or perhaps to be given a plot by his wife's family. In one of these cases the young husband had already found land and was in the process of building a house for his new family. One head of a household had two married daughters living with him and I was never offered a very satisfactory explanation of their permanent residence in the paternal home. Some informants suggested that it was because their husbands were sick and unable to work in their own fields. Others suggested that it amounted to a temporary separation, or that it was a matter of convenience since the husbands' houses were situated at too great a distance from the market. In the remaining four cases the decision to remain in the paternal home was not due to exceptional circumstances but was based on common agreement that this was the most convenient arrangement for both parties, and would probably be permanent.

It is clear, therefore, that an analysis of each of the categories in Table 1 shows that the nature of the cases is quite different. The expected pattern under normal conditions is for a son upon marriage to reside with his bride in his father's house until such time as his own house is ready. It is special circumstances that determine whether a new household is built, or whether residence is established in the house of a close kinsman.

Table 2, which indicates the circumstances of residence with other kin, shows more clearly the factors that determine residence after marriage and later in life.

When a spouse dies while the children are still very small and help is needed in their upbringing, the widow or widower returns to his or her parents, if the latter are still alive. In the 5 cases where the widow, and in the 11 cases where the widower remained alone, the decision was taken either because their parents were dead, or because some of their own children were old enough to help bring up the younger ones, as well as to contribute to agricultural and domestic tasks. I know of only one case where a young widow decided to remain along with her two very small children in spite of the fact that her mother, though old, was still alive. She counted on the help of her sister's illegitimate son who lived with her most of the time. She preferred to remain on her own land to avoid the risk of having a neighbour confiscate it.

If on marriage the young husband has no land two choices are open to him: he can leave the community and work as a labourer or he can move in with his wife's family. Formerly, new land could be cleared and a new field planted. Nowadays every piece of land has an owner who is not very likely to part with any of it on a permanent basis. It is possible, but not very likely, to borrow land from a friend or a relative; and it is relatively easy, but not very profitable, to obtain permission from a white settler to cultivate a small plot on his property.

Table 2 lists a category 'by choice' which means simply that

Table 2. Factors determining residence other than neolocal

		Residing with				
Factors	*Neo-local*	*Husband's parents*	*Wife's parents*	*Other kin*	*Own children*	*Brother*
Death of wife	11	2	—	—	—	—
Death of husband	5	—	1	2	2	—
Illness of wife	—	—	—	—	1	1
Separation	2	—	—	—	—	1
Landless husband	—	—	3	1	—	2
Recent marriage	—	3	—	—	—	—
Illegitimate children	2	—	3	—	—	—
By choice	—	3	1	—	—	—
Illness of husband	1	1	1	—	—	—
Totals	21	9	9	3	3	4

none of the circumstantial factors mentioned apply. Four cases fall into this category, and in three cases the parents controlled a fair amount of land. Cuello (family 8) had two small brothers at the time of his marriage and remained in his father's house. Iuue was the youngest of all the sons; the rest were married and settled on land of their own. Both Urriaga's daughters were married, one to a man who had a considerable amount of property, the other to a very poor Indian who decided to move in to Urriaga's household. This man also had two sons, but the eldest had left the community and the youngest was only eight years old. In contrast with the above cases Akino (family 3) controlled very little land which would certainly pass to the eldest son since the only other child was mentally deficient. It is possible that the decision to remain in the house of the parents was based, in these four instances, on the possible chance of inheriting a larger proportion of land than they would otherwise have inherited. (The question of land inheritance is complex and will be discussed in a separate section.) In any case, the father-son or son-in-law relationship should be close enough to make economic cooperation based on common residence successful, and to increase the son's chance of inheriting the remaining property on the death of the head of the household.

I should make clear that although a house may be shared by two nuclear families, each has a separate fire and, where possible, a separate room. This is not so if a woman with children returns to her parents, but it is true of recently married couples for as long as they remain in the parental house. Though the two domestic units are relatively independent a considerable amount of cooperation is expected by each of them.

THE DOMESTIC UNIT

As in some cases a house contained two separate domestic units, each with its own separate landholding and budget, I shall henceforward refer to domestic rather than residential units. It will be understood that the core of these units consists of a family of procreation and that only occasionally are other individuals included. It will also be understood that these are landholding and production units, though as we shall see, land partition may take place shortly before a new domestic group is formed from the parental stem. Nevertheless, for the sake of clarity, once the development and operation of the domestic unit has been outlined, in this section I shall use the term domestic unit to refer to the minimal economic unit.

Size of the domestic unit. In 91 per cent of the cases size of the domestic unit varied only with the number of children born of each marriage; the other 9 per cent has already been discussed in Table 1. Páez families are not large. Often the number of children born in marriage number no more than four, and at the present rate of mortality[6] the number who reach adulthood is often less.

[6] The mortality rate in the municipality of Belalcázar, which should be similar to that of San Andrés, was 74 per 1000 according to an unpublished study by the 'Comisión Nacional de Rehabilitación y Servicio Nacional de Asistencia Social', 1959. Census data indicate a mortality rate of 16 per 1000, *Anuario General de Estadística*, Departamento Administrativo de Estadística, Bogotá, 1959.

According to calculations from genealogies the average number of live children per married couple is three, but it is impossible to determine the average number born. As sons work independently soon after they reach the age of 20, the average potential labour force available to any father at any one time is lower than the number of children born of the union. The average number of children younger than 20 was 2·7 per family and in considering labour potential we must remember that 40 per cent of this figure represents female children.

Development cycle of domestic unit. An individual marries, builds his house, brings up children and the cycle ends with his death. The time-span of the life cycle of the domestic unit is not very long, usually 20 to 30 years. Sometimes, by continued residence in the parental home, a three-generation depth will be achieved. But we have seen that there are very few cases of this kind. The house itself is not a durable construction; 30 years is a fair life before the canes begin to rot and the roof caves in. Within this mud and cane shell there is nothing which can be considered worth inheriting, no furniture, no objects of value, no religious objects. Land is the only permanent value attached to the household, and this is divided among the sons, together with any animals owned by the father.

Subdivision of land controlled by the household is a slow and continuous process which begins when the sons grow old enough to learn how to plant and harvest manioc and maize, as will be seen in chapter 4. In this way they gradually begin to break their dependence on the parental household. They still share the same house, eat from the same pot in which the mother has cooked the maize and the manioc that both the son and his father have brought from their fields. The son, however, is no longer expected to turn over the harvest to the father and work all the time in his father's field. Father and son help each other with agricultural tasks, the degree of cooperation depending on the closeness of the relationship and the number of younger brothers on whom the father can still depend for help.

The purchase of land by the white settlers in the area and the planting of coffee plantations big enough to require hired labour for their maintenance has in the last 20 years or so had an indirect influence on family relations. Young people can now hire themselves out as day labourers within walking distance of their houses;

previously the few who attempted this had to go much further – as much as a day's journey – and they also had to pay for food and lodgings, which left them with little financial reward for their effort. Finding work for any number of days has become very easy and is often resorted to when the land available for coffee planting is insufficient to satisfy the need for cash. The possibility of working for cash gives more independence to the young sons who remain at home. At the same time it permits families to stay together even though land is not sufficient to feed them all. Previously, all or part of the family had to emigrate seasonally or permanently to work for wages. Nowadays they can remain at home while working nearby. It would be interesting to determine whether there has been a decrease in the number of young people who have emigrated from the San Andrés community. I can only say that at present the situation is as follows:

Table 3. Residence of unmarried sons

Number of unmarried sons over 18 living at home	20
Sons over 18 who have left the community	4
Unknown cases	2
Unmarried men over 18	26

Some of the sons who had remained at home were either working for other people and/or in their own fields. Unfortunately it is very hard to determine to what extent the sons become economically independent and whether the field they cultivate produces sufficient for their own needs. At least 10 of the 20 adult sons were cultivating land of their own, and three others, who had no land, worked as labourers.

Availability of work, it is true, helps to solve domestic economic problems, but at the same time it affects the balance of power within the household. A father can no longer keep his sons at home by delaying the subdivision of the family property. If he does, his sons will refuse to work for him and depend for their subsistence on cash earned as day labourers, while waiting until the father yields to their demands. Under the threat of losing his sons who are a convenient labour force the father might decide to allot to each a piece of land sooner than he had planned, in the hope that a more peaceful cooperative arrangement of labour exchange might be worked out. At the same time the possibility of making a living while remaining at home helps to keep together families short of land, whose unmarried sons would otherwise have had to move out of the community.

Slowly the parental home begins to diminish in size and as the children marry or move out it loses its labour force and its land. This process of subdivision continues usually until the parents are left alone in a by then crumbling house, very often with little land for themselves. Sometimes, but not very frequently as we have seen, the last child to marry may decide to stay with them. Usually the old widowed father or mother continue alone as best they can. Only if ill will a parent be invited by his children to stay with them; old people are hard to live with, it is said, and parents are expected to move out as soon as they are capable of remaining alone again.

The development of a domestic group where there is a large gap in age between the children is quite different from one where the sons are born at close intervals. The rhythm followed in the process of the formation of new households from the parental household is quite different in each case and imposes special problems on the domestic economy. If the sons marry in rapid succession, the father is forced to part with a large section of the land he controls within a relatively short period of time, and may as a consequence have to find alternative means of feeding any children remaining at home. This point is further discussed in chapter 4.

Marriage and the formation of new independent domestic units. When a newly married couple build a house they become independent of the husband's family. The two families continue to visit each other, more or less frequently, depending on distance and on how well they get on with each other. The son might exchange labour with his father, and they might borrow food from each other while waiting for the corn and manioc crops to mature; but the son no longer has any obligation to work in his father's field. Often ties are maintained with the wife's family. In one instance, when an Indian had been imprisoned for having killed a woman, his wife's relatives walked more than a day over mountain roads to visit him. In another instance, however, a married woman had not troubled for many years to visit a brother who lived only half an hour away.

A son looks for a bride, perhaps with the help of his mother, but he needs the approval of the father when a formal approach is made to the bride's parents. A visit to the future in-laws by the young man and his father is the rule. They bring with them several bottles of purchased liquor, containers of home-fermented drink and perhaps a present of food, such as a chicken or other meat. If the proposer is acceptable to the bride's parents they invite him in and the ritual of drinking begins by offering first a bottle to the father, then to the mother, and last to each of the elder brothers of the bride. After all-night drinking, and perhaps dancing, the bride moves to the home of her intended husband's parents where the couple build their own fire and stretch a hide round it in a separate corner of the house. They continue to share the same roof as the husband's parents until the husband decides to build his own house. In the meantime they depend on their own efforts, their own tools and their own land to feed and clothe themselves. The new house is not usually built until the marriage is registered with the local church authority. If the couple decide that Inzá, the chief town of the municipality, lies too far away, and if the priest does not visit the nearest town at a time when they are free to be there, they might move to their new home before receiving the blessing of the Church. Pregnancy permanently binds the couple, whether they have been married by the priest or not, and from that moment separation is unthinkable. Until the woman is with child the man can return her to her family, or perhaps she may leave on her own initiative. Since no property, money, or wealth of any sort has up to that point been transferred, no problem arises when a break between childless couples takes place. This period before the union becomes final is referred to as *amaño* or 'getting used to each other'.

The length of time between marriage and the completion of the house by the husband depends on the time, money, and the source of housebuilding material available to him. It may also depend on how well the couple get on in the parental home. Very few husbands whom I questioned could remember how long they had remained in the house of their fathers before moving to their own; but some specified that it was a very short period because they could not get on with their fathers or mothers.

Only sexual relations between parents and children and with brothers or sisters are considered incestuous. There are few marriage prohibitions. The most important is the rule that one should not marry a woman bearing the same patronymic. In the one case of which I knew, where the rule had been transgressed, an attempt was made to hide it. Data obtained from records indicate another five marriages of people with the same surname, out of a total of 289. It is considered objectionable for first cousins to marry, and for uncles or aunts to marry nieces or nephews. When first cousins marry it is simply said that it is not a good idea; furthermore, the priest will charge a higher fee. Bernal Villa (1955, p. 183) mentions the belief that the tiger will eat them if married cousins cross the high altitude plain. No rule of preference is otherwise expressed and a young man may look for a bride either in his own community or in any other of the surrounding Indian settlements.

Table 4. Original residence of spouses of San Andrés families

	Woman from San Andrés	*Woman from other communities close to San Andrés*	*Woman from other communities*
Man from San Andrés	56	8	28
Man not from San Andrés	6	—	—
	—	—	—
Total	62	8	28

Partition of the domestic unit through divorce, death of father or remarriage. Once a household is established it continues to operate until the death of either or both of the spouses. Páez tradition highly disapproves of separations and Colombian law and religious precepts make divorce impossible. If tension between the spouses leads to violence the injured party first lays a complaint before the reservation council which will attempt to mediate. If the council is unsuccessful the matter then passes to the local civil authority. In my area of study there were only four cases of permanent separation. All these separations occurred long before I arrived in the community, and thus I am not in a position to offer reasons for the failure of the mechanism to prevent separation. It was said that in two of the cases the man had left the woman. In one case the woman had married a man residing in another community and after giving birth to one child had either been thrown out of the house or had moved out of her own accord. She returned to San Andrés, built a hut, and cleared a small field in the land left by her father to one of her two brothers. She had not obtained permission from her brother. A long fight between the two of them ensued, and either because she had a vile tongue or knew how to manipulate the municipal authority he was forced to let the matter rest and barely managed to restrict her to a very small plot. She kept the daughter born of her marriage, and the two, with the help of a second child born to her illegitimately, led a precarious life cultivating a very small piece of land and selling prepared food on market days. In another case, a young girl had left her husband but managed a much more comfortable arrangement, temporarily at least. Her brother (family 11) received her and her young son into his house. He felt sorry for her and for the child, but also looked forward to the time when the child would be old enough to assist him. But the child died, and the arrangement deteriorated until she finally moved out. I could never discover where she went. In the third case, the wife was left alone with a small daughter when her husband left the community with another woman. She managed to remain alone in the house her husband had built, and to work the small plot of land he possessed. It was a small amount of land and this may account for the fact that he never returned to claim it. The separation had taken place long before, the daughter had grown up, married a landless Indian and lived at her mother's house. Not so fortunate was the Indian woman in the last of the cases of separation. While her husband was away in jail, which frequently happened, she had an affair with another man. The husband, who on his return had become aware of her infidelity, left her and the child. Her companion also left her. She shifted aimlessly from place to place until she finally settled in the house of a mestizo earning her keep as a servant. The husband in the meantime had found another woman and raised another family.

Two other separations seemed about to occur while I was living in the community, but they resolved themselves, at least temporarily. In both cases the woman had run away from her husband. Each wife had been subjected to insult and injury, and even though by local standards the two had good reason to leave their husbands, their action was highly disapproved and they were forced to return to their homes while their husbands were fined for their behaviour.

In the previous section I discussed only the cases where the domestic unit remained together even after the death of the husband. More often, however, the wife remarries and moves in with her husband, either taking her children with her or abandoning them to different fates. Abandonment of children, who are later picked up by friends and relatives or by White families who need the help of a young child, is quite frequent. It was difficult to determine exactly how often and in what cases it had happened as people were reluctant to talk on the subject. Of nine widows who had either remarried or lived with another man four had abandoned their children; in a fifth case it was the grown-up children who had decided not to accompany the mother to the house of their stepfather.

It is very hard to keep the family harmoniously together when remarriage takes place. The Páez are quite aware of this and many a lonely widow or widower complained that it was better to put up with the extra work of housekeeping without the help of a spouse, than to add complications by finding another husband or wife; remarriage does not often take place until the children have themselves married. If at the time of the mother's remarriage one of the sons is married, as happened in one case, he is left in charge of his deceased father's land. In this instance the other younger children moved with the mother to the home of the stepfather.

A wife, even if she does not remarry, has not enough authority to keep the children from fighting, and taking upon themselves the settlement and distribution of land. In spite of a great deal of affection that, in one case, three grown sons had for their very old mother – a woman who commanded respect as a wise, strong and kind individual within the community – she was unable to keep them from fighting, dividing the land, and moving away from her even before they themselves married.

We have so far discussed how the domestic unit may be disrupted by either separation or by the death of the family head before the domestic unit has completed its full cycle of growth. As we have noticed, no provision exists to delegate authority to another member of the household or to a kinsman structurally capable of assuming a position of authority. The wife, though often well versed in economic activities and perhaps more capable than the husband of dealing with White traders, is never in a position of authority over her grown-up children. All male sons are considered equal and ties with father's and mother's kin are not very important. An uncle may help and advise if asked to do so, but he has no authority over his brother's or sister's children. With the death of the head of the household it becomes very difficult to keep the children together and it is only possible nder certain special circumstances, such as either the extreme youth of the children, or their sex, where competition for authority is minimized.

Authority within the domestic unit. We have said that the household is the unit of production and consumption; its adult members are obliged to share in productive activities: tilling the fields, harvesting the coffee, and manufacturing cloth and utensils. At the same time they receive benefits in the form of food and clothing provided by the head of the household. The land and the tools of production, either purchased or manufactured by the head of the household, are under his control yet he exercises this right only as the guardian of the family property. The right to cultivate certain fields is registered under his name, and he may transfer it without consulting or seeking the approval of other members of the household. Sometimes the wife may inherit property – most frequently animals – which theoretically she may dispose of as she pleases. Actually, she has to have her h sband's approval for any transactions, and it is understood that at least part of the profits, in the event of her property being sold, should be invested in food or household utensils.

The father, as the head of the household, has authority over the wife and children and he may punish them with moderation if they challenge his authority. He is expected, however, to be benevolent, and often he prefers to let the mother discipline the children while they are still small. A strong unyielding father, it is said, will cause his children to run away and become drifters. But even though the husband's and father's authority over his wife and children is an accepted fact, sympathy will be very often with the one who receives his angry beating. He may even be fined if the punishment is considered unnecessary or out of proportion to the transgression; but the wife or the child who has run away to avoid his beating or his machete is always forced to return to him. A wife must return home to work for her husband and raise his children because, in their own words, a man cannot live alone and the wife's place is by his side. An illustration of this is the case of Vicente who had married a hardworking Indian woman from another community and had had three children by her. They did not agree; quarrels were frequent and neighbours often had to interfere to protect her from his pointless beatings. In spite of strong disapproval from the rest of the comm ity he maintained an illegitimate relation with a young girl and to everyone's surprise brought her to his house. The already tense relationship between husband and wife exploded and one night with the help of a neighbour she ran away. Each partner complained to the local authority. He was fined but she was forced to return. As she meekly walked behind Vicente they passed a group of Indians who were sympathetic to her case but nonetheless all commented that it was only right that she should return.

Wife and children, according to their capabilities, have to work in the fields or perform domestic duties. Job allocation rests ultimately in the hands of the head of the household; a woman has to have his permission before she sets up the loom to start weaving an *anake* (long skirt) for herself or *ruanas* (ponchos) for the children. He monopolizes the labour of the family and maintains this privilege until the sons, at approximately the age of 18, begin to question his authority. As they grow older, whether married or not, sharing his food or not, they lead a more independent life. The final break is reached when the father gives consent to his son's marriage. Before marriage young men start working as wage labourers now and then, and keep the money they earn. Property acquired by their own efforts can be disposed of as they wish; the father has no control over it. Wife and daughters are always expected to hand over most of their individual earnings. When a business transaction involving a woman's labour takes place, it has to be carried out with the husband, who also receives any money obtained in payment. But both husband and wife always insisted to me, very vehemently, that the money earned by the wife was hers, and that she could buy with it whatever she wanted. When pressed further they indicated that, of course, she was expected to buy sugar, potatoes, meat or candles whenever she happened to have a few coins in her hand. Her obligations towards the household seemed to be so obvious that there seemed to be no need to state them. Perhaps also the obligations of each member of the household to the common budget are too subtle, too involved and too dependent upon conditions, to be stated in terms of precise patterns.

The head of the household is expected to provide the family with food, clothing and fuel either obtained from his fields or purchased in the local stores. Very often, however, the money is spent on liquor before he has carried out his good intentions to purchase something for the family. The more aggressive woman bitterly complains when her husband lies drunk by the side of the road, but she has no authority to prevent him from drinking and no mechanism has developed to control the situation which has resulted from the introduction of purchased liquor. The husband takes the coffee harvest to sell in the market or in one of the stores, and on the same day may spend most of the money he receives on farming equipment, animals, food, clothing and liquor, without previously consulting his wife. If he has a horse, he leads the way mounted when he goes to town, while his wife and children walk behind laden with bags full of coffee beans and food to sell. Only when the load is really too great and the wife and children cannot carry it all does he strap a loaded *jigra* across his chest. The wife seldom stays at home and certainly not when there is to be a *fiesta* or a drinking get-together. A small child is usually left behind to keep the fire going and frighten away a possible thief, while the rest of the family file down the narrow paths towards the town or the house where the celebration is to take place. If the wife remains at home when her husband goes to town to drink, it is because she is sick or prefers not to join him. On occasions other than social he might decide that she must remain at home while he departs alone or with a child, to work in another field, to complete a business transaction, or to hire himself out as a labourer in the same or another community.

FRIENDSHIP AND KINSHIP TIES

Páez Indians are excellent walkers. But too much time and energy can be spent in distant visits and even these Indians are not willing to visit friends and relatives in other communities too frequently, unless they deem it necessary. Everyday contact is restricted to immediate neighbours, if any, and if they are on speaking terms. Carelessness in the use of a common water source, shooting a pig that has just finished consuming a supply of manioc, unintentional burning of the neighbour's coffee grove while preparing a field for planting, are a few of the many tensions that can sour a previously friendly relationship.

A Páez family is up by four o'clock in the morning. In the semi-darkness one can hear them march down the road probably going to work in a field far from their houses. A man is accompanied by his wife and children, walking fast and silently without greeting, as they pass the house of a friend. They do not return until sunset. After a long day's work visiting is rare, unless the families live next door to each other and are very good friends. This working schedule continues indefinitelywithout any patterned break. I was never able to count on finding anyone at home and a house often had to be visited four times before I met with success. Not even market days are reserved as a day of rest. With no official day of rest, Indian families often have the same bad luck as I had when they decide to visit a friendly household. As a result, visiting is perhaps most frequently left for special occasions when a family has been invited to share a prepared measure of fermented drink, or when *mingas* – work parties – are called. Attended by neighbours, friends and visitors, *mingas* end in drinking, eating and dancing.

Situations in which social contact between households take place are as follows: the market place, the trading stores where people go to sell their coffee and then remain for several drinks, business contacts in the household, work parties or *mingas*, funerals and marriages, and drinking parties at home. All these situations are very different and they reflect different aspects of the social ties between households.

Visiting involves virtually the whole family. When the Indian family arrives at the household they intend to visit they sit outside and wait until the host comes out and extends a formal greeting. Drink and food are brought to them, or some other gesture is made to indicate that the visit is appreciated. This makes the opening for communications and the visit may last all night if drink is available. Visits are expected to be returned. Some of the Indian households are known for planting sufficient cane to be able, occasionally, to grind and ferment sugar cane juice for parties. These gatherings are not expected to be returned or repaid in kind. Friends and close relatives are invited and at the same time the word is passed round so that acquaintances feel free to drop in. When I asked a woman whether she was in close contact with the only cousin she had left in the community she told me that they did not get along very well together and never really visited each other. She only saw him when he came to join a drinking party at her home. Inter-household visiting, on the other hand, is a reflection of a close friendship or close kin tie. It takes place between two families with all its members participating. The contact is intentional and has to be reciprocated on two levels. Food, drink or a small parting gift must be offered and the visit has to be returned eventually.

Not all Indians attend the market place with the same frequency, and distance has something to do with this. Seldom more than 40 families are seen to congregate by the side of the church where the traders come to display their wares. Individuals remain quite aloof from each other in spite of ties of friendship and kinship. Greetings are exchanged and sometimes a young man may ask for a blessing from his god-parent; but soon afterwards each one drifts away. Each Indian stands alone surrounded by wife and children most of the time as if in search of a profi able business opportunity, though this of course is seldom the case. Only rarely do groups of friends or cliques develop. I was able to gather only negative information, that is, to determine unfriendly ties between close relatives who refused to greet each other. Social contact in the market takes place by chance and with anyone except enemies.

Late in the mornings when the market has finished, if an Indian has any money left from a sale, he drifts to one of the many houses where beer and hard liquor are sold and may spend most of his money there. If he has seen a special friend, or an Indian with whom he wishes to transact business, or a relative seldom visited, he invites him to join him. After purchasing the liquor they join the circle of attendants and a constant exchange of drinks keeps the group together either until a fight scatters them, or the beer supply, or the money, is exhausted. If possible, they avoid entering a store where they might find an unfriendly face and if once inside they notice an enemy they leave as inconspicuously as possible. Women, on occasion, drink as much as men. They do not, however, always join the husband when he is drinking with a friend. This type of social contact does not necessarily involve the whole family, but is carried out between individuals; nor does it involve an obligation to reciprocate at a future date. For every beer that an individual receives he has to buy one in return, but is not obliged to invite the same individual again.

When an Indian needs to purchase food or wishes to sell an

animal, he visits the person with whom the business transaction is to be carried out. He goes alone, perhaps carrying a small present if a service is to be requested. The two Indians involved in the transaction will be good friends or relatives; a stranger or a very slight acquaintance is seldom approached in these matters. Most of the time, especially if the two individuals do not see each other frequently, the business contact ends in a long visit.

Work parties, *mingas*, are attended by friends, neighbours and relatives and their families. The work in the field stops early in the afternoon when a big meal is served. This is followed by drinking and perhaps dancing that might continue all night long. An invitation to work in a *minga* does not imply that the host must reciprocate and offer his labour at a later date, though in practice he might do so, because he forms part of a circle of friends who depend on each other for labour in *mingas*.

It is through these different types of social contact that friendship ties may develop and be maintained. Until a pattern of inter-household visiting has been established exchange of food and services between two families is not expected.

Proximity of residence makes it easier for two families to maintain social contact. At the same time it offers a possible area of conflict; I found that bitter enemies often proved to be neighbours. When quarrels and arguments are averted between neighbours, the families concerned are brought together by a series of mutual obligations necessitated by their close proximity: for example, the path has to be constantly cleared and sometimes after torrential rain has to be re-opened. The channel that brings the water close to their households has to be cleaned so that the water can run freely. It is difficult to evaluate the importance of the ties between neighbours and how influential they are in the development of friendship ties. I knew the close friends of 35 household heads and in 11 of the cases both were close neighbours; five others lived between half an hour and an hour away from each other and the remainder were close relatives.

It is harder still to evaluate the respective influences of friendship and kinship ties. At times of crisis a Páez Indian might turn to a close relative and ask for his help, but in many situations it is a friend who comes to the rescue. Answers to questions on this subject were vague and often only incomplete information could be gathered. The most frequent situations that were observed were cases of sickness or injury serious enough to need the help and cooperation of another individual. In one instance the Indian in question seemed to be at a complete loss as to where he could ask for the help he needed.

Nevertheless, we cannot overlook the fact that in 19 instances the close friend was also a close relative and that only 11 other cases were immediate neighbours. If a relative, he was most probably either a brother of the head of the household or his wife's brother; the friendship continued even after the death of the wife. Contact with close kin was maintained, the frequency of visits depending partly on distance. What concerns us here, however, is how far ties of cooperation between households are based on kinship rather than on friendship and proximity.

It seems best, therefore, to describe first those situations in which cooperation is necessary to the life of the household. We exclude those situations which arise exclusively from the close proximity of two households, that is where maintenance of a common road, and water channel, etc., are necessary, because here the situation itself defines which household can provide the necessary cooperation.

In its everyday effort to procure food the household often needs outside labour. It is easier and quicker to clear a field when several adult males are helping, and weeding is a troublesome job which a Páez prefers to do with the help of others. I shall not discuss here why no outside help is sought when coffee is harvested, or the economic considerations that arise in all these cases, but rather the source of labour when the decision to call a work party has already been made. It is true that the Indians who join the *mingas* are those who have no urgent work to do, and that a household head cannot count on a kinsman who lives too far away. Nevertheless, in spite of these difficulties, most of the Indians asked, suggested that kinsmen would be the first to be invited to join a work party. It is impossible to confirm this statement with meaningful statistics. For very specific economic reasons not many people can afford to call a *minga*, and of the 26 families whose economic activities I followed closely very few had actually done so. If an insufficient number of kinsmen is available then friends and neighbours are called in. There is little reluctance to accept the invitation, since feasting and dancing always follow the work. It is harder to persuade friends to help with the weeding when the only inducement is repayment in kind. If a household head cannot afford to call a *minga*, he has to depend on close kin with whom he is in close contact or, more often, to resign himself to working alone. Of the 26 families I studied, eight had done all the work alone – two because of hostile relations with all living close relatives, and the remainder from preference and practical convenience. Four other families either preferred, or were forced in the circumstances, to hire labourers by the day and to pay them wages. Three other families invited only friends and neighbours to their *mingas*, one because their relatives lived too far away, and the other two, for unknown reasons. The remaining eleven families depended mostly on relatives who were either invited to participate in a *minga*, or asked to work on the basis of labour exchange.

The basic crops that serve as staples in Páez diet do not mature at the same time in all households, partly because of the difference in altitude, and partly because they are not always planted at the same time. When a household runs out of food, another might have enough to spare and it ought not be too difficult for anyone to find an Indian who might be willing to sell or exchange manioc; yet it is difficult. Indians often have to depend on obligations arising from friendship or kinship to be able to purchase food for their families while waiting for their own crops. None of them liked to talk about their specific food transactions, and therefore it is hard to determine whether they depend on kinsmen more frequently than on neighbours and acquaintances for their purchases. I have, however, a strong suspicion that the first was the case. At least this was so in most of the cases I observed.

When he visits another community, or if night falls before he can reach home, an Indian feels free to approach the house of a kinsman and ask to be allowed to spend the night there. A kinsman can also be expected to come when a member of the family has died, so as to attend the funeral and help with the burial. Only if the deceased is in the immediate family does an Indian spend money on candles and liquor and thus contribute to the expenses incurred on the occasion.

In situations where help and cooperation is urgently needed owing to sickness of serious injury, close kin do not always offer to help. I found many puzzling cases of this kind. Information was easily gathered since all cases of serious injury and most cases of serious illness came to the attention of the resident nurse and myself. Páez attitudes to medicine and sickness may be relevant here, but I believe the question goes deeper than that. I remember one night when the *cabildo* officers brought in a seriously injured Indian and then left to inform his wife and mother. I discussed with him the possibility of finding a friend or relative who would help to transport him, and he laughed very bitterly and said that it was unlikely, since people in San Andrés seldom bothered about anyone else. It proved to be true, at least in this case, and after a fruitless day's search and after discussing with his godfather and friends, I had to make other arrangements. It should be noted that a *fiesta* was being held in the town at the time of the accident, and this would make the case rather a special one; but in most of the cases observed special claims could also be made.

Brothers and their parents do stand together when an outsider accuses any of them, or attempts to confiscate some of their land. If a brother is jailed, the others will stand by – except in one inexplicable case – and probably help the wife and children. If brothers or parents are killed it is difficult to establish whether any other kin seeks vengeance. Eight years ago an Indian went to jail for avenging the death of a cousin. It was a rare and involved case that was still very much talked about at the time of my study.

3

The Cost of Bringing Up a Family

TO BE AN INDIAN

Barefoot, clad in store-purchased cotton pants and shirt, protected from the sun and dew by an old felt hat, which seems through age and wear to have acquired the personality of its owner, the peasant walks to and fro between his house and fields. If the peasant is wearing a shor home-made *ruana* or poncho blanket, then we can be sure that he is an Indian. He never takes off this garment even in the heat, and he always carries with him the small decorated knotted woollen bag in which he keeps his coca, lime, and a few coins or other small possessions. His wife weaves his ponchos and laboriously knots the woollen threads which give shape and colour to the bag.[1] On her home-made simple loom here is always a length of cloth to be completed. It will either make a poncho for her husband or sons, or a skirt length for herself or her daughters. In San Andrés women do not make any other item of their clothing for they are otherwise fully occupied; even when walking they either spin wool or fibres, or knot the small decorated bags or the larger carrier bags made of local fibres. The bright blouses they wear, and the Indian-style long, decorated straps with which they tie their babies to their backs are made by the local White peasants and sold in shops. The black shawls they wear for warmth are manufactured in the big cities and sold locally.

It is only the Indian who aspires to become a White who will buy a manufactured poncho, while his wife will purchase a cotton dress, thus becoming indistinguishable in a crowd of peasants. A wide choice of clothing and luxuries is open to him if he has the money: shoes, cigarettes, ear-rings, flashlights, cotton ponchos, dentures, etc. All these expenses are impossible to estimate and useless to express as a normative quantity.

[1] For a detailed description of Páez handicrafts, see Bernal and Nachtigal 1955.

An Indian who has money will purchase more; if he has no sheep of his own to provide him with wool, he will either buy it, barter it, or go without a new poncho until he can afford it. His status in the community does not depend on how well dressed he and his family are, nor on the elaborateness of his dwelling and furnishings. There are individuals, however, who from personal preference take care in the way they dress and who find it more cheerful to sit in front of a framed photograph of the Virgin. But if they want to be respected by their White neighbours, Indians must buy some of these luxuries and have a 'decent' house, neatly arranged with photographs and small ornaments.

Before dawn and just before leaving for their fields, Páez peasants have their first meal. It usually consists of a plantain and manioc stew, or, when maize is available, of a special meal of ground and spiced fresh kernels. If money is available, the Indian housewife may prepare a breakfast of sugared water, fried plantains and perhaps a piece of bread. Ideally, Indians like to eat a midday meal, or at least a snack of fruit and roasted manioc; it is not always possible because of work and poverty. The main evening meal is different only in that, when there is sufficient food available or money to buy meat, the stew will be richer and more plentiful. During harvest time the variety of ingredients added is greater. Blanched maize, dried and ground maize, cabbage, manioc, arracacha (a tuber similar to manioc), beans, plantains and yellow marrow, which are added to the pot, come from their own fields. The food is spiced with onions, parsley and hot peppers from their own garden, and with purchased garlic and cumin; it is often coloured with wild *achiote*.[2]

Other more elaborate dishes are prepared for special occasions and require the purchase of sugar, fat, etc. Indians like to eat well and to consume large quantities of roast meat or chicken. During the coffee harvest when there is money available, they buy one or two pounds of meat a week, or at least some blood for sausages. Between harvests the meat consumption by Indians is nil. Occasionally a trader brings dried fish, which is highly desired by Indians, but purchases are small and only when there is money to spare.

Luxury foods available at the local shop are numerous: candies,

[2] *Achiote* (*Biza Orellana*), the seed of a wild shrub which, when soaked and crushed, produces a yellow pigment used for colouring food.

bread, fat, sardines, rice, noodles, potatoes, sugar, soft drinks, etc. Expenditure on alcohol can be quite heavy; during harvest-time when Indians have money from the sale of their coffee, a visit to San Andrés or Inzá means spending several hours drinking with friends. From November to February, Wednesday market visits last until late in the afternoon. An Indian friend complained that he could not come to market very often because he had too many friends and so he would always get drunk. I had noticed that this Indian often sent his nephew to sell his onions, instead of going to market himself. It is not expected of Indians that they visit the hamlet to drink, but once there, an invitation cannot be refused and has to be reciprocated. It is impossible to calculate expenses of this nature, as not all Indians equally enjoy drinking.

REGULAR DOMESTIC EXPENSES

I would have liked to gather information on daily and weekly expenses in the form of budgets from all my informants, but this task proved impossible and I soon discovered that the information gathered on weekly and fortnightly bases was incomplete. To gather accurate information on patterns of expenditure would be a project in itself. I shall not attempt to analyse income and expenditure here, but only to give a rough idea of basic cash requirements. Investment in tools, equipment and improvements can be more easily obtained and will be discussed in a later chapter.

Table 5. Minimum yearly household requirements for two adults and three children, and cost of purchased items

Items	*Amount*	*Cost (Colombian $)*
Kerosene	50 l.	25
Candles	240	24
Soap	20 bars	28
Salt	56 lb.	20
Cumins	—	26
Raw sugar	312 lb.	140
Total purchased	—	$263
Plantain stems	52–100	—
Manioc plants	500	—
Arracacha plants	300	—
Maize	900 lb.	—

The items listed in this table are those considered as absolutely necessary weekly expenditures. The food indicated is also used to feed chickens, and it is impossible to calculate what proportion of the food brought to the house is used only for cooking purposes. The calculations are based on average estimates so as to give a summary idea of household expenditure among Páez families.

Meat is purchased when there is money available, most frequently during the coffee harvest. The amount purchased during this season depends on whether the family employs paid labour and on the cash income of the farmer; some families purchase 6 lb. of meat – those with large coffee plantations – but more frequently 1 to 2 lb. a wee . After the coffee harvest is over meat consumption decreases considerably; among the 27 families studied 2 purchased 2 to 4 lb. of meat fortnightly, 7 purchased only occasionally,[3] 11 purchased no more than 7 lb. each between coffee harvests, and 7 did not purchase any meat in the same period. Any other meat consumed by these families was of animals owned by them.

Driedfishisstocked by one trader from December to July and only sporadically during the rest of the year. It is unli ely that a family of four to five members purchases more than 1½ lb. monthly.

The purchase of other luxury foods is too irregular to calculate. The prices are disproportionately high when compared with the daily wage of an Indian. A worker earning $2.50 to $3 (Colombian pesos) per day has to pay $1.10 for a pound of rice, $1.70 for a pound of meat, $1.70 for a pound of fat and 40 to 50 cents for a pound of sugar (see appendix for a more complete list of prices).

The amount spent annually on lothing depends on whether traditional dress is worn,[4] where the garment is purchased and the quality desired. Among 14 of the 27 families for which budget information is available, expenditures varied from 30 to 300 Colombian pesos. The highest amount was spent by a wealthy Indian. The average per family for the year was 96 Colombian pesos. But it must be remembered that not all families buy lothing annually.

[3] These families bought meat at other markets and I was unable to determine the amounts or the frequency of their purchases.

[4] Among the married women who lived in the area studied, 109 wore traditional dress most of the time and had a cotton dress for special occasions; five women wore traditional or cotton dresses indiscriminately, and 32 wore only cotton dresses.

THE COST OF BEING A PARENT

Children are born and have to be baptized; they grow up and marry; members of the family fall sick or die. Each one of these recurring incidents or crises in the life of the Páez is marked by ritual, and requires expenditure of money or of food. In the case of sudden sickness or death, planning and preparation to meet the added expense is impossible. The immediate family has to shoulder the responsibility as best it can, either by forgoing other expenditure or by borrowing from traders and repaying later with labour – borrowing from friends or kin is very difficult as very few Indians have spare cash available. A trader will lend money to an Indian if a crisis has afflicted the family, but it is unlikely that he will do so to allow the Indian to celebrate a *fiesta* or a marriage feast. The amount spent on life-cycle ceremonies depends on the source of credit available to the Indian, how far ahead planning is possible and on family savings in cash or cattle.

Birth and baptismal ceremonies. When a child is born no outsider, either specialist or kin, is called to help. The only expense incurred is the special diet of the mother. A chicken is killed to make a mild soup with rice and potatoes; manioc is substituted for other foods. One Indian spent $3.20 (Colombian pesos) to buy rice and potatoes, while the chicken killed was his own. Another Indian spent $9.00 and bought canned mackerel, bread, potatoes, noodles and chocolate.

One or two months after the child's birth it is baptized. The godparents accompany the father and mother to Inzá and the afternoon is spent drinking together if the two *compadres*[5] are old friends. A few months or perhaps even years later a *cuido* or feast is given for the godparents. In some cases the feast assumes large proportions and a small calf is killed for the numerous guests. In other cases only the godparents are invited. In addition to the food provided for other guests, the godparents must be served half a chicken each, a small sponge-type cake and a glass of home-made wine. One particular *cuido* I attended cost $60, but most of the food required came from the Indian's own farm and he had, in

[5] Parents address the godparents of their own child as *compadres* (co-parents). This term is also used by the godparents. Though this mutual relationship is not as important as in Spain, it does entail reciprocal obligations.

fact, to spend only $6. Another Indian purchased most of the food to be consumed and spent almost $50. A third Indian killed one of his calves and purchased a large quantity of store liquor. The godparents usually give the godchild a dress and hat and, if it is a girl, a pair of ear-rings as well.

How much a father decides to spend on a baptismal *cuido* depends on whether he has animals to kill, whether he has money, can borrow it, or can buy on credit; it also depends on how many children he has and how close in age they are to one another. Among the Páez there is no strong social pressure to spend a stipulated amount of money on any ceremony and the more expensive feasts are not always given by the wealthiest families.

Marriage. The only expense incurred is for the gift of drink and a small amount of food given to the bride's family by the groom's family, as well as the feast which the bride's parents have to give in honour of the godparents.

The gift offered by the groom and his family when the marriage is arranged amounts to $10 to $20 (Colombian pesos) in liquor, and the rest is food from their farm. I cannot estimate the cost of the feast as only one marriage took place while I was in San Andrés, shortly after my arrival.

Death. The burial ceremony is very simple and requires only the purchase of a few yards of white cloth in which to wrap the corpse, and candles to burn during the wake. Flowers are given by friends or White neighbours and the priest is not called to give the last rites. The only expense is for entertainment.

Close kin and friends, if they live nearby, are expected to attend the wake and to accompany the family to the cemetery. All the attendants have to be fed and entertained with purchased or home-fermented liquor. The amount of food and drink served depends on the suddenness of the death. Once, when I was asked to visit a sick Indian I noticed that a number of friends of the family had already started to grind cane in preparation for the burial. The food served comes from the fields of the parents of the deceased, if he was single, or from his own or his spouse's fields, if he was married. Close kin and friends make contributions of food and liquor. The general confusion that reigned in all the burial ceremonies I attended made a calculation of cost and extent of kin contributions impossible. It seems unlikely, however, that cash expenses are higher than $30 to $70 – depending on whether meat is purchased. In one exceptional case a coffin was purchased and the priest was called on to give a Mass. When a child dies only the immediate family attends to the burial, perhaps accompanied by the child's godparents.

Illness. Minor ailments, that is, those that cause little pain and discomfort, are treated, if at all, with potions purchased from ambulant traders. Medicine for intestinal disorders is provided free of charge by the government nurse in residence in San Andrés. Indians go to her also in case of serious accident. For other serious ailments a Páez medicine man or a Sibundoy is consulted. There are two medicine men in San Andrés who perform the necessary ceremonies; they do not receive payment, but the Indian has to provide the required food, drink and coca which in some cases may amount to a considerable expense. Bernal Villa (1954a, pp. 219–67) has studied in detail the curing techniques of the Páez and there is no need to repeat them here. The Sibundoys are southern Colombian Indians who travel throughout the country selling herbal medicines and curing all types of ailments; every few months two Sibundoys visit San Andrés, but they are very secretive and I failed to gain any information from them. As not all cases of sickness, even when serious, are treated, and as I have no exact information on the frequency of curing and medical expenses incurred by each family, a detailed account of costs would be meaningless.

THE OBLIGATIONS OF BEING A CATHOLIC

Contributions to the Church

Money contributions by the White community cover the cost of the monthly Mass, the candles and other expenses. Each Indian family contributes between 50 cents and $1 to the annual collection. Very few Indians give more and they are usually to be found among the wealthier 'progressive' families.

The offering. Once a year offerings of food are made to the souls of dead kin. Each family brings bags full of cooked and raw food, piles it on the church floor and surrounds each neat stack with lighted candles. The priest says Mass and after the congregation has left the church he locks the main entrance. The souls of the departed Indians feast on the offering made by their kin, who in the meantime wait quietly outside the church. The doors are later opened and the priest proceeds to sell all the food to the White settlers. In 1960 this ceremony was celebrated in San Andrés for the first time in eight years. The decision to celebrate it was taken by the priest at the last-minute and special preparations – planting extra food or purchasing meat – could not be carried out by the Indians. The food was what each Indian was able to harvest the day before; except for an occasional bottle of beer or soft drink no purchased food was offered. It is impossible to list the items, and quantities, found in each of the piles.

Fiesta expenditures. Nine days of *fiesta* were celebrated in 1960–1. The Indian families who attended the Mass and the procession spend money on drink and food; but the costs of the *fiesta*, that is the Mass, candles, games and decorations are met by the volunteer *fiesta* officers. Each day of *fiesta* is organized by a *fiestero* and his helpers. Two or three consecutive days of *fiesta*, each organized by a separate set of officers, celebrates the day of a saint or the Virgin. The day of the patron saint is celebrated by three days of *fiesta*, less important saints are celebrated only one ay. Not all Indian families attend every *fiesta*, or spend any money and only friends or neighbours visit the house of the *fiestero*.

When the *fiestero* volunteers his services he has to invite three to five friends to be his helpers. A small feast or *cuido* similar to that offered to godparents is given in their honour by the *fiestero*. Half a chicken, rice, wine, cakes and other foods are set in front of each helper. The *cuido* is considered by the Páez to involve considerable expense, but most of the food comes from the family's farm.

Two to three weeks before the day of the *fiesta*, the *fiestero* and his main helper begin to prepare the drink and food that each will offer their guests. Friends and kin of the *fiestero* and main helper visit the respective houses, help with the grinding of cane, and in exchange are fed by the host. Firecrackers are burned and plenty of drink is dispensed to all occasional visitors.

On the eve of the *fiesta*, the *fiestero*, his helpers and the *cabildo* come to church and make an offering of food to the priest. Evening prayers are held in the church, softly lighted with numerous candles he d against the walls. Firecrackers, music from the Indian band, and the ringing of bells deaden the noise of drunken talk and baby cries. After prayer there follows a display of fireworks and, sometimes, a game of *vaca loca* (crazy cow) is organized. An effigy of a cow is made with the skull of the animal and old cloth or plantain leaves. Rags moistened in kerosene are tied around each horn and lighted. An Indian, usually a *fiestero* helper, wearing the effigy, tries to attack another Indian who provokes him with a torch. When the game is finished the *fiestero* and his helper return to their respective houses followed by numerous guests, and dancing and eating lasts all night.

Next day Mass is celebrated and a small procession round the church ends the *fiesta*. In Table 6 the expenses of the *fiestero* and his helpers are calculated. Cash expenditure depends on the amount of sugar cane planted by the Indian and on the need to purchase meat. An Indian *fiestero* estimated hat he would have to spend $300 while another was prepared to spend $700. A helper of a *fiestero*, who owned a large sugar cane plantation, spent $100 on food and fireworks, and one poor Indian was trying to raise $120 to pay for his share of a *fiesta*. Table 7 indicates how often Indian families assume *fiesta* responsibilities.

San Juan and San Pedro fiestas. These two *fiestas* are celebrated with music, drink and food in the houses of the Indians; there is no church celebration and no fireworks. Sugar cane juice is fermented, food is cooked and musicians and friends are invited. Guests may sometimes bring bottles of purchased liquor as a contribution. Expenses, if all the items are purchased, range from $70 to $90. In 1961 six families celebrated San Juan and two celebrated San Pedro, but most of the families who celebrated the first *fiesta* served only drinks.

SUMMARY OF EXPENDITURES

A family of two adults and three to four children has to spend annually a minimum of $353 on food, small household expenses, clothing and replacement of tools. Meat, other luxuries and drink are not included in this calculation of annual expenditures, and would add another $100 to the budget.

In addition, each family will eventually have to pay for three to four baptismal ceremonies, probably two marriages and at least two burials, and will have to serve as a *fiestero* or helper to a *fiestero*

Table 6. *Fiesta* officers' expenditures*

	Expenditures of voluntary officers		
Items	*Fiestero*	*Main helpers*	*Minor helpers*
Cuido to helpers			
Wine container	$20	$—	$—
Wine and fermented cane juice	21	—	—
Chickens	36–50	—	—
Cakes	5–10	—	—
Other food	4	—	—
Sub-total	86–105	—	—
Food for guests			
Sugar cane for fermented drink	60	60	—
Calf	150	—	—
Other food	70	30	—
Sub-total	280	90	—
Church ceremony			
Mass	25	25	—
Candles	4	2	4
Firecrackers	40	28	28
Sub-total	69	55	32
Offering to priest			
Chicken	—	12	—
Eggs	—	1	—
Rice	—	1	—
Manioc, plantain, corn, etc.	—	3	—
Sub-total	—	17	—
TOTAL	$435–454	$162	$32

* Not all items listed have to be purchased but calculations of cost are based on the price of the item if purchased.

Table 7. *Fiesta* offices held by each family in the area studied from 1951–61; number of times and type of office held

Times and types of office held	Held in combination with offices: Main helper	Minor helper	No other	Total number of families
Once *fiestero*	3	1	16	20
Twice *fiestero*	2	2	1	5
Once main helper	—	1	14	15
Twice main helper	—	2	2	4
Once minor helper	—	—	12	12
Twice minor helper	—	—	1	1
Total number of families who held office in 10 years				57

Note: Out of a probable 250 Indians who held *fiesta* offices during 1951–61 only 57 lived in the area studied, which comprises 149 families. The rest lived in other neighbourhoods of San Andrés reservation. Most of the families held *fiesta* offices only once during a 10-year period and they represent about one-third of the population. For a longer period we can assume either that the other two-thirds of the Indians paid for other *fiestas* or that the same one-third shouldered most of the *fiesta* cost.

at least once. To meet these expenses the head of a Páez family saves and invests in cattle.

The impossibility of collecting a number of budgets does not permit me to discuss the actual range of expenditures. I have, in this chapter, at least tried to outline the expected pattern of expenditure and to indicate the variations observed. After all, not all Indians eat the same amount, or offer equally elaborate *fiestas* or celebrate the same number of ceremonies. The tables are not to be taken as trustworthy accounts of family budgets, but are intended as guides to expenditure, to be compared, in the following chapters, with agricultural production and wage-labour activities.

PART II

THE PÁEZ PEASANT AND HIS LAND

4
Land Tenure

SOURCES OF INFORMATION ON LAND TENURE

It is hard to convey in a few words, without visual aids, the difficulties encountered when size and ownership of land have to be established. No aerial photographs are available and the only map on which the settlement of San Andrés is indicated is so vague and incorrect as to be completely useless. The territory of the reservation is large and spreads over innumerable mountain slopes. Even the section selected for this study is too extensive for estimation.

When I arrived in San Andrés I intended to map and pace the fields so as to check the information gathered from the Indian families. A first look at the steep slopes with Indian houses scattered over a wide territory discouraged me from attempting an accurate map. Pacing was completely out of the question. Most of the fields were too steep and I had frequently to jump or involuntarily to slide over loose gravel or mud. Pacing would have been possible in too few fields to make it at all useful. Visual estimates are extremely inaccurate owing to the irregularity of the fields planted. A field is cleared of the heavy brush, whenever it is present – not very frequently nowadays – and then fired to destroy the dry wood and weeds. But the irregularity of the terrain, heavy boulders, the direction of the wind and carelessness in the burning procedure often result in very irregularly shaped burned areas. These areas are then planted without any further recording. Three further points make estimates of the size of fields almost impossible: only a small section of the fields that a family controls is planted, and though every Indian is aware of the boundaries of the area where he is allowed to plant, and can point out the rocks, trees, streams and ditches that serve to define it, the irregularity and extent of the area make any accurate estimates of size almost impossible.

The second problem is that a family often has several plots of land dispersed over a wide area. It would have been a complete project in itself to visit with each farmer all the fields he tilled and then to estimate their size. The third problem is that none of the Indians had any idea of the size of a field other than to indicate that it was or was not sufficient for his needs, or that it was so much bigger or so much smaller than someone else's. This is not at all surprising considering that rights in land cannot be sold. Erosion is a major problem and the wea th of a family does not so much depend on the extent of the land as on its fertility and the steepness of the terrain where the field is located.

No official records offered information that would be helpful in estimating the size of the landholdings. Indians living on the reservation do not pay tax, and, unreliable as tax returns may be, they at least provide a helpful guide. While I was in residence in the community a census-taker collecting information on agricultural production appeared in the area for a short time. The information obtained by him came from only one source, the *gobernador* of the Indians of San Andrés, who supposedly knew by heart the number of animals each family owned and the number of bags of coffee harvested. This will eventually form the only census for a community that does not even record the number of births and deaths.

Owing to the many difficulties mentioned above I cannot present accurate tables listing names of heads of households and acreage of fields, to substantiate the discussion on land tenure. Sufficient information was gathered, however, to enable me to determine the relative size of the fields held by members of the same family and by the heads of different households.

Having listed the difficulties encountered I now list the sources and types of information on which my analysis of land tenure is based, and the relative size of fields determined.

(1) Genealogical information for each one of the families residing in the area studied, with precise age indicated in most cases. This information was compiled from baptismal records and from informants. It helped to determine the exact age difference of siblings, and to account for every individual resident in the community and for those who had decided to emigrate.

(2) Documentary information providing incomplete details of old land disputes.

(3) Information on the relative size and wealth of Indian families

obtained from three informants. Interestingly enough each one proved to know little outside the immediate area where he lived except in the case of friends who lived on other mountain slopes.

(4) Records obtained by thorough interviewing of 26 families where at least the size of the area cultivated could be determined.

(5) A complete census of households drawn up with the help of the secretary of the reservation council.

(6) The remaining information was gathered *ad hoc* through informal conversations and direct observation during my period of residence in the community.

PRINCIPLES OF LAND TENURE

In 1593 it was ordained that titles to land be formally given to the Indians (Fals-Borda 1955). The land was to be given not to an Indian chief or individually to Indian residents, but to the community of Indians as a whole. It has been said that the purpose of this measure was to maintain the traditional Indian social system; but this grant system was applied throughout the Spanish colonies irrespective of existing systems of land tenure. The lands thus granted are known as reservations; some of them still exist, amongst them the Páez reservations.

The San Andrés reservation should, according to law, have received a document of legal validity stating the boundaries of the land granted to them. I was unable to find such a document either amongst those stored in San Andrés, or in any of the archives or government departments. This, of course, does not mean that the boundaries are not known; some of the older Indians are willing to point out precise ridges and rock formations that still serve as boundary markers. This oral tradition has been passed down from officer to officer and was finally recorded during a court dispute with one White settler. Most of the boundaries are natural topographic features, except for a ditch mentioned in the document. I was unable to find the ditch, and was surprised that no artificial markers had been erected at the more accessible and populated boundary areas.

The rights over a territory to which each Indian community was entitled according to the law of 1593 are not absolute. The community may not sell, pledge, or mortgage the land.[1] Any contract to that effect would be invalid even if the transaction was supposed

[1] Decree 90, 1859, article 10, Colombia.

to refer to the sale of an improvement. Furthermore, the boundaries had been established only until such time as a new official revision changed them. In other words, while on the one hand titles to land were not to be held in perpetuity, on the other, no definite period of tenure was established. If the population in any one reservation decreased, the Crown could sell the surplus land and the profit would revert to the royal treasury, that is, the land was ultimately the property of the Crown. Many of the Indian reservations lost most of their land in this way. The Tierradentro reservations suffered less, because of their relative isolation, and the warlike attitude of the Páez which made Spanish settlement difficult.

Under the Republic new legislation somewhat altered the laws regulating the legal rights of the Indian communities. In 1890 it was declared that all of the then existing Indian reservations should be divided, and that titles of individual ownership be given to each family head who was a member of the community. The Guanacas reservations were divided in this way, but the Páez reservations of Tierradentro were left untouched, and the old laws regulating reservation land were upheld. How long this situation will continue is not certain.

Rights over land rest with the community. The *cabildo* and its officers can only administer the land and their administrative powers are prescribed by law. The *cabildo* cannot retain all the land or have it worked communally. Each family has to be assigned a piece of land sufficient to build a house and plant crops; common pasture land for cattle and other uses must also be set aside. Since *cabildo* officers are elected for only one year, there is no governmental élite with direct control over the administration and distribution of the land that belongs to the reservation. Furthermore, while in office, an Indian is not allowed to acquire more land. One of the *capitanes* actually had to rent land from the municipality as he did not possess enough for his own subsistence within the reservation.

The *cabildo* was allowed to lease reservation land only in very special circumstances. When plots of land had been assigned to all the resident families and sufficient pasture land for the number of animals in the community had been allocated, the remaining land could have been leased by public auction in the presence of the governor of the province and the protector of the Indians.[8] The

[8] Decree of 1828, article 20, Colombia.

cabildo could also lease forests and other exploitable natural resources for a maximum of three years, but only if not used by any members of the community. In these cases the *cabildo* had the power to administer the profits ar sing from the lease.[3] There were no other regulations indicating the manner in which the *cabildo* could have administered the funds obtained through these leases. The reservation of San Andrés has not for some time had either forest or unallocated land available for lease. Salt pans within the reservation be ong to the nation.[4]

The above outline shows that the rights over a territory granted to the community are limited; that land is to be administered by the officers representing the community and that there are a number of regulations which check the administrative powers of these officers. The laws on the one hand encourage the communal use of the reservation land,[5] but on the other hand protect the right of every individual to cultivate sufficient for the subsistence of his family. The balance between communal and individual agriculture rests on the administrative powers of the *cabildo* officers and on their ability to exercise them.

The *cabildo* of San Andrés has not retained any land to be used as common pasture. It is true that not all families have cattle or sheep, but it could be argued that if there was pasture land available more families would be encouraged to purchase animals. The reservation of Calderas has maintained common pasture lands.

No communal fields have been planted to meet expenses which may arise in the course of administering the reservation property. Money has been needed to pay for the legal proceedings necessary to protect the reservation land from intruding White settlers, but the law has not been implemented. When money was needed, the *cabildo* officers sold the cattle belonging to the church. No ledgers or records of past accounts and transactions have been kept by the secretary, thus I could not determine whether the *cabildo* had ever received any rent from land, or whether communal fields had ever been cleared for planting.[6]

The main reasons why the *cabildo* has given all the land to

[3] Law 89, 25 November 1890, article 7, Colombia.

[4] Decree of the Department of Cauca, no. 162, 28 April 1920, article 85, Cauca, Colombia.

[5] Decree of 15 October 1828, article 21, Colombia.

[6] By Decree 74 of 1 January 1898, article 26, the secretary of the *cabildo* is expected to keep a register of all transactions or other business of the *cabildo*.

individual families are: the limited authority that it has at present (see chapter 1), and the pressure on the available land resources. In fact the acreage held by any family has probably decreased by one-third between 1938 and 1961. It will continue to decrease for the male population is increasing at the rate of 5·9 per thousand inhabitants.

If land is short and a newly married man requires a plot to support his wife, the *cabildo* has the right to require the return of land previously granted from those families who control more than sufficient for their own needs.[7] In San Andrés, in spite of the shortage of land, the *cabildo* is neither willing nor powerful enough to do this. Many Indians complained that the *cabildo* should take action and redistribute the land, particularly where it remained unused or when it had been acquired by pressure or illegal means. Only once did the *cabildo* confiscate land which had been abandoned, but even then his action did not interfere with three Indians who controlled vast areas. Though it is understandable that the prestige, wealth and power of these three Indians made intervention difficult, it is nevertheless surprising that the *cabildo* does not act in other cases. One of the reasons is that the Páez peasants conceive the relationship of a man to the land he cultivates as a permanent one which defines both his status in the community and ensures his own survival.

In other communities the *cabildo* is stronger and re-allocation of land does occur quite frequently. Conflicts between families and *cabildo* are often brought to court in neighbouring communities; for example, in Guambiano reservations and in those near Silvia. A decree of 1937 enables the Indian to present a complaint to the municipal authority within four months of any action taken by a *cabildo*.[8]

The subtle distinction between community rights and conditional usufructory individual rights on the one hand and of a permanent relationship of a man to his land as a symbol of his right to membership and adulthood within a community can best be discerned when analysing documented land disputes.

In 1940 two disputes about land already occupied and tilled were brought to court and each time the *cabildo* won the case. From

[7] Decree of the Department of Cauca, no. 162, 1920, articles 77 and 78, Cauca, Colombia.

[8] Decree of the Department of Cauca, no. 50, 1937, article 88, Cauca, Colombia.

studying these cases we can conclude that (*a*) settlement had to be achieved through court action; and that (*b*) the *cabildo* land is indivisible. A dispute over a small area controlled by an Indian family means a dispute with the whole community. The *cabildo* is always referred to as the legal representative of the Indians on whose field the boundary is disputed. The cost of court action has to be borne by the *cabildo*. A dispute tends to group all the White families as the opposition. An Indian will not say the *cabildo* is disputing land with such and such families, but that it is disputing land with the Whites. The other point is that, in spite of the fact that the area of conflict is phrased in terms of one community versus the other, action is taken and pressure exerted by one family: the Indian family working the land under dispute. The *cabildo*, primarily as a result of inertia, does not often wish to become involved in a court battle. Cost ought not to be a problem,[9] and money had been spent by the community in previous cases. There may be other reasons for the *cabildo's* apathy, such as ignorance of court procedures, discomfort in dealing with higher authorities and fear of failure. What usually happens is that the cases of the more sophisticated or more aggressive Indians have a chance of being brought to court, while the Indians least capable of bringing pressure on the *cabildo* are ignored. In 1961 a young married Indian was disputing with a White neighbour who was a litigant in a previous feud, the site of a house he had built. The Indian approached the *cabildo* about the matter, but nothing definite had been decided when I left San Andrés. The *cabildo* had assured him a plot where he could build a house in case the White settler evicted him by force; otherwise it was suggested that he shou d continue to live where he was until something else developed.

The complaint that Whites encroach on reservation land is a very frequent topic of conversation. The Indians are fully aware that they are allowing themselves to be pushed bit by bit off the land instead of fighting for it. Blame is not ascribed to the *cabildo* but to the Indian families who give up their land without a fight. Yet, the land which is in dispute is not said to belong to the Indian family in question, but is always referred to as *cabildo* land.

[9] The law considers the Indian community as paupers and thus all court cases to defend their property or any other reservation affairs are free of charge and defended by the protector of the Indians or lawyer appointed by the court. Law of 23 June 1843, articles 3, 4 and 5, and Law of 2 June 1834, article 16.

Church land. The priest and the Indian protector were supposed to encourage the Indians to work communally a piece of land within the reservation by the 'softest possible means'. The products of their labour were to be used for the benefit of these same Indians.[10] What was actually meant by this was that the church could make use of some of the reservation land for the planting of what was normally called the 'field of the saint' and could demand for this the labour necessary from the Indians of the community. The last harvest of maize belonging to the church was gathered in San Andrés in 1958; the failure of the crops and the low profit from the venture convinced the priest that it was not worth the effort. The money from this harvest was not collected until 1961; it consisted of barely $316 (Colombian pesos). No efforts were made after this to cultivate any crops, or to raise cattle. I was informed that at one time the church had had several cows and horses pasturing within the reservation. The administration of the property rested in the hands of the *cabildo*, but either through lack of interest or mismanagement the number of animals began to diminish; supposedly they died, but some were sold for community or personal profit; in 1961 the priest was only able to realize $1,230 out of total assets of $6,000 (Colombian pesos). The story of the lost animals goes back several years and it is very hard to establish the truth of the many versions current in the community. Each story stresses the fact that the church had the right to use some of the reservation land as pasture land for its animals, and to grow sufficient corn to help meet the expenses of the church. Accepted also was the right of the priest to demand labour from the Indian community to plant and harvest the crops, tend the animals and administer the property of the church. The treasurer, whom the priest had eventually removed, accepted this as a just and lawful principle. Difference of opinion centred round the use to which the profits should be put. The treasurer said that the community should benefit from the effort and agreed that it was just for the community to have sold some of the animals to meet the cost of the land disputes with neighbouring Whites; the church should profit only to the extent that the community itself profited.

There is another area called 'the hill of the Virgin' over which the church exercises some rights. It has a monopoly over the tall grass which grows on the slopes of this hill and which serves to

[10] Decree of 15 October 1828, article 21, Colombia.

repair the thatch of the church roof. The Indians are not allowed to plant or to burn grass in this area. However, there are two small fields on the hill. Whenever I asked who had planted them I was told very vehemently that nobody was allowed to plant on the hill of the Virgin. Yet, when on one occasion I passed these fields with an Indian, I was told the name of the owner of the plantains growing on the slope. The cultivation of the fields was not meant to be a secret, since they could easily be seen from the main roads. The whole affair was in fact considered as two distinct factual situations which contained no contradiction: the *cabildo's* permission for the use of a section of the slope was due to a diminishing interest in the upkeep of the church by each of the two communities, the Indians and the Whites. The Indian community was tired of being held solely responsible for the thatch, and for labour in the upkeep of a church which was used by both communities. The priest and the White community were ashamed of the church and had tried several times to modify its peculiarly Indian character; a zinc or tile roof would have made it much more respectable, they thought. Neither of the two parties is thus really interested, or cares whether the grass grows or not, and the rule is allowed to be temporarily forgotten. Only when one of the Indians who planted on the hill of the Virgin very carelessly burned a large section of the grass while preparing to plant his own crops did the *cabildo* report him to the municipal mayor. The Indian was fined, not for planting on the hill but for burning the grass when it was needed for thatching.

If the church has now no land for cultivation and no animals, it should be understood that this arises from the decision of the church, and not as a result of successful opposition by the *cabildo*. San Andrés is, I believe, the only Páez reservation in which the church does not exercise its prerogative of having cultivated fields or grazing its animals.

HOW INDIANS ACQUIRE LAND FOR CULTIVATION AND HOUSING

Any adult member of the reservation has a right to claim a piece of land where he may grow sufficient food to feed his family; if his claim is denied he can always appeal to a higher government officer. Once he starts to cultivate a field he can continue to do so for as long as he wishes, but if he ceases to use the land, except when it is said to be resting, his rights revert to the community. There are certain exceptions to this rule. If, for example, the head of the household has to be away for a couple of years, or is serving a ja l sentence, he is allowed to claim back the land when he returns. The number of years' absence allowed is not clearly fixed; in some cases Indians have re-established their claim to their land after 10 years' absence.

Although the head of the household has only rights of usufruct over the land, permanent rights over crops he has planted are acknowledged. Land with coffee trees cannot be taken away from the man who planted the trees because the latter are his. He is thus allowed to protect them by constructing fences or stone walls around them. The same principle of ownership applies to any building or construction that the individual has erected on the land assigned to him; no prior permission to build is required from the reservation council.

Any natural resources found within the area to which an individual has claim may not be kept for his exclusive use. Any other family may gather the loose branches of small trees and bushes that have naturally grown on the land, may divert water from a stream crossing another family's land, pick lime rock for using with coca leaves, or take white earth that might be needed to whitewash their houses, so long as no damage is done to the crops growing close by. In practice, the right to the common use of wood and water resources causes much friction between neighbours, and it would be much worse were it not for the fact that streams are numerous, and intentional planting of trees to shade the coffee bushes provides sufficient wood for household needs. The law now forbids Indians to cut down trees for clearing, or to set fire to the underbush, without first seeking permission from the local authority, but restraint is only shown when a government inspector is visit ng the area.

According to the law, an Indian can only be allocated land if he is a member of the community in which it is situated. Membership rests on birth and residence. If ego's father is born in another community and then moves to the community where ego is now in residence, whether as a labourer, or cultivating borrowed or leased land, ego has the right, when he comes of age, to ask the *cabildo* for a piece of land. He cannot go to his father's community because his father's membership will have lapsed through absence.

If ego was born in another community, owing to his parents' temporary presence there, but was brought up in his father's community, he has the right to ask for land in the latter and not in the community in which he was born. Membership in a community must be activated before it is recognized; ego must participate in any communal work whenever the *cabildo* requests it. Membership of the community is a principle very strictly observed and can normally be circumvented only by adoption or by marriage into the community. The few outsiders who have land in San Andrés have acquired it by means other than by directly petitioning the *cabildo*. I do not know of any outsider who had been adopted into the community and only 3 per cent of the Indian residents have acquired land by marrying into the community.

In principle, all that an Indian needs to do if he wants a piece of land is to clear virgin soil and then announce his intention to the *cabildo*. The labour required to clear the land of heavy trees limits the area a household head can accumulate; the law has not considered it necessary to set any other check on this right. At present there is no virgin soil available.

Nevertheless, on occasion, unused land reverts to the community. Twenty years ago an epidemic of dysentery killed a high proportion of the population, more ambitious neighbours took advantage of this opportunity and added large shares to the land they already held. Indians are aware that such opportunities are rare, but emigration of a widow with children, as happened when I was in residence, must occur from time to time.[11]

When an Indian knows of the existence of abandoned or untilled land, he visits the *cabildo* officers and invites them to see the land. He prepares fermented drink, purchases liquor and cooks a few chickens. Theoretically this is not necessary, but I was often told that it is helpful to feast the visiting officer, and ensures that the request will be considered. The prospective farmer has to prove to the *cabildo* that he needs the land and that he has the labour resources to use it. In effect, the chances of receiving the vacated lot depend on whether he is a good talker; on whether his relations

[11] The secretary of the *cabildo* did not keep a copy of all land allocations and hence I was unable to check whether land has passed from one family to another. Some heads of households are beginning to register their land in their own names; although this does not establish ownership it at least formalizes their claim. Out of 77 families 53 have received a certificate specifying the amount and the boundaries of their holding.

with the *cabildo* officers are good; and whether he is in a position to exert any pressure or offer any *quid pro quo*.

The formal petition for land is never drawn up until long after the *cabildo* has allowed the Indian to cultivate it. It is indicated in the petition that the farmer has used the land for a certain number of years, the location and boundaries of the lot are specified as also are the names of the farmers whose lands border on it. Nowadays, the petition is addressed to the Minister of Agriculture, but it seldom leaves the house of the Indian concerned and the old trunk of the secretary of the reservation. Though these petitions may be stamped with the municipal seal, they do not constitute legal titles to land. Recently the local government has encouraged Indians to make a formal petition for the land that they have cultivated for many years, and to have this petition stamped by the municipal authorities and approved by the *cabildo*. The Indians are convinced that it is a sign that the government intends to disband the reservation system and some are going to the expense and trouble of obtaining the formal certificate in the belief that their rights over the land they hold will thus be better protected.

Though the land is assigned to the individual he holds usufructory rights as the head of the household and his descendants have a claim to it. The rights of inheritance will be discussed later in chapter 5.

Purchase of land. An Indian who holds usufructory rights within the reservation is not allowed to sell the land or alienate it in any way, even under the excuse of selling improvements made on the land. Colombian law very clearly specifies that improvements made on reservation land are considered accessories to the land and cannot be sold or rented.[12] The *cabildo* is given the right to interfere in the illegal transfer of land, and to declare any contract of sale or rent invalid, and to refuse to allocate more land to an Indian who has been a party to a contract of this kind. I was given to understand that the *cabildo* never interferes when a sale of land within the community takes place, but that permission and 'talking to the *cabildo*' is necessary if an outsider wishes to buy land. I do not know whether permission for a sale is ever refused. These transactions are

[12] Decree 74 of 1 January 1898, article 80. Law 89, 1890, article 40. Law of 6 March 1843, articles 1 and 2. Decree of the Department of Cauca, no. 50 of 1937, articles 1, 2, 3, 10 and 11.

not recorded, but, when outsiders are involved, are a matter of common knowledge. The established legal procedure for circumventing the law is to make the White buyer a member of the Indian community. He is then known as a *comunero*[13] and has to contribute either money or labour when community projects require it. Most of the *comuneros* do not nowadays contribute either money or labour to the *cabildo*, and never trouble with community affairs.

Six outsiders have purchased land either directly from the *cabildo* or from an Indian family. Two of these families were Indians from other areas, one a Páez from Mosoco, and another a Guambiano from near Silvia. Three of the buyers were wealthy settlers, one a trader and the other two landowners. The land they bought was used only as pasture land. The last buyer was a very poor Ecuadorian trader. The Indians complained very bitterly about this kind of sale and about the *cabildo's* conduct in allowing it. Only one of the purchases involved a large amount of money, by local standards; the others had taken place some time before, when buyers had taken advantage of the Indians' lack of knowledge of land prices in the surrounding area. Two of the sales were carried out by fathers who wanted to dispose of the land so that their children would not inherit it. Another was transacted directly with the *cabildo*. In the other cases the Indian owner either wished, or was forced by circumstances, to move out of the community and sold his land to help himself get established elsewhere.

Sales between members of the community were perhaps more frequent and did not encounter so much opposition. It is almost impossible to compile a complete list of sales of land between the Indians themselves. Since these are illegal they are never recorded and no Indian could possibly know all the types of land transference that had occurred since his childhood. I heard of eight Indian families who had sold most or all of their property to other Indians in the past 30 years, but there re probably more cases than that. Five of these families did not wish to cu tivate the land or to stay in San Andrés and sold the property in order to le ve the a ea. Another Indian sold his land just before his death because he did not want his only son to inherit it. Another Indian sold the land while he was se ving a jail sentence for murder. And in the last case

13 One should be careful in the use of this word, as the meaning can vary widely from region to region.

the Indian sold his land but remained as caretaker for the new owner. It is interesting to note that sales are not used to obtain better pieces of land, or a piece of land more suitable to the family's individual needs, but as a final break with the community. I have not heard of an Indian selling a small plot because it was too far away and inconvenient. The price of the land amounts only to the value of a cow or other animal.

Borrowing of land. In a very few cases Indians with either insufficient land or with no land at the proper altitude to allow them to grow certain crops, received permission from a *compadre* to use a portion of the land that was not under cultivation by the lender. Only four such cases were known to me. In none of them was payment in the form of labour, money or goods expected. The rule, however, is for the borrower to make a gift of food at harvest time to the owner of the plot. This gift serves to acknowledge that the rights of usufruct lie with the lender and not with the borrower, and is in keeping with the tradition of gift-giving for any service or advice rendered. But not many Indians have spare land to lend. If there were adult sons in the family resentment on their part would be very strong if their father offered the use of some of his land to an outsider. An informant had managed to borrow some land from a *compadre* on which he had planted manioc, maize and plantains, and had also built a house. When I met him he was, however, living in a small shelter, and explained that his house had been burnt down because of jealousy. He talked at great length about how lazy, mean and jealous people in San Andrés were – he himself was from Tumbichukue. His co-parent is old and cannot work the land, and being a generous man allows my informant to use it. My informant was very cautious about specifying who might have been so jealous of his manioc field as to want to burn it. Much later I understood the reason for his reticence. His old *compadre* is lame owing to an accident but is still an active worker; he has several unmarried sons and a 16-year-old grandchild. It was one of his sons who had burnt down the house of my informant, Jacinto. I suspect that Jacinto's co-parent did not get on with his sons, and had shown his displeasure by allowing Jacinto to work the land. Both Jacinto and his co-parent lived at a distance and the old man never came down to San Andrés. It was difficult therefore for me to know them sufficiently well to confirm my suspicions as to the reason which moved the old man to give a piece of land to Jacinto where he could build a permanent house. He must have been quite aware that it would be very difficult for his descendants to make effective use of the land he had given away. It should be remembered that the use of a piece of land enables an Indian to establish a claim to it, and is proof at the same time that the original owner was in no need of the land if he could so spare it. Having known Jacinto for some time I cannot discount the possibility that he in some way forced his *compadre* to give him a piece of land. He was a very shrewd talker and negotiator and had a reputation as a diviner, and he was not above exploiting these gifts for his own ends.

There was another case where the lending of a piece of land to build a house and for cultivation led to the burning down of the house in order to force the user to give up the property. The Indian in this case had no descendants, though he had been married for a long time, and he had not inherited the land from his father. His wife received a small plantain grove and with this and another small piece of land he had borrowed from a co-parent he built a house and planted enough crops for his survival. While he was in hospital having an arm amputated, jealous neighbours – I suspect the *compadre's* sons – burned down his house. He returned to San Andrés during the last month I was there and then moved to the higher mountain slopes where his brothers gave him a small share of the family land.

Two other similar land transactions were successful. Domingo had received from his father more than sufficient land (family 20) but the land was located at a high altitude and was unsuitable for growing certain crops. His wife preferred to live closer to town so that their child could go to school easily. They built a small hut, their second house, on the land of a friend, a woman with five small daughters, whose husband was working far away most of the time (family 23). It was a very close friendship and the arrangement was helpful to both; their houses were next to each other; Ercilla could call on Domingo if she felt she needed the help of a man, and Ercilla's children could keep an eye open for thieves when Domingo's family had to go and work in the fields farther away. The friendship broke up rather suddenly while I was in San Andrés because of some supposed interference in family affairs. The land was retained by Domingo, however, and vengeance on the part of

Ercilla towards him seemed unlikely. More probably Domingo, with sufficient land and only one son to inherit it, will leave the borrowed plot and build on his own land. He had already spoken of this, saying that he wanted to try to build a tiled-roof house on the higher land.

Pascual (family 22) had a niece who had married a landless Indian from another settlement. He was not a very capable man so my friend took pity on his niece and lent them a small piece of land on which to build a house and plant a few maniocs. It was understood that the young couple would earn a living as labourers and they were given the land as a place to live. The arrangement would not be permanent. Though building a house on it was sufficient to establish a claim to the land on which the house stood and a man could defend himself against eviction, this Indian couple was not very intelligent and could very easily be made to move. They had previously been offered a home among other families and had subsequently been evicted. As outsiders in the community they could enlist little support from their Indian neighbours.

In another case an Indian family lent land to a White neighbour. The arrangement was made partly in exchange for the use of a water source – the White neighbour had spent a considerable amount of labour and time in building a canal from a spring to his house in order to have a safe source of clean water. The arrangement also specified that only temporary crops were to be planted, and knowing the settler in question, the Indian had the assurance that this particular man had no interest in remaining there for any length of time. Arrangements with outsiders are not favoured, but they are safer, since a non-Indian cannot establish a permanent claim to reservation land. This case was unique in the reservation and only a small plot was cultivated.

I know of only one other case where a relative lent a very small plot of land for a year, to allow the planting of a special kind of crop. There may have been more cases of this kind, but their incidence was still sufficiently low not to be considered a ready source of expansion. As we shall see later, out of 27 cases, only twice was land belonging to someone else cultivated.

Tenant farmers. There are cases of Indians with tenant farmers, where use of the land has been granted in exchange for labour. Some of these tenants on an Indian's land are farmers who have sold their property to other wealthier Indians, and have then remained on a section of their original land as tenants or caretakers of the buyer's cattle. For the most part, however, they are landless Indians from other communities. Within the area I studied only one Indian has tenants on his land, though I knew of another very similar case in another section of the reservation. The Indian in my area has succeeded in gaining control over a considerable amount of land and using it profitably by planting coffee, and as pasture land for some of his animals. Enrique is very different from the other Indians and is in a sense considered as an outsider by the rest of the community. His father and grandfather had been born and lived in San Andrés, but Enrique had broken with Páez tradition, associated little with the other Indians, and expressed stronger loyalties to the White settlers than to the *cabildo*. He is, however, a member of the community and the priest had forced the *cabildo* to make him *capitán*. It was partly through his tenure of office that he had managed illegally to expand his original holdings. He has three tenant farmers, two of whom are old couples who serve as caretakers on land which is too far away from Enrique's main household. In exchange for their services, they are given enough land to build a house and plant a little food.

For the most part, tenancy is an institution used by White settlers to attach to themselves Indian families as labourers. There are four White settlers with tenant farmers distributed as follows:

Table 8. Indian tenants

	Number of Indian tenants	
White landlords	*With no other land*	*With other land*
A	4	4
B	—	1
C	—	2
D	13	—
Totals	17	7

Two of the four White settlers have shown interest in having more tenants, but have been unable to find any. If at all possible Indians prefer to remain on their own land, or to leave the community in search of better wages. The 13 tenants attached to family D were originally from the reservation of Santa Rosa which borders on that of San Andrés. They have been included in the study because they have lost all ties with their own community and now live very near to San Andrés where they sell their coffee and buy their provisions. There are three other White settlers with large extensions of land who have tenant farmers; but strictly speaking these tenants live outside the boundaries of the area study, that is, they are neither attached to San Andrés, nor do they use its market.

Under the terms of tenantship the Indian family is theoretically allowed to plant as much as it can cultivate in return for three days' work a month on the plantations of the owner. The tenant family can build a house and plant permanent crops. They are free to sell their products in the open market. Security of tenure is assured by law and a tenant cannot be forced to sell his improvements on the land. In San Andrés the White settlers are more interested in attracting tenants than in evicting them. There is a real shortage of labour, particularly of reliable labour. A tenant is obliged to work or to send a replacement, thus ensuring a full crew of coffee-pickers at harvest time. If the size of the plot utilized by the tenant is very small only two days' labour a month may be required. In one instance, for two days' labour an Indian family had been allowed to build a house and to have a garden plot with corn and gourds. Another Indian family, in exchange for three days' labour planted 2½ acres. A third family also worked three days a month but managed to plant only about three-quarters of an acre of land. There is no strict correlation between the labour owed to the owner of the land and the area planted. As a general rule three days' labour a month is required, but the tenants are then allowed to plant as much as they need. The Indian who planted only three-quarters of an acre did not plant more because his services as *pailero*[14] were requested so frequently that he had no time to work on his own land – any days in excess of the three days required are paid at the local rate of wages. The other Indian who managed to plant 2½ acres is not allowed to plant any more permanent crops. The demand for their labour by the owner of the land is constant and often hard to refuse. Some of the landlords also stipulate that

[14] *Pailero*, a specialized worker in raw sugar production, in charge of the boiling of the sugar cane juice to the proper point. This is highly skilled work and demands a longer working day.

the tenants sell food to them before selling it to anyone else, and at a much lower price.

As indicated in the previous table, 17 tenants have no land of their own. None of them became tenants because they were originally landless. Two generations ago the land they now occupy had belonged to the reservation, and through the legal device of declaring it *baldío*[15] it came on to the open market. The land was bought by White settlers and the Indians automatically became the tenants of the new owners. Landless Indians prefer to work for wages rather than become full-time tenant farmers.

In Table 9 below is listed the proportion of Indians who only have access to leased land and those who expand by borrowing or leasing. The table is based on a population of 149 domestic units which is also the population of this study; Indian families originally from San Andrés are differentiated from those who came from other reservations.

Table 9. Sources of non-allocated land

	Percentage of total domestic units	
Source	*San Andrés*	*other*
Borrowed from other Indian	2%	2%
Lea ed plus other land	5%	—
Leased land only	3%	9%
Total	10%	11%

Most of the non-San Andrés families are from Santa Rosa and some from Calderas, both neighbouring reservations.

ACQUISITION OF LAND BY 27 FAMILIES

In the previous discussion I have indicated the different legal and illegal methods used to acquire land, the problems involved in each case and the principles which either substantiate or contradict them. We shall now turn our attention to specific cases in order to indicate the relative importance of each method of land acquisition.

[15] *Baldío*, a Spanish term denoting untilled land which may be cultivated by anyone, the cultivator th s acquiring a right to it, or purchased from the state.

Table 10. Sources of family's land

Family	*Inheritance* (1)	*Age* (2)	*Land given to sons* (3)	*Acres cultivated* (4)[i]	*No. of plots* (5)	*Source of Land* *Inherited* (6)	*Allocated* (7)	*Rented* (8)	*Leased* (9)	*Purchased* (10)	*Borrowed* (11)
1[a]	N	—	—	½	1	—	—	—	—	—	—
2	N	C	n	1	2	2	—	—	—	—	—
3x	N	C	n	1	—	—	—	—	1	—	—
4	N	B	n	1–2	2	1	1	—	—	—	—
5	N	A	n	3	3	3	—	—	—	—	—
6x	N	C	n	3–4	1	—	—	—	1	—	—
7	Y	A	n	3	2	2[b]	—	—	—	—	—
8	Y	B	n	3–4	2	2	—	—	—	—	—
9	N	C	y	3–4[c]	2	2	—	—	—	—	—
10	Y	A	n	3–4	3	1	1[d]	—	1[e]	—	—
11x	N	A	n	4	3	—	—	1	—	2	—
12	N	B	y	3–4	4	3	—	1[f]	—	—	—
13	N	B	y	4–4½	2	2	—	—	—	—	—
14	N	A	n	5	1	1	—	—	—	—	—
15	N	B	y	5[h]	2	2	—	—	—	—	—
16	N	A	n	5–6	2	2	—	—	—	—	—
17	N	C	y	6	2	—	1	—	1	—	—
18	Y	A	n	6–6½	2	1	—	—	—	1	—
19	N	A	n	6	1	1	—	—	—	—	—
20	Y	A	n	3[g]	3	2	—	—	—	—	1
21	N	A	n	7	3	2	—	—	—	1	—
22	N	A	n	7	2	1	1	—	—	—	—
23	N	A	n	7–8	1	1	—	—	—	—	—
24	N	A	n	8	2	2	2	—	—	—	—
25	N	B	n	8–10	3	1	1	1[f]	—	—	—
26	N	A	n	9	4	—	1	—	—	2	1[i]
27	N	A	n	12	1	—	—	—	—	1	—

x indicates the Indian families from other settlements.
N indicates that the families cannot hope to receive any further inheritance.
Y indicates that either because the families have not yet received any land in inheritance or only a small part they can still expect to receive a portion of land retained by the father.
n indicates that head of household has not yet allocated any land to his sons.
y indicates that the father has already subdivided the land or allocated it to those sons who have reached marriageable age.
A indicates not the exact age group of father but that his sons are still very young, younger than 17.
B indicates that the father has sons of marriageable age.
C indicates that the father has married sons.

I selected 27 families whom I was able to study closely. The selection of this sample was based on ability to establish a friendship between them and myself w ich would allow me to ask them continual questions and to be sure of receiving truthful answers. Henceforward I shall refer only to these same 27 families. I was interested in being able to follow all their productive activities and thus I had to select a sample on the basis of practical problems. They could not live farther than one hour's walk from my residence, as otherwise I could not see them often enough to be able to question them about their crops, harvest, and sales. I had to be able to establish a friendship early enough in my stay in the community to be able to follow their activities for a significant length of time. Geography and circumstances beyond my control determined the sample selected. I tried as far as possible to make friends in different areas and among different groups of people. In this I succeeded. In the sample are cases both of what we may call very 'conservative', and of very 'progressive' Indians. There are significant differences in wealth between the members of the sample though the two wealthiest families are not included. But it is not a random sample

---

Notes:

[a] Household headed by a divorced woman who established herself without permission on her brother's land.

[b] One of the plots inherited is within the area of settlement which requires the payment of rent to the municipality.

[c] This Indian family has considerably more land, but the head of the family is too old to work it and refuses to subdivide it amongst his sons.

[d] Actually the land has not yet been allocated and lies within disputed territory. Half an acre of plantains has been planted, as well as corn, yuca, and beans. So far no conflict has arisen.

[e] A plot of land where family 10 built a house and planted a small garden plot. A White settler who insists that it lies within her boundaries demands two days' labour a month for the use of the land. The Indian seldom works his debt because, supported by other Indians, he insists that it lies within the boundaries of the *cabildo*.

[f] These lots lie within the area of settlement and they are rented from the municipality for $5.00 (Colombian pesos) yearly.

[g] This Indian family had a large plot of very good land on which it did not make use.

[h] This Indian family had a large extension of land used as pasturage, most of its land was too high to be used efficiently for agriculture.

[i] This Indian cleared a field together with his father-in-law, a very old man who helped him with the heavy work and in planting semi-permanent crops.

[j] The acreage listed refers only to the amount under cultivation. In a later chapter we shall discuss the relation of used to unused land.

and the categories (wealth difference, ideological differences, etc.) are not proportionately represented. The study of land tenure is not based solely on the analysis of the 27 families sampled. My knowledge extended much further than the families tabled here and this knowledge enables me to qualify and expand some of the data that emerges from the tables.

In Table 10 I have indicated the source of land cultivated by each of the 27 families and have tried to correlate it with other factors which might have a bearing on the question. I have listed them according to the number of acres under cultivation. The area under cultivation is, except in unusual cases, in direct proportion to the land the fa ily controls; but this will be clarified and expanded in later chapters on land use.

The following table gives a summary of Table 10:

Table 11. Sources of family's land

Sources of land	*Number of plots*	*Percentage of plots*
Allocated by *cabildo*	6	11
Inherited	33	59
Purchased	7	13
Leased	4	7
Borrowed	3	5
Rented	3	5
Total	56	100

From Table 11 we can see that most of the land controlled by a family is received through inheritance. Purchasing of land is next in importance as a means of acquiring land and will probably become more so since the *cabildo* has no more land to offer and some Indians have sufficient money to purchase land. The price of land depends on the astuteness of the purchaser and the experience of the owner. One of the sellers was a White and the rest were Indians, who for the most part sold all they had and left the community.

The figure of 11 per cent of plots received from the *cabildo* (Table 11) requires explanation. Most of the plots were received years ago when land was still available. In two instances the plots received were small and were extensions of original holdings. All the rented land was rented from the municipality and it is unlikely that any more will be offered for rent since all that is available at present is small plots for house-building. Of the land borrowed, family 20 had built a house on the land of a friend, a case mentioned before. In the other two cases land was loaned in order to plant temporary crops (see note i, Table 10).

Comparing column 3 of Table 10 with columns 7 and 11, we can see that the heads of all those families who purchased land in order to expand their holdings were under 40 years of age or at least with children too young to demand land. The purchases occurred between one and ten years ago. The families who borrowed land on a temporary basis were again of the same age group, and all of them were among the families who already had extensive fields. When they borrowed land it was for very special purposes and in very special circumstances.

Table 12. Sources of family's land

				Source of Land					
Family	*Acres cultivated*	*No. of plots*	*No. of sons home*	*Inherited*	*Purchased*	*Leased*	*Borrowed*	*Allocated*	*Rented*
4	1–2	2	3	1	—	—	—	—	—
5	3	3	2	3	—	—	—	—	—
8	3–4	2	1	2	—	—	—	—	—
12	3–4	4	7	3	—	—	—	—	1
14	5	1	3	1	—	—	—	—	—
15	5	2	3	2	—	—	—	—	—
16	5–6	2	1	2	—	—	—	—	—
18	6–7	2	1	1	1	—	—	—	—
19	6	1	1	1	—	—	—	—	—
21	7	3	1	2	1	—	—	—	—
22	7	2	1	1	—	—	1	1	—
23	7–8	1	—	1	—	—	—	—	—
24	8	2	2	2	—	—	—	—	—
26	9	4	4	—	2	—	1	1	—

To buy land a family has to have money. A young couple cannot aspire to save enough cash in their first years of marriage.

This is the case of family 10; instead of buying, the young Indian decided to lease land. Land is leased only by young people or by those who have spent long periods in jail (family 17), that is, by those who have not been able to accumulate the capital necessary for purchase. But tenantship exposes the Indian to labour demands from the landowner, which compete with his own labour needs. He must therefore decide upon the priority of his needs. Families 4, 8, 12, 13, who still had dependent children to help with farm labour, preferred to work as wage-labourers than to expand their fields by leasing from a White landlord. They needed cash rather than food, and, furthermore, working as wage-labourers they had greater freedom in the decision when to work for money and when to work in their own fields. The head of household 13 had been ill at intervals for many years and could not consider expansion.

Summarizing, it can be said that the most available avenue for the acquisition of land is inheritance. If an Indian cannot inherit, he either migrates or becomes a tenant farmer. If he wishes to expand his holding he either leases or purchases more land. If he is poor, he will lease a small lot for special crops. If he can accumulate some cash and is a competent manager, he may be able to buy land; but land for sale is not readily available and he must be clever and quick to seize or create an opportunity. Indians frequently express a wish to accumulate more land, but most of them see it as improbable, other than by inheritance. Expansion is most often discussed in reference to the relationship between father and son and not in the context of land required to realize some of their projects; this point will be discussed again in the final chapter.

5

Inheritance of Land and Other Property

Usufructory rights granted by the *cabildo* to the head of the household can be transferred to the grantee's children. I have indicated in the preceding chapter that the *cabildo* does not, even if it has land available, assign a plot to a young man until it is shown that the father's land is insufficient for him and his descendants. I have also indicated that in most cases the land used by each family is acquired through inheritance. Inheritance, then, has a very special importance, and for this reason I have left it for separate discussion. I shall deal first with the inheritance of land, and then the inheritance of any other property held by the head of the domestic unit. Land is actually the only property significant enough to give rise to problems of transfer. Other inheritable property might consist of a crumbling house, a few chickens, and perhaps a few animals. Unharvested crops will for the purpose of the discussion be considered as part of the land; any necessary qualifications will be indicated in a separate section.

CONDITIONS NECESSARY FOR THE INHERITANCE OF LAND

Ideally all children inherit equally. Land is, however, a very special type of inheritance, since it is not the land which is inherited but the right to use it. Certain conditions relating to the use of the land must be met, in order to receive an inheritance and in order to keep land thus received.

The first is that of membership of the community. Those children who for any reason leave the paternal house, and have not returned at the time of the death of the head of the household, lose the right to receive their inheritance. Temporary absence during the father's lifetime, arising from his inability to provide enough land for his children, is allowed. But once land is available for them they must return immediately if they wish to retain their membership of the community. Decisions by the *cabildo* as to lapsed membership through absence are never clear cut. The factors motivating departure seem to be given serious consideration. One of my informants, an only daughter, was very young at the death of both her parents. She was brought up by an unmarried sister of her father who feared that she might marry an Indian more interested in the land she had inherited than in her well-being. In order to protect her the land was placed in the care of the *cabildo* until she came of age. As a young girl she left the community in order to work as a maid for a White family, and did not return until much later, by then a mature woman with children. She was given back her land, but she had to struggle for it. Frequently a young man goes to work in Popayán or Cali, if he does not get on with his father, or, if the paternal holding is too small for him to have a share in it. The death of the father may occur during the young man's absence in which case the *cabildo* will recognize his right to work some of the land his father once worked. The only strong and difficult opposition may come from his brothers. In one notorious case a man had long before killed a fellow Indian, ambushing him as he returned home late at night with provisions. The family of the victim swore vengeance on all the remaining sons of the culprit. The tension increased to an uncomfortable pitch and most of the sons decided to seek a future away from San Andrés. Vengeance was satisfied with the murder of the remaining descendant, the offender was jailed, and calm was restored. Some of the sons who had departed had returned periodically for visits, and one of them spoke of the offer the *cabildo* had made to give him the land that his father had once worked; in other words, the land that, had events followed their normal course, he would have received in inheritance. Even in such a special case as this, if membership is not reactivated, rights to the paternal land lapse and descendants cannot claim them.

A second requirement for inheritance of land is that the sons should have adequate labour available to cultivate both the land they already have and the new plot. A serious problem arises when the plots inherited are very distant from each other. If the distance is great enough, it will prevent one person from working the different plots with ease, and may render acceptance of the land impracticable. If the plot lies in the colder regions suitable for pasture, and if the Indian can afford to buy an animal, he will accept the land. But if, on the other hand, he lives in the high colder region and the inheritable plot is in the lowlands and is too small to warrant a move by the whole family, he might not trouble to claim it; it would be too difficult to visit the field every day and as a result most of the food crops would be stolen. Other factors may be carefully considered when brothers discuss the distribution of land left by their father.

The third condition to be met is that a man's descendants should not already have sufficient land for their livelihood. This condition leads to many subjective interpretations. In most of the cases in my sample this condition is irrelevant, since the Indians seemed to have no land other than what they had inherited. It was implemented in the case of daughters. Theoretically a woman has a right to inherit; however, if she is married, the *cabildo* might deny her the inheritance on the ground that her husband has sufficient land; if she is unmarried but of marriageable age the *cabildo* might deny her the inheritance on the ground that she will soon marry and will have no need of the land. She might also be denied her inheritance on the ground that she might marry an Indian from another community and move away; that she would then cease to be a member of the community and that her sons would belong to the community of her future husband. Of the 27 families studied only two (7 per cent) had received land from the wife's father. The percentage notwithstanding, actually when a daughter receives land it is for very special reasons, such as:

(*a*) She may be an only child, as in one of the cases in the sample. She might then be allowed to work the land once held by her father with the help of her husband, but only as long as they remain in the community. In San Andrés there are only five instances of daughters who are sole heirs. One has a very young girl of six and lives in the house of he grandfather. In the other four cases the land has been inherited by the daughters.

(*b*) If a girl married a landless Indian her father might give them a piece of land to work. This allocation of land is considered an inhe itance and not a dowry, thus admitting the implicit right of a daughter to inherit equally with her brothers. There are a number of cases of women marrying Indians with little or no land. In 11 of the 108 marriages (which excludes the eldest living generation) the husband had little hope of acquiring land, and in seven of these cases the wife's father offered the husband a piece of land on which he could work. In the other four cases land was not offered, either because the wife's father was already dead, or because the relationship between the two was very strained, or the young husband had other prospects in mind. It may be that if a father cannot assure his daughter of a piece of land he will not allow her to marry a landless Indian.

(*c*) A daughter may be unmarried and have children of her own. It is very likely then that she will stay in the paternal house, her father assuming responsibility for the children. If she is still without a husband when her father dies, she is likely to receive a small piece of land to enable her to plant subsistence crops; she is not likely to inherit as much as her brothers. Her father may on the other hand not be willing to forgive her and she may be forced to leave the house.

Whether in such case a woman receives land or not depends on a number of factors: how much land the father has; how many sons he has to provide for; the closeness of the father-daughter relationship; whether she is likely to find a husband; and how traditional are the moral standards of the father. I was able to obtain information about 22 women who, in the past two generations, had had illegitimate children, but reluctance to discuss the subject warned me that the information may not be complete.

Table 13. Inheritance of land by women with illegitimate children

Women who left home	11
Women residing at home	4
Women with own house and land	3*
Women who received land from father	4
	22

* These are women who were either illegitimate children themselves or themselves managed to acquire land.

RULES OF INHERITANCE OF LAND

(1) On the death of the head of the domestic unit the administration of the land passes to the wife of the deceased and she continues to cultivate it. As the sons of the deceased husband grow up and need land to establish their own independent households, she assigns to each a suitable plot. What proportion of the land a widow can retain for her own subsistence is never specified, nor is

the amount which she must assign to each of her children as they come of age. Limits are naturally fixed by physical and social circumstances. Cultivating, cooking, and bringing up children is a considerable burden for one person. Often her only available labour is her own and that of her own children. It is difficult for her to establish reciprocal labour exchanges because she is tied down by household work. Being able to work only a very small amount of land alone she has little interest in retaining a large area for herself, and willingly allows her sons to cultivate most of the land. One young widow was left with a considerable amount of land and with three sons and a daughter to bring up. When the two elder sons came of age they began to work the land themselves and left her and the remaining children with a miserable portion. The sons made no attempt to help her by assuming any responsibilities within the household. The mother could do little but complain. Eventually the daughter married and the youngest son was left with the one small plot which the mother had been able to retain. This is an indication of how minimal is the authority that a mother has over her grown-up children. She is unable to retain her sons for any length of time and unable to demand of them the labour she so desperately needs. Her authority is so weak that her wishes have little influence on the eventual distribution of the land.

How often do a widow, and her children, receive the land left by her husband? There is always the possibility of opposition from her husband's brothers, or, more likely, from her husband's father. They do not question the validity of the rule of inheritance, but add certain conditions before the widow is allowed to assume control of the property. If she is too old to consider remarriage or has children approaching maturity no problem arises; but if she is still young or has no children by her husband (an extremely unlikely case) she may find herself forced to demand the protection of the *cabildo* against attempts to usurp the land on the part of her deceased husband's family. A young woman might easily remarry; it is often feared that the children in this event will be abandoned – as frequently happens. In this case the land cannot be retained by her second husband, but will likewise be lost to the abandoned children. There are good grounds for the belief that children of young widows might be abandoned. A year before I arrived in San Andrés a son of one of my informants had died (case 12)[1]. My

[1] Case numbers refer to Tables 10, 27–32.

informant, an old man, was all alone and thus not so interested in his son's land. Of her own accord the widow abandoned the land, gave away her children, and wandered about San Andrés and other communities, only returning to harvest her coffee. She did not allow the old man to have either the land or the grandchildren and he feared that the land would be lost both to the grandchildren and to the family. This is one of the main reasons why a woman who has lost her husband while still young, and who has young children from the marriage, has difficulty in retaining the land. She is not pushed out of house and land, but if her husband's father or brothers are still alive they may start using her land, and bit by bit move the boundaries until she is effectively left with very little. Only one case came to my attention, where a young widow had been forced from her property by her husband's family. With two small children she wandered from house to house after her husband's death (case 13). His death had occurred shortly before I arrived and while I was still there the *cabildo* helped her to regain her land. On closer investigation the case proved to be much more complicated. The widow, it was true, had been deprived of her land when her husband died, but the relationship between father and son, efore the death of the latter, had been very strained and difficult. The young man had been living with his parents while suffering from a serious tubercular condition. Disagreement broke out between the father and son, and both the son and his wife had had to move to a shed, where he eventually died. This was by no means in keeping with traditional solidarity of the Páez immediate family at times of serious illness or death. Neighbours expressed their disapproval of this treatment by the father. In spite of the fact that the widow was not well liked, she was given lodgings by friends until the land was officially handed back to her.

When a young widow has only young daughters at the death of her husband she will certainly have to be firm in order to retain the land. In one case, when a young mother was left with three daughters (case 15) the land was taken away by her husband's father and her children went to live with their grandparents. Eventually she regained control of the land but only after promising that it was to be held in trust for the three daughters. She did not keep her promise; she sold the land and left for the city with another man.

If there are sons of the marriage, and it is certain that they will not be abandoned, a second husband is allowed to cultivate the land until the sons are old enough to cultivate it themselves.

Usually when the husband dies the widow is left with at least one son old enough to undertake cultivation of the fields with or without the help of his mother. Thus in half of the 18 cases where a woman was left as head of the domestic unit there was no reason to question her right to receive the land that belonged to her husband. In the other nine cases inheritance of rights to land was rather more problematic. The following table illustrates these points:

Table 14. Land inheritance by widows

	Widow retained land		*Widow did not retain land*	
	Hu's-Fa	*Hu's-Br*	*Hu's-Fa*	*Hu's-Br*
			Da_3	Da_3
			S_{13}	S_{13}
			Da_{15}	Da_{15}
	S_8	S_8		
	S_{12}	S_{12}		
Above line		Da_7		
kin alive		S_4		
Below line	Da_7			
kin dead	S_4			
	S_2	S_2		
	S_{11}	S_{11}		

S indicates there are young sons and perhaps daughters.
Da indicates there are only daughters.
Number below letter refers to code of the case.

(2) If both the parents are dead the land has to be subdivided equally amongst those children who are still under parental protection.[a] In other words, all sons who have already received their allotment and become independent farmers are excluded from receiving land in inheritance. I have already discussed this point in the section about conditions for inheritance (see pp. 109–12).

[a] Decree 74 of 1898, Chapter 4, articles 89, 90 and 91.

The relevant decree states that the parental land should be subdivided equally amongst all the children; a point which the Indians of San Andrés never fail to mention. Equality in inheritance does not imply equality of size, but of potential productivity of the land. None of the sons should be placed at a disadvantage with either poorer or very specialized land. I found that this principle was seldom adhered to, not because it was not firmly held or because of a father's preference for particular sons, but rather because of complications in the process of land transfer, which I discuss later in this chapter.

(3) If the land left by the deceased is not sufficient for all his descendants some of the allocations are made from unused *cabildo* land.[3] This has long been impracticable as all the land has long been distributed. In fact the rule is no longer mentioned. The land that the head of the domestic unit was allowed to cultivate in his lifetime now has to be divided among all his sons.

(4) If (as sometimes happens) before a household head dies, he is cared for by another Indian living with him, the *cabildo* will allocate the land to this other Indian.[4] Usually the only person who will care for an old man or woman is one of his or her children. It is very common for old people to live alone and only in the case of illness or for visits do they stay with one of their children. I know of only one case where a grandson went to live with his grandfather on the death of his own father. He had been taken in by the old man to help in the house. At the death of his grandfather the boy inherited such property as remained. No resentment was expressed by the one surviving son of the old man; the grandchild had worked for many years caring for his grandfather and the land therefore was his by right.

An older unmarried woman assumed responsibility for the upbringing of an orphaned girl, a child of her brother, and of two of her deceased sister's children. When the three children grew up they left San Andrés. Only her brother's daughter (now a married woman) returned to live and care for the ailing woman. She received the land and the house when the old woman died.

Since the arrival of many White families, child labour is in great demand and when young children are orphaned a White family will offer to bring them up. Small children are very useful to run

[3] Decree 74 of 1898, articles 89, 90 and 91.

[4] Decree 74 of 1898, article 94.

errands, bring wood and water and care for babies. Only infrequently now do kin of the deceased bring up the orphans in their home, so that this rule is no longer effective. At present, for example, all the old people remain alone, and only periodically visit their chi dren.

(5) If the head of a domestic unit has no descendants at the time of his death, the land reverts to the *cabildo*.[8] Land cannot then be inherited by any other kin with the exception mentioned in rule 4.

INHERITANCE OF PERMANENT AND SEMI-PERMANENT CROPS

There are no specific written or unwritten rules governing the inheritance of crops growing in the field at the time of the father's death. If his wife survives him no problem arises, since she continues to administer the property; but with the death of both parents the situation changes. We have mentioned that frequently crops are considered as part of the land on which they grow and are subdivided accordingly. The procedure of subdivision is outlined in the next section (subdivision of land). For the most part crops are not extensive or important enough to matter greatly if the father dies an old man, since he will not have had the energy to plant large areas, or even control enough land to be able to do so. If he dies when he is still young and healthy and no wife survives him, the children will be too young to profit and the crops will probably be stolen by neighbours or harvested by whomsoever assumes the responsibility of feeding the orphans; or they will be used to feed the guests attending the wake and the burial.

The only valuable crop left at the death of a young Indian might be his coffee plantation. As this is a crop introduced only 30 years ago there are no customary laws regulating its inheritance; the rules are in process of being formulated. Each case poses specific problems and solutions and it will be some time before any general rules can be used as guidelines by the Indians. At present, every farmer questioned expressed a different opinion and suggested a different general rule. More often than not the coffee plantation is next to the main house; hence it is usually the youngest son who is still at home who will also receive the coffee. If the owner of the plantation dies an old man, his descendants will show little interest in coffee trees which are a ready wilting.

[8] Decree 74 of 1898, article 94.

APPLICATION OF THE RULES OF INHERITANCE

I have so far enumerated the rules governing the inheritance of land and crops and discussed the conditions for their application. This information is based both on edicts of Colombian law and on oral information supplied by the Páez. It may be significant that though people talk a great deal about land and have constant feuds over it, they are seldom explicit about the rules that govern the inheritance of land. If asked, they will reply that all children inherit equally and leave it at that. When I confronted them with possible qualifications they were never ready to answer and never very sure of their answers. After much thinking, they made statements which coincided with what I had already gathered from reading the relevant body of law. There was also a high degree of agreement amongst opinions collected from Indians. It must be remembered that the system of inheritance cannot be said to be traditionally Páez. With the establishment of the reservation system the previously existing social and political organization was disrupted and hence we cannot infer how land was controlled or transferred before the late 1700s.

When checking what happened on the ground I discovered that, contrary to what was said, not all sons inherited equally. In order to clarify the factors that affect the implementation of the rules of inheritance, I shall first discuss the process of transference. This process does not occur in a vacuum but is part and parcel of other social processes, which condition the implementation of the rules of inheritance. For this reason, I shall now describe the contextual situation of most of the inheritance cases. I am concerned not only with the social and economic status of the grantee and the recipient, but also with the conflict between them. It is the task of the anthropologist to explain the cases that do not fit the rules; as Firth has warned us, 'an understanding of the dynamics of a social system needs in addition a constant study of observed behaviour' (1954, p. 8). The rules serve as guidelines and limit the choices open to an individual; they are seldom so binding as to preclude an alternative. Within this universe defined by rules and by opportunities each Páez Indian operates and manœuvres so as to maximize his productive capacity and ensure his membership and assert his adult status within *his* community.

PROCESS OF SUBDIVISION OF THE PATERNAL LAND

The land that belongs to the head of the domestic unit at his death reverts to the *cabildo*, but only for division between and allocation to the legal descendants, in accordance with the rules of inheritance outlined in the first section of this chapter.[6] The *cabildo* takes into consideration the possibility that some of the sons have already inherited their share, in which case they are excluded from the subdivision.[7] They are also excluded if they have already been allotted land by the *cabildo*. The *cabildo* must then administer and subdivide the land among the surviving sons. It is expected that in so doing it will consider the needs of each one of the sons as when normal petitions for allocation are made to the *cabildo*. Furthermore, it is stated that if the land left by the father is insufficient for all the children, some of them should be assigned new land still held in common by the community. In other words, according to the law and principles of rights to land, inheritance is not conceived of simply as the transfer of the father's property to those descendants who have a claim on it, but also as a manner of redistributing the land that has been vacated through the death of the man who cultivated it. The sons who have remained in the household as dependents of the deceased now have to be given the land.

This law was enacted in 1898. By 1961 there remained no common land held by the *cabildo*, and new grants could only be made from the land that belonged to the deceased head of the domestic unit. Furthermore, the *cabildo*, as previously mentioned in other contexts, did not interfere in land matters on its own initiative. The distribution of such parental land as remains undivided is left to the surviving sons, and only after they have settled their differences – a process frequently requiring many years – do they apply to the *cabildo* for separate allocations. For example, only in 1960, two brothers petitioned the *cabildo* for property inherited and subdivided about seven years before.

The unwillingness of the *cabildo* to administer the land, the lack of unused land, and the prevailing opinion that though land belongs to the community it also belongs to the individual who cultivates it, all add a number of complications to the question of the inheritance and subdivision of land.

[6] Decree 74 of 1898, article 93.
[7] Decree 74 of 1898, article 92.

Land is given to a son at three or four different points in his life. At a very early age he is given a piece of land on which to play at farming; at about the age of 16 he receives land, wh ch marks the beginning of his independence. The third phase occurs at about the age of 20 when he marries and receives another plot. Finally, he may again receive land when his father dies. Stage one is unimportant since the amount of land transferred is small. Stages two and three are perhaps the most important, and determine the outcome of the distribution of the inheritance. We shall therefore begin with stage two and describe each stage in detail.

Stage 2. It is at this point that the first sizeable plot is given to a son. It is not a formal transfer of land. A son is allowed to clear a plot for planting in a section of his father's field, when he begins to manifest impatience at not having land of his own. This lot becomes the first instalment of his future inheritance. It is likely to be small, constraining him to plant a mixed crop of manioc, maize, beans and arracacha. Very seldom will a young man begin by planting coffee trees on his new land. I knew, however, of a young enterprising 17-year-old who had planted 1,200 coffee trees, none of which bore fruit and which had to be replanted later. The size of the land received at this stage, which will be only as large as the son can plant alone, is not of great importance. After he has received a first plot, a son knows that he will probably soon receive the rest, and that he may not have to wait long in order to marry.

At this stage he has no commitment to feed anyone. The food he harvests goes in part to his parents and the rest is sold or perhaps exchanged for animals. A young Indian aspires to acquire a horse, not as a productive asset, but as a means of showing off before h s age mates. Selling or exchanging the harvest is not the only way of acquiring a horse; it is not even the best or the most frequently used procedure. A young man very often, at this age, works as a day labourer in the fields of White settlers. Instead of wages the young Indian frequently makes an arrangement with his employer to receive a filly for a certain period of labour. For the next few years he spends his time partly in his own field, and partly working as a labourer to earn enough money for drink, clothing and the trading of animals. Sometimes he helps his father, mostly during the coffee harvest, but he has no strong feeling of obligation to help in the parental fields. If a son remains in his father's house he contributes food from his own fields, but not necessarily labour.

Some fathers are not very willing to part even with a small piece of land which they could use themselves. But if he does not give his sons land they may resent this sufficiently to refuse their co-operation. An old half-blind widower who had too little land to subdivide amongst his several sons was left to work alone while his eldest son worked elsewhere and seldom stayed at home. The contributions that his sons made were on the level of a bag of sweets and similar small purchases brought from other towns. Help in clearing larger fields and in planting them was not offered.

I knew of a young Indian of 20 who had not yet received any land and who had left for Neiva, a big centre in the lowlands, to look for well-paid work. He returned disappointed and without money. His wages had been low and had all been spent on food and lodgings. He had learned a lesson, he felt, and mentioned that he would probably stay at home and perhaps work only close by. A few months later he was on the road again, full of hope to work in La Plata for a few months. San Andrés bored him, he explained. As he was the only son he needed only to return home from time to time to ensure his inheritance at the death of his father. His departures were in no way intended to put pressure on his father to give him land. He was in no hurry to get married, laughed at the possibility, and was much more eager to look for adventure. Had he decided to marry, his father would certainly have given him part of his land inheritance.

Tense relations with the father may have the same effect as boredom for a young son. A son who is badly treated by his father does not wait very long before leaving home. There are a few families who have lost their 12–14 year old sons after too many beatings and it is unlikely that they will return to receive their inheritance after their father's death. Others with more patience or endurance remain in the area and work as steady labourers though seldom setting foot in the parental houses. The son has to make sure that his departure will not so anger his father that in turn he may give a larger share of the land to a younger brother.

At the time when the son should receive his first piece of land the father must carefully consider whether he prefers to retain his land or his son. If he procrastinates too long his son may become impatient and move away. The father then loses not only his good-will but also his immediate labour and future cooperation; if they do stay at home sons are likely to help with the harvest, though this depends on the quality of the relation between a father and his son. The son has also to consider the possible consequences of his departure. If he moves away for too long his father may give a larger first share to a younger brother. If the next oldest brother is much younger, then the latter has a few years in which to exert pressure on the father or to enjoy himself without great risk of losing his inheritance. The potential loss of a son's labour during the coffee harvest exercises a considerable influence on the father's decision and at such times a father will avoid a complete rupture with the son. If several brothers are very close in age they will all range themselves against the father rather than compete among themselves.

In reviewing and analysing the 22 cases out of 30 young unmarried men aged 17 onwards, I have noticed the following points:

(*a*) Six sons have left the community for good with no intention of returning. Only one of these had any hope of inheriting land as he was the only son of a wealthy Indian. The remainder came from poor families with several sons. However, I should not like to suggest that this was the only reason for their departure. Whenever I asked about them, fathers and neighbours described the young man as a 'vagamundo' or a worthless drifter.

(*b*) Land sufficient to enable them to become independent was not allocated until the sons were over 19. There was one case of a 19-year-old who did have land; the father was a sick widower and depended on the help of his only son to do the heavy labour which he himself was no longer capable of doing.

(*c*) The sons who worked full time and spent little time at home were either only sons who had no fear of losing their best land to another brother, or unmarried men over 20 years of age whose fathers had almost no land.

(*d*) Sons and brothers normally remained at home, only occasionally working for White settlers. There is one curious case of a rather poor Indian with 12 children who had given land to his 21-year-old son, but has succeeded in retaining the labour of his other sons of 17 and 18.

Talking to married and settled heads of domestic units, I was consistently told of the struggle between father and son during the stage previous to marriage and the difficulties that each encountered. The fathers constantly complained that children would not help or contribute to the family upkeep and that they spent all their time either working in their own fields or working for outsiders rather than helping their fathers. The fathers also complained that they never benefited from the proceeds of their son's efforts in cash or in kind. The sons complained that their fathers held too tight a hold on the land as long as they could. Since it was not possible to estimate the exact area of the land controlled by the father and his sons, any reliable, objective discussion of the above complaints is impossible, but serves to indicate the tensions that arise in the transference of land at this first stage.

From the cases studied and the problems briefly mentioned we may summarize three points:

(*a*) Independence of the sons is not reached until the ages of 19 to 21, after a period of pressure by both parties.

(*b*) A son does not completely break with his father and work full time away from home unless he sees no hope of inheriting land until the death of his father; or does not care to work the land in any case; or is an only son and therefore runs no risk of losing his claim to the paternal land (recently, however, fathers have sold land rather than let their only son inherit it).

(*c*) A father will give land to a son when he is young in order to keep the son working in close cooperation with him, particularly if he has no other children to help him and too many children to feed.

Stage 3. At marriage or when an Indian finds a marriageable woman, he needs to receive land from his father in order to be able to set up an independent household. If the father denies him land and he cannot persuade the *cabildo* to intervene, the resulting difficulties may prevent his marriage. I know of five young men over 21 years of age who had not received any land and who had not married, and of four others who had married, but who, in spite of all their coercion, had not received land. In all these instances the fathers had originally very little land, and had still less after they had allocated part of it to the older sons. In other instances failure to receive land was due to the early death of the father and allocation was not made by him on the basis of need. Of the five young men who did not marry I cannot tell whether they did not marry because they had received no land or whether they did not receive land because they appeared to have no prospect of marriage. The other four cases are more important to this discussion because here in spite of their marriage and demands, these sons were unable to force the father to give them their due inheritance. A closer examination of these cases will provide a clue to the explanation of this situation.

Domingo had a brother of about the same age, also married, but who had left the area long before. He also had two other much younger brothers, aged 14 and 4 years. The old head of the domestic unit was a very strict, tight-fisted individual and the father of many children. He had little land and tried to keep it in his own hands as long as he could. Were it divided into four the land would not have provided a plot sufficient for each son. Domingo settled on a small plot of land given to him by his wife's father. All the land that the now aged father of Domingo possesses will pass to the two younger brothers. Domingo, it must be said, was not a very capable person; no one thought much of him and in my opinion he was somewhat retarded. Probably he was incapable of exerting the necessary pressure on his father.

Juán is quite different from Domingo; he is sharp and hard-working. His father is, however, very much like Domingo's father. As a matter of fact both old men get on very well with each other and are very good friends. Juán is the youngest in the family and has three older married brothers whose ages are 46, 40 and 33. He is 29 years old and married, with two children, but he has not received any land from his father though all his brothers have received their portions. The father still retains some land and in spite of all his son's complaints he has not parted with more. Juán will probably receive a plot but not until his father dies. His elder brothers were aggressive and succeeded in getting what they demanded, so that little was left by the time Juán came of age. He has solved his immediate land problem by working with his wife's mother and leasing a small plot from one of the White settlers. Contact with the father is maintained, in spite of a rather strained relationship, so as not completely to lose his future inheritance.

Jacinto is an older man, the eldest of five brothers. When he married he settled on the land given to his wife. They never had children and it was thus difficult for him to claim more land. He broke off relations with his family and on the death of his father received no land. His brothers, who had remained at home, divided the land among themselves. Now, at 53, his house burnt down by neighbours and the small field he had borrowed pillaged, he has been given a small plot in the mountains by the youngest of his brothers. With no children, and only one arm left as a result of an accident, he cannot expect more than this small gift.

In the last case, an Indian was left landless owing to the early death of his father (who was murdered), and the abandonment of the land by his mother. The land has been allocated to other families and the Indian finally succeeded in acquiring a small plot from his wife's father, but as it is not sufficient he is trying to acquire more from other sources.

Usually a son will not marry if he has no land. In 4 per cent of the cases, young men married without any prospect of land. They solved the problem by either borrowing, leasing or obtaining land from the wife's father.

In 96 per cent of the cases, land was received by the sons at marriage, either because of their pending marriage or because they had forced the unwilling father to do so by refusing to help him and threatening to work as wage labourers. The question remains, however, whether each son receives an equal share, and whether he receives the full amount of land due to him at this stage. In the examples mentioned we saw how a son might be left without any land while his brothers had received their share. Examples of unequal allocation of land abound, and are a source of constant complaint and fighting. I have already indicated some of the manipulations that arise in connection with the allocation of land to descendants, the reasons that motivate a father to withhold land from some sons and to grant it to others, and the reasons why a father might allocate more land to the first or last son than to the others. Also described are the schemes a son might employ to force his father to give him land. To what happens in the second stage is added what happens during the third stage. As a result, the portion each receives as his share of land is not simply what is due to him, but depends on the circumstances prevailing at the time he demands his land. The second stage is the more critical, since final independence is achieved at this point, and future prospects may depend upon the amount of land so far received. There is no possibility of further allocation of land before the death of the father. Tensions and fighting between brothers, and sons and fathers are greatest at this point. The second stage is only important insofar as it is a preview of what might happen in the third, and directly reflects the outcome of how much land each son might receive.

Stage 4. On the death of both parents all the land which has remained in the possession of the deceased father is distributed. Those sons who have already received their share on marriage are excluded from this distribution. But the question arises who is to judge whether they have received their share? The brothers who have received land and become independent will have broken away completely from the parental household. Subdivision is then carried out amongst the sons who have remained at home. It is quite possible that some of these are still young, and are not yet concerned with or capable of claiming their share. If the *cabildo* follows the prescribed procedure it will claim the land and then subdivide it equally, thus protecting the rights of the younger children. Allocation of land is by no means carried out on a fair basis by the family itself. The oldest son remaining at home, who is most capable of working the land, will take most of it. If his brothers are still very young he often, but not always, accepts the responsibility of supporting them; otherwise the young orphans are brought up by a relative or a White family. Once the land is subdivided, it is difficult for these younger orphans to claim, when they reach adulthood, the land that was once due to them. If they are prepared to fight their case and if they have enough influence in the community to bring pressure to bea on the *cabildo*, they may eventually succeed.

In one family both parents died when the children were still very young. The two eldest worked the land and when the third came of age he had to leave the community and look for work elsewhere. He was old enough to want to be independent, but too young to influence the *cabildo* and prompt it to interfere. He worked in La Plata for some time and then returned to the community and married. His next elder brother, the more aggressive of the two, had expanded his fields and now controlled most of the land their father had once worked. Owing to his long absence, and the influence of his elder brother as an officer of the *cabildo*, it became impossible for the youngest son to claim a plot of his deceased father's land. He had to purchase land from other Indians and resign himself to losing his inheritance.

In another household a number of small orphaned children remained alone under the care of the eldest brother. He took care of them until they were old enough to be independent. Then he built himself a house and left the paternal house to his younger brothers. In so doing, however, he took most of the land and left only enough for two of the brothers.

In another household the mother remained as the head of the domestic unit after the death of the father. She had three sons and when the eldest came of age he started to work some of the land himself. In a few years she was left with very little land and with still a daughter and son to care for. When she died the youngest son inherited the land that she had retained. It was very little, since most of the original inheritance had already been confiscated by the elder brothers. The mother could not retain the land, even as head of the domestic unit, since she lacked the necessary authority and could not attempt to allocate the land as the father would have done.

The above example demonstrates that the death of the father is more critical than the death of the mother. For all practical purposes the land is divided when the father dies, and only if the children are very young does the mother assume direct control over the land left her by her husband. Her survival ensures that the land continues in the family so that the children may inherit it when they come of age. If the children are old enough, however, her survival is not important and the land passes almost immediately to the sons who are capable of cultivating it.

SUMMARY OF THE FACTORS DETERMINING AMOUNTS OF LAND RECEIVED IN INHERITANCE

Inheritance of land is the transmission of parental usufructory rights to immediate descendants. This transmission, as we have seen, is carried out in stages and does not occur simply at the death of the parents. It is, then, necessary to describe the rules of inheritance, and also, as I have done, the process of transmission and the factors which affect the application of the rules. These are as follows: the amount of land that the father controls; configuration of the sibling group, i.e. the number of brothers and the age differences between them; time of death of the father; diminishing authority of parent; present lack of authority of the *cabildo*.

INHERITANCE OF PROPERTY OTHER THAN LAND AND CROPS

Generally, the possessions of an old Páez are few. Apart from his land he has little of inheritable value other than animals, a house and perhaps a cane press. Few families have cattle or horses. If there are a few chickens or a pig they are killed to feed the funeral guests. I was consistently told that if the father has cattle or horses each child, including female children, receives an equal share. If there is only one animal and the descendants are a brother and a sister the brother receives it. If there are more sons than animals then one son receives the cane press, another the animals and the others are recompensed with something else. Since there are few families with either sheep, cattle or horses it was hard to determine how exactly this rule could be effective. I heard, however, of several women who had inherited animals from their fathers.

The house and the cane press are the other items of inheritable value. A mud house with a thatched roof remains habitable for no more than 30 years and a house with cane walls lasts a much shorter time. It depends on how carefully the houses were built and on whether the thatch has been kept in good repair. If the father dies an old man, the sons have little interest in receiving an old and crumbling house. If the mother remains she retains the house for herself and her younger children. The sons prefer to build a new, sturdier house for themselves. There is normally no furniture in the house. The sugar cane press is the only valuable piece of equipment. It has, however, its own life-span. The wooden cylinders wear out from years of grinding, but can be reconditioned or replaced. The model at present in use is relatively new and most of the informants remember their parents using a simpler, manually operated version. These older specimens are now non-existent in San Andrés. I was told that the cane press is inherited by the son who remains in the house, but as the new model has only recently been introduced, I could not check whether this was true. Nowadays, a coffee pulper and a grain grinder similar to our kitchen meat mincers can be added to the inventory of inheritable items. Any other personal items, such as clothing, carrying bags, machetes, and tools are disposed of; they are burned after the burial of the deceased.

With the purchase of more expensive equipment such as the coffee pulpers which have in recent years been substituted for the mortar and pestle, and with the building of sturdier tiled-roof houses, inheritance of property other than land might become very important. All these items can be sold and soon find purchasers. Animals can also be sold either to other Indians or to Whites; but the number is unlikely to increase because San Andrés has neither good pasture lands nor a climate suitable to the type of cattle the Indians possess.

CONSEQUENCES OF RULES OF INHERITANCE

The rules of inheritance and the conflicts resulting from their implementation have very far-reaching effects on the productive operation of the domestic group and the unity of the community.

Land is passed down from one generation to the next, never collaterally. That is, a father can transfer land to his own direct descendants, to his own children and through them to his grandchildren, but never to his brothers or his brother's children or to his father's brother's children. Therefore a Páez cannot expect to receive land from his brothers, once land has been subdivided or from his father's brothers or sisters. Inheritance of land does not help strengthen kin ties other than those between father and son. It is understandable therefore that each family makes no effort to keep in touch with other families just because there are kin ties between them.

A young Indian cannot normally receive land from his grandfather though I have described a situation in which this could take place (see p. 116). The ties between grandparents and grandchildren are purely affective. Children are not bound by the authority of their father's father and need only show the respect due to all older people. The grandfather by this time no longer has authority even over his own married children.

Each domestic group remains an isolated residential unit whose ties with other in are weak. With no possibility of receiving land from collateral kin no serious attempts are made to maintain an otherwise weak link for any length of time, nor are attempts made to learn genealogies. Labour requirements, on the other hand, do help to strengthen kin ties.

Present restriction on inheritance of land and the conditions necessary to inherit make it impossible for existing wealth differentiation to become permanent. The amount of land available to a young Indian depends on the number of his brothers, and the number of brothers his father had. Once the inheritance is received, redistribution by sale is not allowed. Since control over land is relative to the amount of land that an individual can cultivate, wealth differentiation between families also depends on the number of sons a father may depend on for help in the fields. Thus in one generation a family might be well off, because it has enough land and the labour of several sons. For the same reasons, in the next generation each one of the descendant families may be poor and with little possibility of increasing its landholding.

Very frequently, if there are many sons, the problem of land shortage is resolved through the migration of some of them in search of work elsewhere. Instead of staying in their father's household and receiving an insufficient amount of land they leave San Andrés. The father in this way loses his immediate labour force. The potential pressure of land in the next generation thus has an immediate effect on the present generation. Migration is counterbalanced by two factors. By moving out of San Andrés the son relinquishes his rights to inherit; it is not always easy to adjust to different conditions and to face the uncertainty of low income without friends and kin to help at times of crisis.

The fact that residence and membership of the community is necessary to receive land either directly from the *cabildo* or by inheritance from the father stabilizes the population. The Indian families of San Andrés were direct descendants of the Indian families who had inhabited that area at least when the reservation boundaries came into existence. Since then, Indian families have moved away and some surnames have disappeared, but there are almost no new surnames. Each reservation is distinguished by a given set of surnames. In San Andrés one finds Pencue, Iuue, Cunacué, Huétocue, Quinto, Lemeche, Volverás, Cuello, Chasky, Cuscue and Piñacue. The Pencues, Cuellos and Volverás are the largest groups. Furthermore, within the reservation each surname appears to be concentrated within a certain area. The Pencues dominate what is called the 'Loma Alta'; the 'Mesón' is cultivated almost exclusively by the Cuellos; the Chaskys are close to the settlement of San Andrés; and the Iuues are found in 'Patucue' and the 'Picacho'. This grouping of names into areas, of which the Páez are very conscious, may very well be a result of principles of inheritance and land tenure. Though it is possible for an outsider to become a resident of San Andrés it is not very easy to do so and is not very likely to happen. It can be said categorically that the population increase in the past 100 years has been due mostly to the descendants of the earlier residents. Kin from other settlements cannot inherit land in San Andrés and vice versa; hence, even when land must have been available, mobility between reservations was very restricted. Unless there is more widespread buying and selling of land the population of San Andrés will remain stable. And this will and does provide a certain unity that the community otherwise lacks. The *cabildo* is not an effective authority. Kin ties are not strong. Reciprocity ties between friends and neighbours depend on permanent residence in the area for a considerable length of time. It is exactly through these ties of friendship between neighbours, and ties of reciprocity between neighbours and kin, that the feeling of belonging to the same community is maintained. Leach (1961, p. 146) has said in reference to Pul Eliya that 'the land is fixed, the people change', '. . . all the time the land is in the same place and the "owner" must adjust his relationships to conform to this inescapable fact'. This is equally true of San Andrés, where the people make their homes in the fields they cultivate, and where the presence of a neighbour on the next plot of land will bring the two families together in some ind of relationship. But the very special rules of inheritance, and restrictions set on the use of land in the reservation of San Andrés, make this neighbour a permanent neighbour; he cannot sell his land and be replaced by new people. When these two neighbours die the successors to their land will already know each other, as the sons of the two families will have played together since childhood. This makes for a greater permanence in the bonds of reciprocity which may be easily continued from one generation to the next. In this way, through the interdependence of neighbours and friends, the unity of the reservation *vis-à-vis* the White settlers and the surrounding Indian reservations is maintained.

I have indicated that as a result of competition within the family for a larger share of the paternal land, friendship between brothers and between father and son in some cases becomes very strained. Assistance in daily affairs is not expected of family members, except for labour exchanges and in any critical situations. Fragmentation of holdings sometimes adds actual distance to the social distance that develops as a result of constant disputes. Brothers thus turn their attention to developing friendships with other neighbours. It is to friends that appeals are most often made for the borrowing of goods or exchange of labour. The permanence of families in the reservation and even in the same neighbourhood allows the formation of permanent bonds of reciprocity. These are as important as bonds of kinship which are themselves too weak to hold together related families beyond the sibling range.

The limited scope of the rules of inheritance, and the conditions prescribed for receipt and control of land, are forcing the Indians to bypass restrictions on rights to land altogether and to turn to illegal purchase as the only means of obtaining land. It is simpler to buy land than to attempt manipulation of a system with so many limitations. Simplicity, however, cannot be the only reason that motivates this change of direction. The number of sales, as was pointed out previously, is still small and the Indians are reluctant to sell to an outsider and do not really approve of sale of any kind. In time and given an increase in money resources available to the Indians, sales may become more numerous. It is also possible that the government may decide to implement an earlier decision to subdivide the reservation and grant absolute rights of tenure and sale to individuals presently farming the land. In this event, the life of the community will be profoundly affected. The right to sell might affect relationships within the family and add to the son's dependence on the father. At the same time the chance to purchase land may reduce competition and friction between brothers. Furthermore, since land transactions must be processed by the municipal authority the *cabildo* will probably gradually lose the few functions it still retains. The Indians will more directly depend on the White municipal *alcalde* instead of on the Indian *gobernador*. Furthermore, sales might take place to White settlers who have more money, and as we have indicated, are short of land and eager to acquire more. There will be an actual intermingling of the two populations which has so far been usually avoided. An Indian family will have to depend on a White neighbour for its source of water and cooperation; the opposition that has so far kept the two communities distinct entities might begin to break down as has already happened in the areas surrounding San Andrés.

The scope for manipulating the amount of land received ensures that more aggressive Indians acquire land at the expense of less confident and competent brothers. This implies that the shrewd farmer has greater resources than the less daring. It remains to be seen whether aggressiveness is an important managerial quality.

PART III
THE ALLOCATION OF RESOURCES

6

Agriculture: Techniques and Costs

I. AGRICULTURE

Preparation of the field for planting. When the dry season approaches fields are prepared for planting. In San Andrés there are now no virgin lands and clearing of the land is therefore not arduous. Low bushes and underbrush are cut down with a machete and left to dry. If transport is not too difficult the wood is used for burning in the hearth; some is also reserved to fence the field. Fifteen days of sunshine are necessary to dry the cut bushes so that they will burn. In some cases the Indian farmer carefully clears a safety zone round the edges of the field before burning it. Fires are lighted on the higher part of the slopes and allowed to burn slowly downhill. But not all Indians are careful or patient; some let the upswinging winds blow the flames up the slopes and accidents would be more frequent if the houses and plantations were not so far apart. Even the more careful individuals do not succeed in clearing and burning a field in a predetermined shape. Every evening during the months of January and February the hills around San Andrés glow with the reflection of the fires that have been lighted in preparation for planting, or to encourage the growth of new, fresh green grass.

The size of the burned fields varies a great deal, but they are seldom larger than 2½ acres. If an Indian farmer has land and labour available to plant more than 2½ acres, instead of burning one large plot he will clear two separate plots at different altitudes, and plant in each of them crops requiring different climatic conditions.

The labour needed to burn a large field is always considerable, and has to be completed before the rainy season starts. If the Indian farmer has enough money and food he invites a *minga* (or work party); otherwise the men and women of his household perform the task alone. To clear and burn an area of 2½ acres, 40–60 man days of labour are required. The exact number of days depends on whether the terrain is rocky, and on the amount of underbrush to be cut. Another important consideration is the type of fence the farmer decides to erect. On the lower slopes fences are usually made by setting up posts 1 metre apart, linking them by interweaving branches and twigs with the wood cut from the field. On the higher colder, slopes more permanent fences are constructed. Parapets of dirt are built round the field and *cabuya* is planted on the top,[1] thus serving a double purpose. Fields that are to be used for several years may be fenced with wire if the Indian has the money to purchase it. It is important that clearing, burning and fencing be carried out during the dry month.

Planting. When the first rains of the season have moistened the soil sufficiently to soften it, planting begins in March; although some families manage to clear a smaller field in late August and plant it in September. June and July are very rainy months and rains continue, though less intensely, into September. The fields are then too wet to burn properly so that September planting covers only a small area. Not infrequently the first rains are unduly delayed or too heavy, and the recently planted crops either dry on the fields or are washed down and a second planting is required.

Men and women help with the planting and no outsiders are called in to help. The only tools employed are the shovel and the metal-pointed dibble.

Coffee cultivation. Coffee plantings are started from saplings growing wild in established coffee plantations. Saplings are given free of charge t any individual requesting them, partly because they grow wild and the demand is limited. Usually a request is made to one of the White coffee growers whose plantations are sufficiently big to have a quantity of wild saplings growing. Planting can be done in any month of the year. Holes to receive the saplings are dug 6 to 9 feet apart; bigger holes are dug farther apart to plant trees to give shade. A variety of trees are used for this purpose: some plantations bloomed red with the flower of the *cachimbó*,[2] while other plantations were shaded by fruit trees or giant bamboos. I have no figures for San Andrés on the labour required to

[1] *Cabuya*, a common American agave (*Foucrea cabuya-trel*). The fibres are used to make rope and carrying-bags.

[2] *Cachimbo*, a local wild tree (*Inga*).

start a plantation, as at the time of my visit the coffee trees had already been producing for several years; from the figures suggested by Jaramillo (1955) for a similar area I have estimated the cost per hectare of coffee planted with 1,000 trees during the first two years when no berries are harvested.

Table 15. Cost per hectare of establishing a coffee plantation

Item of cost	*Labour in man days*	*Cost of labour*	*Cost per hectare*
		$	$
Clearing of land	50	150	—
Preparing holes for saplings	16	48	—
Preparing holes for shade trees	6	18	—
Transport of saplings	4	12	—
Planting of saplings	12	36	—
Weeding for two years	80	240	—
Total	168	504	504
Depreciation and cost of initial equipment			260
Total cost			764

Plantations are started when an Indian is young and most of the labour required, apart from the initial clearing of the land, is his own; hence the actual cash outlay, but not the cost, does not exceed $400.

After the coffee trees have been planted rows of maize, plantains or manioc are scattered between the young saplings. In the second year after starting the coffee grove, food is no longer planted as the amount of shade there inhibits the growth of the crops. It takes 2 to 3 years for a coffee tree to produce berries, though a few may appear in the first year. The yield increases annually and the maximum is reached after 7 to 12 years.[8] The plant will eventually dry and die, but will continue producing for 15 to 20 years.

[8] United Nations, Food and Agricultural Organization, *Coffee in Latin America*, part 1, Colombia and El Salvador, 1958, pp. 1–104. The productive life of trees and yields of plantations are difficult to estimate even in larger surveys, as farmers do not know the number of trees in production, nor do they remember when the trees were planted.

Twice a year the coffee grove is weeded, once during the rainy season and again in October to facilitate the harvest. The undergrowth is cut with a machete and the weeds allowed to rot. The trees are not pruned and no fertilizer is used. The only other care given to the grove is the replanting of dead trees with wild saplings growing in the same grove.

The main harvest starts in November for the plantations at lower altitudes, and in January for the plantations at higher altitudes. The trees bear fruit again in July, though the yield then is smaller and in some years, as in 1961, may pass almost unnoticed. Berries do ripen throughout the year and households with larger coffee plantations always have sufficient beans to satisfy their household needs.

The coffee berries are hand-picked, the ripe ones being carefully selected on each branch, and a coffee grove has to be gone over several times before harvesting is completed. The pulp of the berries is removed to expose the two beans. In San Andrés this process is carried out with the help of hand-turned metal pulping machines purchased from the traders. If the harvest is small the machine is rented or pulping is done on the grinding stone; but all families with a coffee harvest of 250 lb. normally purchase pulping machines. After the pulping, water is added to the beans and they are soaked at least overnight. The beans are then washed and dried in the sun. Whilst the beans are drying, and care must be taken that a sudden shower does not wet them again, children and women congregate around the skins and sacks used for drying and carefully separate the bad beans from the good. The market price depends on the dryness of the beans and on the care with which they have been selected. As coffee beans do not all ripen at the same time, a small coffee grove can be efficiently picked by one member of the family who can organize the time between harvesting berries, husking and washing them, so that the amount of berries to be dried does not exceed the number of skins, sacks or any makeshift equipment necessary for the process. If the harvest is expected to be larger than 20 arrobas (500 lb.), extra help may be needed to prevent the berries from falling to the ground. The critical point above which hired labour during the harvest may be needed cannot be estimated exactly; it depends to a certain extent on weather conditions, since the amount of rain affects the maturation as well as the drying of the already processed bean. A yield of

20 arrobas (500 lb.) can be harvested by husband and wife, while three persons can harvest 40 arrobas (1,000 lb.). A plantation giv ng 120 arrobas requires the attention of five to six persons. During harvest the wife, daughters and young children help, each according to their ability. The mother or an older daughter, at least, has to remain at home drying the beans and quickly putting them under cover if a short shower threatens to wet them. In 1960–1 the rainy season was prolonged and bean-drying then required the full attention of an adult person.

The yield varies from grove to grove, the weight in beans depending on the age of the plants, the amount of shade, the quality of the soil and altitude. In San Andrés Indians plant coffee over the 5,000 ft. limit of the optimum coffee zone. Yield estimates for the area are not accurate because in only a few cases could I estimate the number of trees or the area of the plantation. The larger, better cared for plantations in 1961 gave a yield of 60 arrobas (1,500 lb.) per hectare; others much less. The average estimate of 32 arrobas (800 lb.) per hectare is lower than estimates for Colombia, in spite of the fact that 1961 was a good year for coffee.[4]

In Table 15 labour is calculated at $3 a day, to include the cost of feeding the Indian; the yield estimate is 60 arrobas (1,500 lb.) per hectare, the maximum registered in the larger coffee plantations; the price of coffee is estimated at $40 per arroba.

The figures represent rather the costs incurred and the profits earned by White farmers than by Indians as they are based on a high yield and on the payment of labour in cash. If an Indian uses his own labour his cash outlay will be less than indicated in the table; but the cost of production will not necessarily be less as his own labour must be taken into account. Nevertheless, it is worthwh le to make the point here that the maintenance of a coffee plantation one hectare in size, and yielding an average of 32 arrobas, costs an Indian, who can at least count on the help of his wife, $150 for labour and depreciation of equipment and amortization of initial cost, so that he will make a net profit of $1,120.

Indians had no doubt that of all the crops they planted, coffee

[4] 42 arrobas (1,050 lb.) per hectare is cited for the rest of Colombia and 60 arrobas (1,500 lb.) for the department of Caldas. (See 'Investigaciones Agrícolas en Colombia', *Agricultura Tropical*, vol. xv, no. 11, 1959, pp. 709–806; and Jaramillo 1955. A national survey carried out in 1956 by the Federation of Coffee Growers lists an average coffee yield of 34 arrobas for the department of Cauca. (See United Nations, F.A.O. *op. cit.*, p. 24.)

Table 16. Cost of coffee per hectare when yield is 60 arrobas

Item of cost	*Labour in man days*	*Cost of labour*	*Cost per hectare*
		$	$
October weeding	20	60	—
May weeding	20	60	—
Picking berries	120	360	—
Processing berries	30	90	—
Total	190	570	570
Depreciation of tools	—	—	20
Amortization of initial cost	—	—	50
Total			640
Proceeds of sale			2,400
Net profit			1,760

was the best cash-earning enterprise. There was dissatisfaction with price fluctuation; nevertheless the expected 50 arrobas per hectare (which is higher than the average, but lower than the highest yield) was regarded as sufficient to cover costs and bring in a higher profit than other crops. Few farmers could estimate the number of trees they owned as they replaced and planted a few new saplings from year to year, so that their plantations had changed in size from the time of their first planting.

Manioc. The manioc or cassava (*Manihot utilissima*) grown in San Andrés is the sweet variety and the tubers are rather small, seldom longer than 12 inches or thicker than 3 to 4 inches. Sections of the long manioc stems are usually planted in pairs, and a metre apart from the next pair. Sometimes other crops are planted in alternate rows. Mixed fields of maize, arracacha, beans, and sugar canes are planted in this way, (see p. 199), but fields with nothing but manioc are equally frequent. The stems used for planting either manioc or arracacha come from the farmer's fields or are bought from or given by neighbours or friends. The price varies considerably from case to case.

There are three types of manioc known and grown locally, often alongside each other. Each type has a different taste and matures at different seasons. 'Noli' manioc requires a year for the tubers to attain full size, while 'guaturunga' or 'negra' take two years. Manioc can be eaten at any time, though the longer the tubers are left in the ground the larger they will be. There is no harvesting season and the tubers have to be consumed shortly after they are gathered or they turn black and hard. Once or twice a week the Indian has to go to his manioc patch and harvest no more than his family can consume in the next few days. Longer storage is successful if the tubers are left in the ground, but even so they are not suitable for consumption after a week.

In order to keep a manioc patch productive for more than one harvest, the Páez Indian either replants a new stem every time a plant is pulled up, or he pulls out the top tubers carefully without disturbing the stem. The second planting gives only a small yield but the labour of clearing a new field is thus avoided. After a second planting the field is not used again for two years.

It is impossible to estimate yields in weight as manioc is never measured in pounds and the tubers are harvested weekly throughout the year.

Indians expect all plants to produce. They are aware, however, that unforeseen climatic or soil conditions may affect the yield and thus they consider it possible that one-third or even half the field might not be productive. Such a low productivity, though conceived as possible, was considered a misfortune. I can thus estimate revenue only in terms of the number of plants likely to produce tubers and the price per tuber at the local market. The price varies, according to whether the purchaser is an Indian, and on the quality of the tuber; there are no seasonal price fluctuations.

Calculations in Table 17 are based on a commercial enterprise but the demand was so limited that only one White peasant was successful. Indians are more like y to sell large quantities of manioc in the field at a much lower price ($.08 a plant) thus avoiding the loss incurred if the tubers are not sold within the week; smaller quantities could be sold to San Andrés White peasants at 20 cents a plant. Most Indians can expect a revenue of $400. Hence it is not a commercially profitable venture for most peasants; if we discount the cost of marketing, the profit would be approxi ately $10, and perhaps a little more if he could sell a larger proportion of his harvest to White peasants. But it should be noted that except for the clearing of the land he needs no help and his cash outlay will be no more than $190. The cultivation of manioc, therefore, provides the Indian farmer with an amount of food similar to or larger than

Table 17. Cost of one hectare of manioc under production for 1½ years

Item of cost	*Labour in man days*	*Cost of labour*	*Cost per hectare*
		$	$
Clearing of land	60	180	—
Planting	3	9	—
Weeding, four times	64	192	—
Harvesting and marketing at Inza	120	360	—
Total	247	741	741
Sale of manioc at $1 per plant			2,500
Net profit			1,759

he could buy with wages from labour; but with an income that cannot readily be converted into cash or other foods.

Arracacha (*Arracacia xanthorrhiza*). This is a perennial herb, 2 to 3 feet in height, with large fleshy roots which are prepared in the same way as manioc. It is often planted together with manioc, one row of arracacha to two of manioc, and sometimes in a field with maize. It is seldom planted alone as it is not eaten as frequently as manioc. Arracacha requires the same care and labour as manioc except that only the top parts of the roots, neatly trimmed with a machete, are planted. It takes a year to grow and, like manioc, has to be harvested weekly as it does not store well. Land has to lie fallow for two years after a crop of arracacha. The cost of production is the same as for manioc, but there is no question of production on a commercial scale as there is no local outlet for the harvest of one hec are of arracacha. For an Indian the income from arracacha is similar to that from wage labour, except that the return is in food, not cash.

Maize. Two varieties of maize are planted in San Andrés. 'Capio' grows well in the higher altitudes and colder climates, 'calentano' grows only at lower altitudes. 'Capio' maize takes longer to mature than 'calentano', the ears are smaller and the kernels are

Table 18. Cost of fresh maize per hectare

Item of cost	*Labour in man days*	*Labour cost per hectare at $3 per man day*	*Return per hectare*
		$	$
Clearing of land	60	180	—
Planting maize	12	36	—
Weeding	40	120	—
Harvesting	20	60	—
Tools and seeds	—	17	—
Total	132	413	—
Return from sale of fresh maize			1,000
Less costs			413
Profit per hectare			587

lighter. Both types are grown in other parts of Colombia, but 'calentano' is preferred by the non-Indian buyers.

About 20,000 plants which produce on average 40,000 ears of corn can grow in one hectare; but if the soil has been in constant use the production may be much lower than this and sometimes nil. The yield in weight fluctuates considerably and I was given estimates of 30 arrobas as well as higher ones of 120 to 180 arrobas. These figures compare with other similar areas of Colombia where the average yield is 100 arrobas. If the Indian knows the land will not produce a good harvest he will only plant at most a quarter of a hectare for home use.

Five-inch holes are made with the metal-pointed dibble and five to six selected grains are planted in them. It is expected that two to three will germinate and that each stock will produce one to two ears of maize. The next hole is made 1 metre away and, if possible, a neat row is planted in this way. Very often, sugar cane, marrows and beans are planted between the rows of maize.

Fields have to be protected against birds and small animals. For this purpose scarecrows are put up and a member of the family remains guarding the field day and night. Three months later the field is weeded, a task which has to be repeated once more before the ears of maize are harvested. At the second weeding the dry yellow leaves are sometimes pulled out. Bernal Villa (1954b, pp. 291–367) mentions a different planting technique for other Páez reservations with colder and wetter climates; he mentions that beds are built around the maize stalks, and also lists a number of magical practices associated with the cultivation of maize. This does not, however, apply to the San Andrés reservation.

As soon as the ears are ripe a few are harvested for immediate consumption and the remainder are left to dry on the stalks. This practice of picking and consuming corn before it is completely dry makes exact calculation of yields impossible. By the time the maize is finally harvested a considerable amount has been consumed. The expected yield from 1 arroba (25 lb.) of seed is from 6 arrobas (150 lb.) to 60 arrobas (1,500 lb.). The ears are stored without degraining, hanging over the rafters and protected by the smoke. Maize cannot be planted again in the same field for 6 or 7 years.

Beans. Three different varieties of bean are planted in San Andrés. A very small red bean, planted and consumed only by Indians produces a high yield but requires a great deal of labour for weeding, and the harvest is easily destroyed by birds and small animals. The common red bean is the type preferred by White buyers and has a higher market value. The local variety of bean, called 'cacha', requires little labour and grows wild.

Holes are made with the metal-pointed dibble wherever unburned trunks have remained after burning the field, and these serve as poles for the climbing beans. Only a few pounds of beans are planted in any one field, and are always mixed with other crops. The 'cacha' bean matures before the other types, and the common red bean takes from 8 to 12 months, depending on the altitude. The beans are weeded at the same time as the other crops growing in the same field.

Beans are consumed fresh or dry, so that when the final harvest is completed a portion of the amount produced has already been consumed. Yields, therefore, are difficult to calcula e. Páez farmers do not plant beans for convenience, but because they enjoy eating the red beans and it helps break the monotony of their diet. To plant a large quantity of seed would be too laborious, according to them, and too risky because of birds and animals. Hence, little time is spent on the cultivation of beans; if the harvest is good, a few pounds of beans will be sold in the market and if it is only fair, they will be used to make stews and soups. Occasionally, an Indian tries his luck and plants half an acre or so of beans; the yields obtained in such cases range from 4 arrobas (100 lb.) to 10 arrobas (250 lb.) for every arroba (25 lb.) of beans planted. Only one Indian had planted a small patch of beans during the period of my research; unhappily I learned of it at harvest time and hence calculations of labour input are too unreliable to be taken into account.

The Páez do not appreciate 'cacha' beans as a food. They recognize that the yields in relation to labour employed are good, and that as it reproduces itself wild, it is a permanent available source of food. It is harvested only when needed for food. Thence, yields cannot be estimated.

Plantains and bananas. Three varieties of plantains and one of bananas are cultivated and eaten by the San Andrés Páez. Bananas are not grown frequently because they need a warmer climate. The varieties of plantain differ in size and number of fruits on the stems, as well as in taste. The variety most suited to the ecological conditions of San Andrés is the 'guineo', well known in the rest of Colombia; the plant has a short stock and produces a small number of thick, small fruits. 'Guineo' grows well at altitudes of 6,000 feet, though the yields are then rather lower. The optimum altitude for all plantains is 2,000 to 4,500 feet.

Young stocks are purchased from friends or neighbours at about 50 cents (Colombian cents) each. Holes just big enough to take the young plant are dug at intervals of between 3 and 5 metres, depending on whether other crops are planted together with the plantains. The daughter-plants that sprout round the main stems have to be transplanted once a year and the field has to be weeded twice yearly. Plantains produce a stem once a year, but in San Andrés not all trees produce fruit. The productive life of the original stem is estimated to be about five years,[6] after which replanting is necessary.

The amount of labour required to start plantain production depends on the distance the stems have to be transported, the size of the holes to be made and the use of coffee compost as a fertilizer when the young stems are planted. The yields vary according to the productivity of the soil; Indians often cultivate plantains on the very steep and rocky slopes and reserve the more fertile and gentler slopes for other crops. Yield also depends on the age of the plantation; the Páez replant new saplings so that the same plantation continues to produce for 10 years. They expect only half the trees to produce one stem per year; rains wash down the saplings and without fertilizer productivity is low after the first year. It is impossible to determine the average yield because the Indian farmers could not remember when they had started any particular plantation; nor do they keep count of the number of stems they harvest throughout the year. It is, however, equally important for our discussion to be able to determine what yields the peasants expect. Based on their expectations, and if plantains are planted for sale at Inzá, the profit would be as follows:

Table 19. Cost and profit of plantains per hectare

	days	$
Clearing land	60	180
Transplanting saplings	10	30
Making holes	20	60
Clearing	40	120
Cost of saplings	—	300
Cost of marketing	60	180
Total cost		870
Revenue from sale		3,000
Profit		2,130

The above figures are based on the productivity and quality which are expected on the lower slopes and areas which are easily accessible to the Inzá market. But even on these slopes the quality and size of the fruit could not compare with that produced outside

[6] Departamento de Investigaciones Económicas, Caja de Crédito Agrario, 'Banano y Plátano', *Carta Agraria*, no. 25, 1959.

this region; hence the peasants cannot hope to export and must adjust their production to the needs of the local market. The profit an Indian can expect if he plants a hectare of plantains on the colder slopes is no higher than $700. On these slopes the small 'guineo' variety of plantain grows better than the higher priced 'common' variety. The demand for the former is lower and so is the price it fetched at the Inzá market. With a hectare of 'guineo' an Indian can expect a profit of $300 to $360, whereas if he plants a few 'common' plantains, he can expect about $400. As a cash crop it is not very profitable, but as a subsistence crop it is satisfactory since it requires little labour and only a low cash investment.

Potatoes. This crop is planted mainly on the higher slopes as it is best suited to colder climates. Only a few families in San Andrés have suitable land for potato growing, and in every case only a few pounds of seeds are planted. Potato growing is common in other Páez reservations particularly near Mosoco. (Bernal Villa 1954b, pp. 312–16).

Sugar cane. Four different varieties of sugar cane are planted alongside each other: 'java', 'criolla', 'guineo' and 'Santa Cruz'. No one type is preferred by the Páez, and each has its own particular advantages and disadvantages. For example, 'guineo' sugar cane is suited to higher altitudes, but the canes are thinner and shorter. Each variety matures after a different length of time.

The seed, which consists of sections of cane, is purchased from neighbours or friends, the price depending on the relationship between buyer and seller. Two sections of cane are planted next to each other, sometimes in fields where maize and other crops are planted, and at other times in fields with nothing but sugar cane. If the sugar cane is intended exclusively for the production of fermented drink it is planted mixed with other crops; if it is intended for the production of raw sugar or for sale to White raw sugar producers, it is planted alone.

Sugar cane fields have to be weeded twice a year and produce one cutting a year for three consecutive years, but the yield is lower at each subsequent cutting. Sugar cane does not have to be harvested at any particular season, but if it is allowed to remain uncut for too long the canes will dry, and the yield of juice extracted will be lower. Once the canes are cut they have to be used quickly.

For this reason those families who plant sugar cane to extract and ferment the juice prefer to plant different varieties that will mature at different times.

Grinding is a time-consuming operation necessary for the production of fermented liquor or of sugar. The wooden press used in San Andrés is the same primitive model common in the rest of Colombia. Three vertical cylinders turn in opposite directions by a very simple system of interlocking teeth. The cylinders are connected to a long pole to which a horse is harnessed; as the animal circles the wooden press the cylinders rotate at the same speed. A young boy is in charge of the horse, and two adults, sitting on opposite ends of the press, feed the canes into the moving cylinders back and forth until they are squeezed dry. Sugar presses are locally manufactured by Indian specialists and the wooden cylinders can be reshaped when they are worn out. Most of the White farmers and two Indian raw sugar producers have purchased metal sugar presses of a similar design but faster and more efficient than the wooden ones.

If fermented drink is produced, no more than 50 canes are ground at one time. The juice extracted is boiled, skimmed and then poured into a hollowed trunk or a pottery vessel. It is then allowed to ferment for one or more days.

The processing of raw sugar requires more equipment: a copper vat costing from $100 to $300 depending on size and quality, a home-made strainer and home-made wooden moulds, and a raised hearth built under a shed. After the juice is extracted it is brought to the boil in the copper vat, and constantly stirred and skimmed until the required thickness is reached. The hot liquid is poured into the moulds and allowed to harden. The procedure is simple but requires experience and long hours of work. Not many Indians or Whites are skilled sugar producers and those who know the trade are in constant demand.

From Table 20 it can be seen that it is more profitable to grow cane and sell it to a White sugar producer than for an Indian to produce his own sugar. This is true because White producers have more efficient equipment and higher profits are possible in a larger scale operation.

Garden crops. Around every Indian house there is a small vegetable garden. Red pepper bushes, parsley, tomatoes, spring onions,

Table 20. Cost of planting one hectare of sugar cane and production of raw sugar

Items of cost	*Man days of labour*	*Cost of labour*	*Other cost*	*Net profit*
		$	$	$
Seed, 20 loads	—	—	100	—
Clearing and burning of a field	60	180	—	—
Transportation of seeds	5	15	—	—
Planting	5	15	—	—
Weeding	40	120	—	—
Cost of production	—	330	100	—
Sale of 1 ht. sugar cane	—	—	—	370
Cane production	—	330	100	—
Cane cutting	60	180	—	—
Cane transportation	25	75	—	—
Grinding cane and sugar producing	160	480	—	—
Depreciation of equipment	—	—	50	—
Cost of sugar cane production	—	1,065	150	—
Sale of 15 loads of sugar, $1,500	—	—	—	285

cabbages, *alchuchas*,[6] and cucumbers grow scattered among the fruit trees. Not much time or care is devoted to this small garden, which is usually tended by the women and children. Only one Indian in San Andrés grew spring onions for commercial purposes and he was the main supplier of the White and Indian families. Fruit trees are planted either around the house or in the coffee plantations, but only oranges are offered for sale. The most common fruits are *granadilla*,[7] pineapples, papayas, tree tomatoes, *chachafruto*,[8] avocado pears; fruits are eaten as snacks and never as part of a meal.

Coca (*Erythroxylon Coca*) is a small tree or bush with light green leaves which are picked and roasted over the fire and chewed mixed with lime. This mild narcotic is common to Andean Indians who

[6] *Alchuchas* (*Cyclanthera pedata*), a cucumber-like vegetable, eaten in stews.
[7] *Granadilla* or passion fruit (*Passiflora lingularia*).
[8] *Chachafruto* (*Erythrina edulis Triana ex Micheli*). Trees with long pods containing several seeds which are cooked and eaten as snacks.

will not embark on a long trip or heavy work without a supply of coca and lime to chew throughout the day. Only one Indian in San Andrés had a small plantation of coca trees, all other families merely planted a few trees round the house. The trees produce for several years and the leaves can be picked at any time.

Other minor crops. Four other crops are cultivated in San Andrés, but not by all families: wheat, peas, broad beans and *ullucus.* Thirty years ago wheat was the main cash crop, and the water-powered mill still stands, though broken and in disuse. The few families who still grow wheat have to take it to neighbouring reservations for grinding.

2. ANIMAL HUSBANDRY

None of the Indian families specialize in cattle breeding exclusively, though some of the wealthier Indians or those families with good pasture lands in colder climates have a considerable number of animals. A farmer tries, if he has money, to own at least one cow to slaughter for special occasions, and one horse for transportation. Pigs and chickens are common in most households. Mules are expensive and thus difficult to acquire. Sheep do not fare well in the temperate climate of San Andrés; they are also easily stolen or killed by hungry dogs. Indians prefer to forgo this source of meat and purchase the wool necessary for home weaving from kin or friends in other reservations.

Cattle. San Andrés has no good pasture lands except on the higher slopes, and only Indians with adequate land can raise cattle. Of 80 families out of the 138 studied, 35 owned at least one cow. In Mosoco and Calderas reservations more families own cattle than in San Andrés.

An Indian family which owns 2 horses, 1 colt, 3 cows, 1 calf and 2 sheep has two fenced pasture lands that have to be weeded twice yearly. Salt has to be taken to the animals at least once weekly and if the pasture land is far away considerable time is spent in watching the animals.

A family with six animals can expect to realize an annual revenue of no more than $400: from the sale of one colt $150, one calf $50–160, and wool $40–60 (or, for the sale of a sheep, $50). The original stock, of course, does increase in value.

The above calculations are not in fact very relevant to our case, as very few Indian families had adequate pasture land on which to fatten their animals. Normally, they buy one calf for fattening and resale, or to consume at an annual feast. Investment in cattle is also conceived as a way of saving cash against future misfortune. Breeding is rare as they lacked bulls and it is not easy to hire one,

Table 21. Cost of maintenance of six animals annually

		$
Weeding of pasture land	80 man days	240
Care of animals	56 man days	168
Salt, 144 lb.	—	55
Fencing depreciation	—	20
Total cost		483

except at a high fee from a White farmer. In practice cows belonging to Indians do not calve frequently, and animals are killed or sold before they produce even one offspring.

Poultry. With a few exceptions every household has chickens, ducks and turkeys. Only a few old men or families who live close to the main path do not raise poultry, as it is easily lost to thieves.

Chickens, ducks, and turkeys are allowed to run free and require little care, the task of taking care of them being carried out by women and children who own a number of animals. Poultry is fed on maize, if possible, mixed with chopped manioc or arracacha. If maize is not available, substitutes are used. Poultry is raised for household consumption and not for sale.

It is difficult to calculate the cost of rearing and fattening chickens as the Indians feed them with whatever is most easily available. If a hen is fed half-maize and half-manioc, it will cost $12 for feeding before it is fat enough to eat. A chicken costs the equivalent of 7 to 11 lb. of lean beef and sells for about $12 to $20. A small profit is made, it is true, from the sale of eggs. But Indians do not calculate cost and are not interested in knowing whether there are other cheaper sources of meat. Chicken does not have to be purchased, hence no cash is spent on it, eggs can be sold from time to time and chickens can be killed when there is no food for them. Indians are, in fact, well aware that it is not a worthwhile proposition to raise chickens for sale. Special breeds and special feed may make it worthwhile; but even then it calls for technical knowledge and heavy cash investment. One of the White settlers, known to be a clever businessman, tried it and gave it up soon afterwards.

Pigs are allowed to roam freely, with a metal ring through their noses and a forked pole fitted to their necks, so that they cannot cross a fence and destroy crops.

Young pigs are purchased from Indians or Whites for $20 to $50, depending on the breed and age; mountain pigs are sold even more cheaply. The animals are not fattened for sale and Indians often slaughter them before they become heavy.

Garbage, arracacha and manioc are used as feed in fattening. Pig-fattening is a profitable business and most White settlers keep one or two animals, and eventually slaughter them and sell the meat. Pork is expensive and this enterprise is profitable only if one or two pigs are fattened at the same time, so that most of the fodder consists of household waste.

Table 22. Cost of pig-fattening

	$
Cost of small pig	50
150 lb. corn and 75 lb. of manioc for feeding	110
Total	160
Sale of meat	473
Net profit	313

The above estimates are derived from a White family living in the settlement.

In spite of the high return Indians do not fatten pigs for sale. The main reason is that they would have to sell the animal cheaply to one of the White families, as only they are able to realize a high price per pound. White butchers and traders think of Indians as cheap food suppliers; they do not pay them for their merchandise the price which it would realize in the local market place. Indians cannot hope to sell large quantities of pork to their neighbours at the price estimated in Table 22; and Whites will buy it from them only if it is butchered in the way to which they are accustomed and sold in town, that is, only if the animal is killed and cut by a White. Even including the White settlers the local demand is limited because pork is higher priced than beef. Local traders consider breeding for export a doubtful venture. It is true that traders residing in big cities and with a sure knowledge of consumer demand in bigger centres visit the area in search of a good bargain, but they do so only occasionally.

Guinea pigs (*Cavia aperea*). These animals are traditional to most of the Andean area. In San Andrés few families raise them because they are affected by a local illness and die easily. They are small and are kept within the house. The meat tastes like chicken.

7

Availability and Cost of Labour

Even though the area cultivated by each Páez farmer is small, most Indians prefer, if possible, to do the heavy clearing and weeding tasks with the help of outside labour. These two tasks are considered monotonous and long, only bearable when shared with friends and neighbours. Moreover, some of the Indian families have coffee plantations large enough to require seasonal help if part of the crop is not to be lost. Thus economic and social needs have created an internal demand for labour; a demand that has so far been met mostly by the local population. There is also a demand for Indian labour from the local White sett ers. It is best to describe first the different types of labour contracts as well as the social and economic implications of each type. The demand for and supply of labour are discussed in the last sections of this chapter.

TYPES OF LABOUR CONTRACTS

The minga. Minga refers to a working party.[1] Friends, kinsmen and neighbours are invited to attend. They arrive at the house of their host early in the morning and are first given a meal which usually consists of ground maize and meat. About eight o'clock the guests and the farmer set out for the fields, each one carrying a portion of coca and a supply of drink. They work continuously throughout the day with only short rests, finishing early in the afternoon.

The cooperative character of the party is reflected also in the lack of leadership and direction of the labour activities of its

[1] The word *minga* is used by both Indians and Whites to refer to an invitation to work extended to friends, which ends in a small feast offered by the host. The word has no other meaning in Páez and may very possibly be an Inca word. When used by the local Whit s the word has an overtone of contempt; but this may not be true of other parts of Colombia where this system of labour is also common.

members. They do not start work until all participants have arrived. Each male member is expected to be an experienced farmer who does not need to be told what needs to be done; furthermore he is considered to be equal to any other participant and would thus resent any serious attempt to direct his activity. The owner of the field has thus to trust the good intentions and responsibility of participants as convention does not allow him to assume a supervisor role. The only way in which a farmer can control the quality of the work performed is by making sure to invite those Indians whom he knows from experience to be good workers. He also limits the use of the *minga* system to those tasks where supervision is not of primary importance: clearing, weeding, and harvesting are well suited to this type of working part .

Strictly speaking, members of the working party are not equals, as wives and adolescent sons of male participants are also included. Thus we can see that the exchanges established are not between individuals but between households. The payment for services rendered takes this into account; the feast celebrated at the end of the working day is attended by all members of the participating domestic unit, including those individuals who did not work for the host. The request to participate is based on an already existing tie of kinship or friendship. The use of *minga* fulfills Páez social obligations; those Indians who have become wealthy and have drifted away from traditional behaviour scorn this form of labour, thus denying their community obligations. Conversely, *minga* parties enhance communit solidarity.

Payment for *minga* labour is in the form of a meal before and after the working day, a small package of cooked food given to take home, three balls of coca and sufficient drink to quench thirst during the day. If there are musicians amongst the guests an all-night party might develop, but even without the music the evening meal and drinking continues until quite late. A *minga* is then more than a working part , it is also a small feast.

The cost of a *minga* varies with the resources of the head of the household, but he is expected to be generous with food. I found it rather difficult to establish the cost of food; it comes from the host's fields, and is not kept apart from that used in everyday cooking; furthermore, no attempt is made to calculate or to judge the amount of the ingredients with any precision. Meat is the most important and most difficult item to estimate. A small animal, either calf, sheep or pig, is slaughtered for the occasion. I was able to observe that not all the meat was consumed during the *minga* and enough was left over to feed the family for a few more days.

Table 23. Cost per day of feeding a *minga* worker

1 lb. meat	$2.00
Fermented drink – sugar cane or raw sugar	0.30 – 0.50
Plantains	0.15
Manioc	0.10
½ lb. corn	0.10
Salt and spices	0.10
Coca	0.20
Total	$2.95 – 3.15

I can give only a rough estimate of the amount of food consumed per *minga* worker. Cost is given in terms of the prices that the Indians have to pay and not in terms of local market prices. The amount given in Table 23 must be compared with wage labour, which costs from $2.00 to $2.50 per day, to which should be added another $1 per person for food. However, it is difficult to calculate the actual cash expenditure. It should be remembered that most of the food items listed are grown by the family and therefore do not require an expenditure of money. The same is true of coca and possibly of the meat supply. However, if the host kills one of his own animals meat consumption might be higher than if meat were purchased with cash at the local market. The same holds good for the amount of drink prepared; if the host has a supply of cane and considerable free time, he may try to produce a sufficient amount to fill the hollowed trunk where the juice is fermented. Much time has to be spent preparing the food and drink for the *minga*: one or two days grinding cane, several trips to the fields for food, a morning spent slaughtering and cleaning the animals to be consumed, and the time spent on actual cooking. It is impossible to translate all this into cash terms. I calculated that an informant who had called a *minga* of 30 individuals to work for 2 days had spent $3.00 per head and at least 7 man days in preparation. Another informant, who had no animals and no cane, spent $4.00 per head and only 1 day preparing drink and procuring food. From the above calculations it would appear that the cost involved in calling a *minga* may perhaps be a little higher than the cost of hiring wage labour. The *minga* system may also be less efficient in total output, but it has two advantages: First, it is a form of entertainment, and, second, most of the necessary items can be furnished from the host's own resources so that little cash is needed at the time. This is very important because some *mingas* are held between coffee harvests and shortly after the *fiesta* season, when any previously earned cash has already been spent. Food is substituted for very scarce money and the extra cost is not so important to the host. On the other hand as a *minga* requires female labour in food preparation, it is an arrangement restricted to Indians with a wife or adult daughters at home.

The *minga* is the preferred type of labour arrangement and the only one in which friends and neighbours are most easily persuaded to participate. It is a system reserved for certain tasks; mostly it is used for the clearing and weeding of fields, and the weeding of coffee plantations. Seldom, if ever, is it used for coffee harvesting. The number of participants rarely falls below eight and more often consists of 10–15 persons. The tasks to be performed must be laborious, for example, weeding or preparing two to three acres of land for planting. The number of *mingas* called by an Indian varies with the size of his holdings and the distribution of his food crops. If the distance from his house to any of the fields is too great for the work to be finished in one day, the *minga* system would be inconvenient. The amount of food and drink to be transported would be too large, or too much time would be spent in travelling back and forth to take advantage of the feast. Wage labour or exchange labour, where the amount of food to be consumed is much smaller and can easily be prepared in the field, would then be far more convenient. These practical considerations, as well as the lack of an anima to slaughter, prevent many families from holding a *minga*.

Of the 26 families interviewed only 12 had called *mingas* during the past year. The reasons given by those who did not were as follows: sickness of the head of the household, no animals to kill or no money with which to buy meat, no projects requiring large labour force, too great a distance to the cultivated patches and dissemination of these over a large area. Four families interviewed considered the system inefficient, and were proud of using only wage labour. These families had large coffee plantations and were outstanding examples of what, later, I shall describe as the 'progressive' Indians.

To recapitulate: the *minga* system is a very specialized form of labour, the cost of which fluctuates, sometimes surpassing that of wage labour. It is regarded by the Whites and the 'progressive' Indians as inefficient and expensive, an opinion difficult to test as tasks are seldom comparable. It is, however, preferred by the rest of the Indian families and is frequently used, unless very specific economic reasons proscribe it.

Looking at the *minga* system from the point of view of the individual Indian offering his labour services, the only clear advantage it offers is the opportunity to participate in a feast. It is true that, when calculating cost, the remuneration he receives is the same or more than he would earn as a wage labourer, but it is by nature limited to food consumption and does not bring him any cash. This is not particularly serious as he is unlikely to participate in more than six *mingas* annually. Furthermore, by attending a *minga* an Indian complies with his social obligations of cooperation, and at the same time pays with his own labour for an evening of feasting and entertainment.

Exchange labour. Both husband and wife attend *mingas* and share in the work, while in a simple labour exchange only the husband is involved. Food is provided, depending on how far from the house the field is located. No coca is offered and only enough fermented sugar cane juice to drink while at work. If an afternoon meal is provided for the workers it is much simpler than that prepared for a *minga*, perhaps even without meat.

Exchange labour is resorted to when the help of one or two individuals is required and when the return is feasible and convenient. It is an arrangement used for harvesting coffee in small to medium sized plantations, as the beans do not ripen evenly throughout one plantation, or from plantation to plantation. Labour is also exchanged when help for small tasks is required. It is used for planting and weeding only when an Indian does not have very much land; otherwise the labour in-put required would be too large to make return labour possible.

In some cases, the return may not be made with services alone but may also be made partly in kind. Such arrangements are resorted to when a family has lost part of its maize and can afford the time to help a friend or kinsmen more fortunate in his harvest. One of my informants had received two large bags of maize valued at $2 in return for a day's work; the informant was in desperate need of the grain. This particular return was not considered by the parties concerned as a payment in a wage labour transaction, but as a return in a labour-exchange agreement; both parties frequently helped each other. Since the details of the arrangement depend on personal factors and on other favours granted it is difficult to arrive at a figure which would represent the value of a day's work in this type of agreement. In fact, the success of this arrangement rests on the fact that the giver and receiver of the exchange assign a different utility to the service or goods exchanged. It also rests on the fact that the terms of the exchange are sanctioned by an already existing relationship either of kinship or friendship. As long as Páez remain small farmers who do not specialize in any one particular farming activity and who are short of cash assets, labour exchange will be practised and will serve the idiosyncratic needs of each Indian.

Among the 26 families studied exchanges were not very frequent but the information is too unreliable to be tabulated in quantitative form. For example, when I asked an informant with a very small coffee grove whether he had done the harvesting himself, he answered that he had too little coffee to trouble to get help. Yet I remembered distinctly that the previous week when I visited him, a young widow, and a young man, both relatives, had been helping him; when I mentioned this he insisted that it was not quite the same thing. The young widow was merely paying a social visit and had decided to stay and help, and later eat with them. The young man, according to my informant, came to help of his own accord for the sake of company. This form of occasional unsolicited help is never mentioned and unless I was present to observe, it would have gone unrecorded. It is, however, frequent enough to affect considerably any quantitative evaluation of labour exchanges.

Whether one participates in a *minga* or in a simple labour exchange an implicit obligation to return the cooperation remains. The economic benefits of time and labour spent in another man's field are not realized in return until later. The agricultural function of the labour exchange arrangement is to provide for a better time distribution of the farmer's own labour so that he may concentrate it or divert it in relation to seasonal requirements. Climatic variations within a small area make for the adaptability of the exchange system to local agricultural requirements; but even then the range is relatively narrow.

This form of labour can only absorb individuals who are independent producers. *Minga* participants are, therefore, not unemployed individuals in search of an income but individuals with agricultural demands of their own. The labour exchange system cannot absorb surplus labour in the community. An Indian whose father has very little land at his disposal cannot depend for his subsistence on the feast that follows the *minga*, and still less on straight labour exchanges. Nowadays, these unemployed individuals are absorbed by the local White wage-labour demand; in previous times there was an adequate supply of land, so that the problem of landless Indians searching for other means of subsistence did not arise.

Naturally, inability to harness the community's labour potential militates against its potential economic growth. The issue, however, has to be considered together with three other problems: availability of land, productivity of land and the system of tenure. As has been pointed out, all the land in the area has been distributed and most of it is in use. Though much of the unused land is totally unproductive, some could be exploited by the farmer who controls it if he could attract labourers or if it could be leased to other Indians. Tenure regulations proscribe the latter solution, and the former is only open if wage labour becomes a more feasible possibility. The difficulties are discussed in the next section. Population increase does not result in higher labour-inputs with consequent increase in productivity; it leads to emigration to lowland plantations.

Wage labour. A wage labourer is expected by custom to work from 8 a.m. to 5 p.m. with a rest for lunch. But the hour of the day is judged by the position of the sun and thus a fixed schedule is not kept. Furthermore, Indians are not accustomed to eating lunch when working on their own fields and thus often forgo the lunch break when working for a wage. Indians therefore work a longer day than that established by convention.

The pay for an eight-hour day varies considerably, depending on a number of factors: the person who hires the labour; the skill required in the job; and whether food is included. An Indian feeds his own labourers, but payment is seldom more than $2.00 per day. A White settler pays either $2.50 or $3.00 per day, depending on the labourer and on whether food is also provided. The settlers with large coffee plantations and with a large crew of helpers always pay the same wage, but coffee growers with smaller plantations, who hire two labourers for one day and two others for another day, do not always offer the same wage. I was in close contact with one of these White settlers and observed that the amount of food, its quality or its absence, as well as the pay, varied with the worker hired. A *pailero* (skilled worker in sugar production) is always paid at a higher rate, never below $5 per day, but he is highly experienced and has to work a much longer day.

The work of harvesting coffee is done exclusively by Indians. A few White settlers direct the harvest, assuming responsibility for drying and perhaps for pulping the berries, but none work for wages as coffee pickers even if in need of work; it is an unpleasant task and considered beneath their social position. Coffee groves are damp; the berries must be individually selected and the effort of doing this work in an awkward position results in unpleasant neck strains and recurrent headaches even for experienced workers. Members of the White community work only as house builders, *paileros*, carpenters, carriers, and odd-job men. They are paid higher wages than an Indian doing the same task, i.e. a minimum of $5 a day, and possibly more. The difference in the rate of pay is not based on the greater knowledge or ability of the White labourer, with the exception of house building, but on the difference in social position.

The Páez have little regard for those Indians who do not remain independent and full-time farmers. Ideally, an Indian should acquire sufficient land and work it successfully enough to produce all the food he may need. Those who frequently work as labourers are considered lazy d fters, unwilling to work the land they possess. The families who stay at home take great pride in the fact, though few can afford to rely solely on their food and cash crops; but no Indian, even those in serious need, seeks seasonal work in San Andrés. The White settlers must visit the Indian's home by

3 a.m. and plead for a few days of their labour. At most, an Indian condescends to appear in the hamlet on market days where he knows he will be approached by coffee growers. Sometimes he receives advance payment, yet still waits a few days before appearing for work, working then for a day or two and then perhaps waiting two weeks before fulfilling the verbal contract. The labour team on which a coffee grower can count is very unreliable; one day he may have a full crew, another day only half. The smaller coffee growers find themselves in a difficult situation: sometimes they have large crews when extra labour is not really needed and at other times they are short of labour when they are desperate for it, as at the height of the harvest season. This kind of erratic working rhythm adds more tension to the already strained relationship between Indians and Whites.

The efficiency of Páez labour is low. Páez labourers select coffee beans individually in contrast to the practice of workers in larger Colombian plantations who gather all the beans with one sweeping movement of the arm down the branch. The disadvantages of the second method are that it damages the branches.[2] It does, however, have the immediate effect of requiring less labour.

The Indians constantly complain of the working conditions – that they are not fed properly or that they are not paid enough. However, few complain that they are not given any coca. The Indians begrudge every minute spent in wage labour and the most positive statement I heard was a half-hearted defence of their most frequent employer. Most of the Indians prefer to work for only one or two particular settlers. The strain in the relationship between employer and employee is great and each side complains equally about the other.

With such an uncooperative labour force how does the White settler succeed in collecting a large enough crew? Higher wages or better conditions would not bring more applicants; fringe benefits are considered more important. However, labourers are obtained not by more advantageous contracts, but by placing Indians under the obligation to work. Most of he White settlers are also traders and they are willing to sell food and other goods on credit, especi-

[2] When ripe and unripe beans are picked together they have to be dried before husking. For comparative material on coffee harvesting problems, see Wolf 1956a. Among Mexican peasants ripe beans are picked, dried and then laboriously hulled with a mortar and pestle. (See Foster 1942, p. 24.)

ally just prior to the coffee harvest. The debt is seldom paid in cash. The Indian has little money to spare, and the trader is willing to receive either coffee at a lower than market price or to discount the debt with days of labour, paid at the normal wage rate. Payment in labour is of greater importance to the trader-planter than payment in coffee during harvest time. The system is successful because the Indian's cash needs are greatest just prior to the coffee harvest; *mingas* to weed the coffee groves are usually in progress and meat may be needed; food supplies are running low and the Indians are happy to increase and vary their diet with store-purchased items; the *fiesta* season begins and new clothing may be needed.

Another means of obtaining labour is by extending small loans in the form of advance payments. As we shall see in a later chapter none of these debts are very large or remain unpaid for long. This situation cannot be compared to the extreme indebtedness of the Indians in other parts of Central and South America (Wolf and Mintz 1957, p. 380).

Those settlers who are not traders, but who have enough land, lease it to Indian families in exchange for two days' labour a month and in this way secure their labour force. The labour has to be given when the settler needs it, and extra labour may be demanded at the normal wage rate; a tenant farmer finds it difficult to refuse too often, since he might then find the landowner uncooperative if he were to ask for more land or for the use of wood and water supplies. A White settler with a sufficient number of tenants seldom lacks help. In San Andrés most of the White settlers have small coffee plantations; only one harvests more than 20 loads of coffee during the main harvest. The wealthier land-owners prefer cattle ranches which require less labour, more land and bring higher profits. Nonetheless, only three coffee growers have tenant farmers in proportion to their labour needs. The rest extend loans of money and credit in order to force workers to come when needed. These small loans or credits are considered by the Indians as fringe benefits.

Indian coffee growers with coffee plantations large enough to require constant help during the harvest (there were six such families in my area) could not, of course, attract workers by leasing land or extending credit as Whites do; instead they rely on advances of wages and other fringe benefits. These six families depend almost exclusively on hired labour from San Andrés and other reservations. Some Indians expressed a preference to work for other Páez rather than for White settlers. They are usually given more and better food and drink; breakfast is included as well as two snacks during the day, and a dinner with meat in the evening. This is to be compared with the standard mid-day meal of plantain and manioc offered by the White settlers. If the labourers come from another area they are offered lodgings and find it more comfortable to spend the night in the house of another Indian than in the house of a White settler. Language difficulties are also avoided, though most Indians speak some Spanish and some of the White settlers are fluent in Páez. By offering better working conditions and a more agreeable environment Indians succeed in attracting labourers. Kinship and friendship ties cannot be depended upon to attract wage labour. Indians with large coffee plantations form a separate nucleus within the community of San Andrés, a nucleus that I shall later describe as the 'progressive' Indian farmers. They have broken with some of the ties of tradition, and have moved somewhat apart from the rest of the community.

As a labourer an Indian is not part of a permanent crew or personnel of an organization. No institutionalized procedures involve him in a role relation with co-workers. A Páez Indian does not work for one farmer only. Labourers are extremely mobile; they work one day for one farmer and the next day for another. This shifting from employer to employer is not prompted by a search for better working conditions or higher wages, nor does it make the labour market more competitive. It is the result of the unwillingness of an Indian to work for more than a few days at a time. The short stay of each labourer in any one coffee plantation leaves little opportunity for the development of organized action or corporate bargaining. This lack of commitment on the part of the Indian is only partly explained by the low prestige of labourers. It will be more fully understood when the decision process is discussed.

The individual nature of the labour contract and the amorphous nature of the labour force affects the labour market and the wage rate. Furthermore, the parties to labour contracts usually belong to two very different communities. They do not share the same traditions, the same values or the same economic awareness. Also, the two communities stand in opposition to each other. Mutual resentment and lack of cooperation is always present. It is within this tense atmosphere that wage-labour operates and the negative preconception held by each of the contracting parties influences the fulfilment of their specific roles. To the Indian labour r the employer is a White and thus to be distrusted; in this category the Indian will also place other Indians who depend mostly on hired labour, since they have moved too far away from traditional values. The Indian accepts that he will be cheated and believes he has no means of demanding better terms.

The White coffee growers expect little efficiency and little co-operation from their labourers. As members of the White community they consider themselves socially superior; they treat their labourers with disrespect and manifest antagonism. In spite of the small scale of the enterprises, relations between employers and employees are not of a paternalistic nature, nor do workers feel strong loyalties to any one settler.

The Indian agricultural labour force has no cohesiveness, it is not fully dependent on employment, and does not develop personalized ties. It does not have the bargaining power of industrial workers, but at the same time it is not so dependent upon employment for subsistence. Labour commitments are assumed by a San Andrés Indian in order to satisfy marginal cash needs. For the above reasons it may be better to speak of 'labour pool' or 'labour potential' rather than 'labour force'.

Comparing and contrasting the wage labour system with the exchange labour system it can be remarked that while in one case payment is made to the domestic unit – a feast or labour return – in the other, payment is made to the individual. The wage labourer receives a personal compensation for his effort, and his sharing it with other family members depends on his own decision or on social obligations; unlike exchange labour, wage labour offers the possibility of economic independence. I have already described how the young men resort to wage labour and spend their earnings on themselves rather than in helping with family expenses. I have pointed out how this has jeopardized the authority of the father within the family. When a young man is hired as a coffee picker he is paid the same as his father or any older member of the community. The employers take little notice of social distinctions among Indian employees. In many ways a young man is preferred to an older man because he is stronger, a better worker and has more time available. Though a young man with cash in his pocket may feel strong enough to challenge his father, he realizes that he still depends on him for the plot of land that will make him a fully-fledged member of the community.[8]

Wage earning is not the only means the Páez have of obtaining cash. It is still more profitable to be a large and successful coffee grower. On the basis of the 1961 harvest, a very good year for coffee, the estimated total income from the sale of coffee beans within the area must have been between $70,000 and $90,000 (Colombian pesos), depending on the actual sale price paid to each grower. On the other hand the cash earned from wages could not have been higher than $50.000 (Colombian pesos). Young wage earners are seldom able to compete in wealth and purchasing power with some of the older Indians who have invested in coffee groves or cattle.

Little money circulates within the community through wage labour payment. What an individual earns as a labourer is spent on the purchase of goods produced outside the community and not on food or goods produced within it. Earning money has the effect of raising the standard of living and facilitating the acquisition of tools to improve farming efficiency. However, money so earned and spent does not help stimulate production. Rather it provides a stimulus to the trading activities of the White settlers, who in this way increase their market for purchased goods brought from the cities and larger towns, or for products such as raw sugar which are manufactured locally by them.

Piecework contract. For some jobs such as the weeding of pasture lands or cane fields a White settler usually prefers to contract an Indian for a specified amount of money. In this way he does not waste time in searching for labourers or in supervising them, which is especially important as pasture lands are at a great distance from San Andrés. From November to Febr ary, when the coffee harvest is in progress, White settlers must remain at home not just to supervise work in their own coffee groves, but also to purchase goods from the Indians and to attend to their stores. From March to October business is very slow, since no one has much money to

[8] Páez young men do not monopolize cash resources. Preference by employers for younger rather than older men does not undermine the authority of the latter to the same degree as described by Hogbin for labourers in the Solomon Islands. (See Hogbin 1941, p. 167.)

spend or coffee to sell: traders have to be alert to other small business ventures to tide them over until the next coffee harvest. They travel to other reservations to buy cattle or laurel wax and to sell their own goods in small quantities. Others have to attend to large cattle ranches far away from San Andrés. The upkeep of small pasture lands and cane fields would require their presence if they were to assume the responsibility of supervision. By hiring an Indian who agrees to assume complete responsibility they are free to attend to their own business needs. There is another reason for this choice: it often costs them less. White settlers are much better at bargaining than Indians who have very little entrepreneurial experience. I discovered that frequently Indians agreed to highly disadvantageous contracts.

When payment for the contract is agreed upon the Indian must either decide to do the work himself or with the help of labourers. What he decides to do depends on the time he has available and on the form of payment he is to receive. If the Indian has asked for a small calf or a horse instead of cash he will have no money to spend on labourers and has the choice of either calling a *minga* or of fulfilling the contract alone. If he is to receive money he may ask for an advance payment and with this pay others to help him. The first procedure is comparatively frequent and is the easiest way for an Indian to acquire animals.

On what basis is payment established? How does an Indian calculate the time he will spend in weeding the field and the margin of profit deserved? He seldom does so. I was present at some of these transactions and could observe the haphazard way in which they were conducted. The White settler approaches an Indian informally wherever they happen to meet, and mentions that he needs a certain job done; depending on how shrewd he knows the Indian to be he either quotes a price or asks the Indian for a bid. The settler already knows the Indian and is quite aware of how low he may bid. Estimates are exchanged, but final settlement is usually left for a later date when, as if by chance, they meet again. When I asked an Indian how long he thought it might take him to weed the pasture land, a job that had just been offered to him on contract, he answered that it was hard to calculate and he really could not tell. They are not accustomed to estimating costs and yields beforehand in terms of weights and prices; their productive decisions are made within a different context and their calculations are not intended to evaluate productivity, as we shall see in the concluding chapters. Lack of experience with a system where products of labour are sold for cash, and a decision-making process where the selected factors are different from those chosen in a market economy, explain the answers received; it is not a question of *irrational* economic behaviour. The Indian's bid is not established on cost and labour but rather on how much cash is needed at the time, or on how much he thinks he can get. At this early stage of the bargaining procedure I was able to press the informant for a time-estimate using peons, and then to help him translate the calculations into cash; it turned out that he would lose money. The reaction was immediate and with an injured air he answered: 'You see how the Whites always take advantage of us'. I could not discover whether my calculation had any influence on the final price settlement. When by simple calculation I could show the Indians that they had made a disadvantageous contract, they would rather exaggerate their helpless position in avoiding exploitation than admit that they were poor or inexperienced bargainers in this type of contractual relation. For this reason it is impossible to rely on verbal account from Indians of past transactions. Information obtained from Whites is equally unreliable, because they either exaggerate their generosity or boast of past business exploits.

One should not conclude that Indians are always poor bargainers within the context of a market economy. In some situations they proved to have a good business sense. I wanted once to buy a small decorated woollen coca bag. It was unusually beautiful and I was glad that the Indian was willing to sell it as they are not normally made for sale. He offered it to me for $60 (£3). I preferred not to bargain in general, but the price shocked me. Very carefully he itemized the price of each one of the yarns, the time his wife had spent in making it and even the amount spent on feeding her. His calculations were correct and the price on this basis was justified, but I withdrew my offer. It would be interesting to know how many Indians follow Juan's careful method of calculation, and how many calculate not in terms of cost but in terms of need. It is possible that if once an Indian asked for a fair payment the White settler might try someone else. Together with a sharper business sense the Indian, however, is also likely to have developed greater business reliability. A cheap contract might take longer to finish and a White settler might prefer to pay more but to deal with a reliable Indian who *would* finish the work much more quickly.

I knew of a considerable number of contracts below cost and of some involving Indians who, I thought, had more experience. Competition for this form of labour is not keen. The less efficient workers restrict themselves for the most part to working on a day to day basis. Only six Indians in the area I studied prefer piecework contracts as a means of earning cash, though occasionally contracts are accepted also by other Indians. This preference seems to depend upon physical fitness, a greater capacity to work and more experience in estimating cost.

Non-agricultural jobs such as roof-thatching, carpentry, and house-building, are usually carried out on a contract basis, but only occasionally are such jobs available. Indians build their own houses, except in the case of women who are living alone. White settlers are now beginning to build sturdier houses with cement floors, and tiled roofs; they contract members of their own community to do the work. There are only two private bridges in San Andrés that need repairing every two years. Skilled contract labour available to Indians is restricted mostly to small repair jobs on fences, doors and roof-patching.

LABOUR DEMAND OF INDIAN AND WHITE FARMERS: THE LABOUR MARKET AND TRADITIONAL LABOUR SYSTEMS

The largest demand for wage labour is from the White settlers, which amounts yearly to about 4,000–5,000 man days (the figure, however, excludes the demand for labourers in sugar processing industries). The eight Indian big coffee growers required only about 1,400 man days annually. There was a further demand for labour from other Indians with coffee yields of three to four loads and from two Indian families with extensive sugar cane plantations who also processed sugar. Thus the intra-community wage-labour demand must be considerably higher than 1,400 man days, but never as high as the White demand for Indian labour.

It is difficult to determine exactly how many of the less wealthy Indians hired labourers. Out of the 22 families studied, who had smaller coffee groves and a little sugar cane, only three hired labourers to work in their fields. One was a widower, another was an Indian who had married into the community, and the third was the *capitán* of San Andrés reservation.

Labourers are also hired between harvests on short piecework contracts or for small garden duties by the White settlers or by the Indians, in order to ensure the quicker completion of a contract undertaken by the hirer. But though competition for labour is not so keen between harvests, the wage remains the same throughout the year.

Wage-labour demand is mostly seasonal. This is partly because of the character of coffee agriculture, but also because of shortage of cash on the part of Indian and White employers between coffee harvesting seasons. This makes it difficult to undertake small and not very profitable agricultural enterprises that require much hired labour.

Effect of White labour demand on Indian agriculture

I have calculated that 72 Indians are willing to work as wage labourers, usually because they are economically compelled to do so, either because they are short of land or are in urgent need of money. Normally they work 3–4 months during the year.

Table 24. Degree of personal commitment to labour pool

	No. of male Indians	
	Frequent wage-labour	*Infrequent wage-labour*
Fathers with sufficient land	4	40
Fathers with insufficient land	25	9
Tenant farmers	23	—
Unmarried young men	20	—
	—	—
Totals	72	49

The above table takes into account only adult male Indians, for the area of the reservation studied, and excludes all those individuals who are either too old to work or who are chronically sick; it also excludes married or unmarried women who only work occasionally during harvest or as domestic help. From Table 24 it appears that the total labour pool of the area studied consists of 121 able-bodied men; there were 17 other male Indians in the area on whom there was insufficient information as to their economic need and who only rarely worked as wage labourers.

These and the other Indians, men and women alike, who work for only a few days during each harvest, do not satisfy the local demand for labour. Outsiders come to San Andrés to help with the coffee harvest; some of them are also Páez Indians from other reservations. Most of the labour potential in the area studied (138 males over 15 years of age) is devoted to cash labour activities from November to February. The Indians' time and physical effort are diverted during these months from their own plantations to those of the White coffee growers. Labour is hence diverted outside the community when it is most needed within it. The demand is not a reflection of the internal labour needs of the economy. The supply is a reflection of the monetary needs of the community. This need could also be satisfied through the expansion of the Indians' coffee plantations but the capital required is hard to obtain. As a result the labour potentialities of the community are drained away, instead of being utilized for higher return within the community.

The response to the outside labour demand is motivated by the cash needs of individuals, yet the wage reward is not related to the price of the goods purchased. While in the surrounding settlements and even in San Andrés a White would not be hired for less than $5 a day an Indian is never paid more than $3. At the same time an Indian is often charged a higher price for goods purchased in the stores. The disparity is easily understandable if one remembers that labour exchange takes place between two different economic systems and under conditions of relative geographic isolation. Furthermore, there is no sharing of the socially prescribed rules to which bargaining is subjected. The wage-labour system is not properly integrated as a free competitive market. Money is itself a very scarce thing; an Indian may be willing to work for even less than the going wage rate so long as he is paid in cash. If a higher wage is offered in another plantation and the Indian is free to move and work there he might do so. The wage level is affected by many local factors affecting free market competition as well as by prevailing prices and costs of production. A careful investigation of factors impinging on the wage level would lead me away from the topic under discussion. The point I would like to make is that the draining of labour away from the community harms the internal production of the Páez Indian economy, and labour expenditure brings to an Indian a low reward in relation to the purchasing power of the money he earns.

Competition of White and Indian employers

How does the economic labour exchange over bo ndaries affect the internal wage labour demand? The few Indians with coffee plantations extensive enough to need a considerable amount of labour (eight families within my area) find themselves having to compete with much wealthier White settlers. Most of the White coffee growers either have large enough areas of land to have tenants, or they are traders and can procure enough men by involving the Indians in debt, as has been previously described. Furthermore, White settlers have other sources of income and a better knowledge of coffee prices. They can afford to pay $2.50 or $3.00 per labourer daily. Indian families short of cash find it difficult to pay the standard wage, and pay from $2.00 to $2.50. However, they offer much better food and lodgings. Páez from a distance prefer to work for other Indians, finding it more comfortable to be among their own people. This is the main advantage that Indian coffee growers hold over Whites. Indians, nevertheless, cannot depend on kinship or friendship ties to obtain help. The eight Indian families who devoted most of their land to coffee attempted to purchase larger extensions of land, and gave up their *fiesta* commitments; by so doing they drifted away from approved economic goals and broke their social obligations to other members of their community. Contact with kin amongst these Indians is often minimal and in some cases even strained. I know of only one wealthy Indian of San Andrés, who lives just outside the area studied, and who is able to depend on some of his relatives for wage labour. He is, however, much wealthier than the other eight Indians mentioned, and has managed to maintain general respect.

Most of the Indians find it difficult to borrow money to hire labourers during the harvest. Only the wealthier ones can purchase meat on credit or borrow cash until the coffee is ready for sale, without obligating themselves to work as wage labourers. The others find hiring help beyond their means and have to harvest as best they can, with the help of their own families.

It can be said, perhaps, that competition with White traders may serve as a stimulus to the more 'progressive' Indians who, in this way, are forced to find new sources of cash to pay for their labour needs. They might, for example, convert more of their land to coffee instead of food production. There are, however, limitations to expansion: first, the necessary capital is difficult to acquire; second, it is illegal and not easy to acquire more land; third, food crops are also needed to feed the labourers that have to be hired for coffee harvesting.

The White coffee growers' demand for labour during the harvest months makes difficult the organization of any form of cooperative or exchange labour arrangement amongst those Indian families who cannot afford cash expenditure for wage labour. Very few households can depend on the help of friends or kin during this time of the year. An Indian's free time is spent working for outsiders either to earn money or to pay a debt. *Mingas* and labour exchanges are, then, restricted to the period between February and October when the outside demand for labour is low.

Effect of traditional labour system on agriculture and wage labour

Unless the Indian farmer can count on a sufficient labour contribution from his son or sons he hesitates to plant too many coffee trees in case he may not be able to harvest the berries before they fall to the ground. Traditional labour is mostly restricted to the planting and upkeep of food crops during the non-harvest months. Outside this season, the traditional labour system concentrates on planting food crops that provide at least a minimum subsistence. The cash expenditure required in exchange labour is low. Thus in San Andrés, where cash income is not on a par with cash demand, there is still an avenue open for agricultural expansion of food crops. Traditional labour exchanges thus have an adaptive function during this stage of economic change. Were labour exchanges also applied to coffee production the gap between the larger Indian producers and the rest of the population might not be so great. It allows for the relatively smooth functioning of the economy in spite of the strains caused by a heavy cash demand, which is only half met through the sale of coffee and labour services.

The presence of an alternative source and type of labour adds another imperfection to the internal labour market. Not only does it block the possible competition of the poorer farmers but also stimulates the continuation of traditional agriculture which provides only a minimum subsistence; at the same time preventing over-dependence on wage income.

Though the use of traditional labour exchanges affects the wage level in the labour market, so that this does not exactly reflect the slope of the supply and demand curve, it also indirectly contributes to the maintenance of wages at a lower level than wages outside San Andrés. Traditional labour exchanges allow the Indian farmers to continue planting and expanding their fields; they do not become completely dependent on wage earning for subsistence and can work for short or long seasons according to the demand of the White settlers. If the Indians were either full-time farmers or completely dependent for subsistence on earned wages, the White employers would either have to offer permanent jobs or higher rates, which would attract outside seasonal labourers.

8

The Páez Farmers: Socio-Economic Constraints and Productivity

In this chapter I shall discuss some of the predicaments faced by Páez farmers as well as their performance as part-subsistence farmers. I hope to show, with the data collected from 26 families, that the outcome of their activities represents a fair solution to some of the problems encountered. The problems to which I refer are constraints on allocation of resources, on availability of factors of production, and on social rewards derived from economic activities. Some of these points have already been touched upon in previous chapters, while those relating to the distribution and marketing of farm products are discussed in chapter 9. It is not my intention to lay greater emphasis on economic determinants of social behaviour, or to treat social factors as inescapable and unchanging limitations on economic behaviour. Social rewards are derived from economic activities and sometimes constitute the main goal of a particular course of action; at the same time one requires goods and labour to satisfy social obligations. I must also remind the reader that, as has been pointed out in the introduction and in the first chapters, social obligations are not inescapable, that sanctions do not always ensure conformity and furthermore that individual and communal aspirations change with a rise in expectations and increased opportunities. The interlinking of social and economic factors is described in more detail when the decision-making process is outlined in chapter 10. In this chapter, I have attempted to present the bare outlines and have thus been forced to disregard a myriad variations and draw them together into general trends.

The farming activities of the Indians can be studied either by carefully analysing individual performances and individual decisions as attempted in chapter 10, or by focusing on the performance of the system. It should not be forgotten in the latter case that the Páez Indian reservation does not operate as an isolated self-contained unit. It is a sub-system of the larger Colombian economy. Although the goals and economic relations differ in each system, one is dependent upon the other. This interdependence is expressed in terms of in-put and out-put relations. The Indian community provides labour and agricultural products and in exchange receives cash, city-manufactured goods and processed foods. The coffee harvest is sold in its entirety to White traders who transport it to bigger towns and cities; on the other hand the food produced remains within the San Andrés Indian community; only a small portion is consumed by Whites. Thus in order to understand the performance of the Páez sub-system one has to take into account the demands of the coffee market and of local traders.

The specialization of Páez as subsistence farmers, and of Whites as coffee planters and traders, as well as the difference between these two groups in regard to contact, knowledge, wage rate, and access to resources, permits us to treat Páez farmers as if they were members of a separate sub-system. The fact that the boundary that separates the two economic systems is also the boundary that separates the two socio-political systems lends support to the conceptualization of the Páez economic activities as a system. It must not be forgotten, however, that each individual Indian stands in a separate relation to this socio-economic boundary.

It is helpful to study the performance of a system, particularly if one is interested in the problems of the economic growth and the contributions which peasants make to the national economy. It is for this reason that, whenever possible, I present data which would make such analysis possible. It is, however, impossible for me to give complete information in terms of aggregate figures; for reasons that must be obvious to the reader they are difficult to obtain. The other disadvantage of the system approach is that it is not always possible to deduce individual behaviour from aggregate behaviour and to understand the observed range of economic activities. Research workers interested in the rise and growth of middlemen and entrepreneurs will benefit more from a close-range analysis of the economic activities of individuals. In this chapter, as well as in the chapters on labour resources and marketing channels, I attempt to bridge the gap between the two approaches and present information which, though structured in terms of the analysis of individual decisions, will permit other research workers to test their own hypotheses.

THE GENERAL GOALS OF ECONOMIC ACTIVITIES

The Indian community is not a perfectly homogeneous community as regards economic aspirations and willingness to comply with certain traditional expenses by each individual family. As far as this is concerned one finds not only individual differences but two general and distinct trends of economic aspirations, which are not, of course, mutually exclusive. At the end of this chapter, I shall consider the large variations in individual goals and efforts, but at present I shall disregard them and describe only the two main goal orientations. I shall refer to these as the 'traditional' and the 'progressive'. These two terms are not to be taken as corresponding to types within a sequence of development, but rather to types which affect, each in their own way, the process of economic development. I have used these terms because they are equivalent to the terms used locally: *indios cerrados* (meaning unwillingness to accept anything new) and *indios racionales* (rational Indians). Each term also expressed in one word the general tone of the ideologies of each type.

The 'progressive' Indians. These families show an interest in maximizing, above all, their cash resources. With more money they can purchase more manufactured goods, some of which have productive utility, while others serve as status symbols. Cash is not earned by working as labourers, an economic role which would put them in a position of inferiority to a White peasant. For economic reasons which will be discussed, food is not produced for export; instead their coffee groves are expanded, and pasture fields are acquired to provide for an increase of herds. In order to facilitate expansion wage labour is hired, and this forsaking of the traditional *minga* and labour exchange systems is motivated by a disdain for them, as well as by doubt of their efficiency and the impossibility of being able to return the labour involved. Not all the land, however, can be converted to coffee production and cattle raising, since food has to be planted to feed the family and the workers.

The money earned by these 'progressive' Indians is not spent in giving *fiestas* except in rare cases when a family accepts the position of helper to a *fiestero* friend (family 21); even in this case the expenses incurred are well below their means. None of them ever become *fiesteros* themselves and very few are willing to be helpers. Instead they make money contributions to the church, spend a large part of their income on better clothing, rice and processed foods, improve their houses, and expand their fields.

The 'traditional' Indians. Though they plant as much coffee as they can they are equally interested in planting more manioc and corn. Their object is not merely to produce enough food to feed the family and labourers throughout the year, as is the case with the 'progressive' Indians, but also to provide gifts whenever the occasion arises and to accumulate the amount necessary for a *fiesta.* Sugar cane is another important crop, and is used to produce fermented drink to serve to friends and neighbours who are invited to an afternoon of drinking. As can be seen, food is reserved for the family's subsistence needs and the fulfilment of social obligations. If a relative or friend loses part of his own harvest it is considered an obligation to exchange, lend or even to sell him what he might need; but the sale of food at the market place is considered a different matter and is not approved by the 'traditional' members of the community. Since food should not be produced for sale there is no point in the unlimited expansion of manioc and plantain fields beyond the family needs specified above. Help for agricultural activities is enlisted by calling a *minga* whenever possible. If there is money available and only a few workers are needed cash payment may be offered. The 'progressive' Indians might be happy to work as labourers if they were hired on a basis equivalent to that of White peasants, but 'traditional' Indians look down on any form of wage labour. This does not mean that they do not often work for wages; on the contrary, since most of the 'traditional' Indians are poor they are forced to work in the coffee plantations around San Andrés. The cash earned either from the sale of coffee or from wage labour, should be spent on agricultural expansion or on fulfilling social obligations rather than on the accumulation of wealth objects. The clothing of the 'traditional' Indians is generally poor and their houses are built without any of the conveniences and luxuries frequently found in the houses of 'progressive' Indians. *Fiestas,* liquor, meat and increased food consumption are the main expenditures. If earnings are sufficient they may be invested in a cow or a horse, or on more and better agricultural equipment. On the whole the 'traditional' Indians are less vocal about their future economic plans than other Indians. When asked how much they thought they might plant the following season, they generally answered that they would plant as much as they would need, no more no less. It was an abstract measure impossible to define with more precision. Sometimes even after planting they had no idea of the number of manioc plants that were beginning to sprout in their fields. A 'progressive' Indian, on the other hand, can talk for a long time on agricultural techniques as well as the folklore associated with it, and on his own plans of production. This difference in approach to management cannot be simply explained by the lack of foresight or lack of ability on the part of 'traditional' Indians. 'Progressive' and 'traditional' Indians could, with individual differences, plan ahead if necessary. The lack of planning and of careful measurement of yields and costs is explained in the next chapter in terms of the internal requirements of the economy, which define the opportunities available to the individual. Aspirations affect actions, but it must be remembered that they are also shaped by the opportunities available to the farmer. The 'progressive' and the 'traditional' farmer must not be taken as two rigidly defined types; they are flexible concepts which reflect the economic situation as much as the personalities and aspirations of the farmers.

The difference between 'traditional' and 'progressive' Indians is one of degree of concern in the general orientation of farming and other economic activities. Each type is interested in increasing productivity, improving the standard of living and achieving greater prestige within their own ranks; the 'progressive' Indians are trying at the same time to align themselves with the White community.

For a better understanding of the possibilities of economic change within the Páez communities of San Andrés it would be interesting to determine how the 'progressive' are differentiated from the 'traditional' Indians, and whether more Indians are likely to become 'progressive' in their outlook. Unfortunately little can be inferred from the life history of the 'progressive' Indians or from accounts by older members of the reservation. Their background varies considerably from case to case. In some cases the

Indians or their parents are newcomers from other reservations, in others they are old-established families. Some have spent a considerable time working outside, but so had some of the very 'traditional' individuals. In some cases only one member of the family had broken away from subsistence agriculture to rely more heavily on coffee growing. To some degree what happens depends on the personality of the Indian. At present the number of those Indians who may unmistakably be referred to as 'progressives' is too small, and the variations from case to case too great, for the social factors that have helped their break from tradition to be isolated and precise hypo heses to be drawn. In this chapter I outline some of the economic factors which have made it possible for some Indians to become successful farmers, as well as the difficulties they have to face when they intend to expand their holding. I hope this discussion will be of help to those who are interested in determining at what point agriculture becomes commercialized.

AVAILABILITY OF FACTORS OF PRODUCTION

Before embarking on an evaluation of the rationality of the outcome of decisions on agricultural production, I shall recapitulate what has been said about the availability of resources.

Land as a factor of production has already been discussed in chapters 4 and 5. In general terms it can be said to be a fixed factor, as the amount of land received in inheritance is all that most farmers can hope to possess. It is possible to buy or lease more land but in the first instance the farmer requires cash to enable him to do so and in the second he must commit his labour to the landlord; both cash and labour are in short supply. Furthermore the land available for purchase is often far from the reservation boundaries and thus difficult to administer.

A farmer controls a minimal amount of labour; he has direct control only over his own and his wife's labour; he can count on the help of his small children, who are capable of performing light tasks, but he has only limited control over the labour of his adult sons and daughters. Furthermore, a wife has other duties to perform and though during critical harvest and weeding periods she may work as much as her husband, she has too much work to do at home to be counted as a full-time agricultural labourer. This basic domestic labour potential can be stored and released when needed through the traditional system of labour exchanges. Extra labour can be hired, but the farmer has often little cash before the harvest and competition for labour is very keen.

Seeds and tools are either purchased or acquired in other ways, for example, seeds may be saved from the previous harvest, or may be received free of charge from Whites or Indians. Tools are often manufactured by the farmers themselves. Details are discussed in chapter 6.

Some capital assets may be acquired by barter with traders, coffee being exchanged for tools or animals, or with Indians by exchanging animals for wooden sugar cane mills. In the first case, Indians are bartering with a crop that has only a monetary value; coffee is grown for the cash market, thus any exchange for coffee is equivalent to payment with money. The productive capital assets that may be acquired by barter from other Indians are limited to what they own or manufacture: animals and sugar cane presses; even in these two cases the seller may choose to demand cash instead of goods. Theoretically the cash which a Páez farmer requires for productive investment can be obtained from income saved, or by means of a direct or indirect loan in the form of a credit sale.

In order to increase investment a farmer has either to maximize his cash earning activities or his saving propensity. I have already discussed in chapter 7 some of the problems involved in wage labour as a cash earning activity; I have stressed the fact that the revenue received is less than if the same period of time had been spent in their own coffee plantations; furthermore the local labour demand, though greater than the voluntary supply, is not enough to satisfy the cash needs of the community. In this chapter as well as in chapter 9 I discuss some of the factors which militate against the expansion of coffee plantations, cattle breeding and the sale of food. I have calculated that the average annual cash income of a Páez farmer is $400, which barely covers all the expenses itemized in earlier chapters. It is difficult to talk of 'inducements to save' when incomes are so low. It is equally difficult to calculate what percentage of their income one could expect them to save. It is true that cash incomes can be forgone, that Indians would survive without many of the items which they themselves consider luxuries. In fact, although most Indians do not earn more than it has been calculated they must spend, most manage also to invest in tools, seeds, and the like. Less than one-third of the families studied made a profit which allowed for investment after meeting family and social obligations in full. The other two-thirds had forgone some basic consumption needs in order to invest in equipment. These are some of the issues which make the discussion of thrift or inducement to save amongst low income families very difficult.

A time element is implicit in any definition of savings, where 'savings' means the forgoing of present consumption. If income is regularly spaced, and the intervals that elapse are not extensive, then the concept of time is useful. But when cash revenue may be the result of the annual sale of cash crops, then it is not present expenditure that has to be considered, but future and past expenditure. Cash resources immediately after the sale of the coffee harvest are much larger than immediate food needs; the money is thus spent in purchasing luxury goods, on entertainment or tools, and some may be saved for future investment and food consumption. Savings in the latter case can be defined as forgoing capital investment for future consumption.

In those cases where it can be said that cash saving is intentional, its purpose should be established, i.e. whether it is intended for the purchase of items of prestige, or whether it is meant for productive investment. If the immediate goal is productive investment, what then is its scope? The nature of the economic action is not the same if savings are used to replace a machete for subsistence production, and if they are invested in labour to expand cash crop production. In other words, one should distinguish between savings to cover depreciation cost, to bring prestige, to increase the standard of living and to increase the productivity of the farm. Furthermore, if savings are used to cover depreciation, does this refer to equipment to be used in subsistence production or cash production? Thus, the nature and aim of saving behaviour has to be examined in the context of economic decisions. In a subsistence economy or in the subsistence sector of the economy, depreciation of productive resources has a social dimension which may be more effective than economic considerations in encouraging the replacement of tools. If shortage of tools limits the amount of food produced, the family may have to purchase from others and thereby lose the respect of neighbours. A similar example would be the purchase of new tools for use by a younger son; not only will the father then be able to ask him to help with the weeding, but this action will contribute to the reaffirmation of the tie and future cooperation between them.

In the above discussion I have talked of savings in terms of the nature of the intended investment, since only in these terms can we discuss saving behaviour among the Páez. It is true that time always elapses between the moment when payment is received and the money is spent. It could be said that money is being saved for a limited period, but it is impossible to account for such short-term savings. None of the Páez families I met saved money from one main coffee harvest to the next. Whether this was due to very meagre income, or to heavy investment in social and productive activities it is hard to tell. It is difficult to talk of savings of food because these assets have mainly a subsistence function and, moreover, storage is difficult if not impossible, given the present technical level of Páez farming. Cattle can be considered as savings which can easily be converted into money, but cattle have also a traditional function which limits the liquidity. Cows are necessary for *fiestas* and for *mingas*. A family which does not intend to save an animal, does not intend to keep up traditional obligations. Cattle, furthermore, once butchered have to be consumed and an animal is too large to sacrifice merely for household use. Hence, the only alternatives are either to save it for a traditional purpose or to sell it for cash. The Indians are not familiar with the current market prices for cattle and are convinced, often with justification, that a White trader will only buy an animal from them at an unfair and low price. It is understandable, therefore, that they prefer to keep the animal, unless they are in distress and need a considerable amount of cash or food. Thus practical and ideological factors militate against the disposal of cattle except for special occasions and ensure that savings accumulate in the form of animals owned.

In practice Indians never speak of savings; they talk about investing or preparing for a *fiesta*. The latter does not entail heavy cash expenditure and preparations do not commence until the planting season prior to the date on which the celebration is to take place. (See chapter 3.)

If an Indian does not realize a sufficiently large profit from the coffee harvest or if he is unable to save enough to cover intended purchases later in the year he may buy from the local traders on credit. On the whole, Indians are reluctant to buy on credit and traders are reluctant to extend it.

Whether a trader extends credit or not depends partly on the reliability of the individual farmer, and on the length of time which the trader estimates the farmer will require to repay the credit. Not all traders agree on how profitable it is to sell on promise of future payment, the difference of opinion being a direct reflection of the trader's capital assets and his reliance on trading as his main economic activity. Traders with small capital and small stock cannot afford to have many outstanding debts. On the other hand, wealthier traders can afford to do so and use credit as a means of enlargi g the market for their products. I found that Indians could not afford to buy meat with cash just prior to the harvest; yet it would be at this time that a cattle breeder who was also a butcher could sell most of his meat. This man encouraged Indians to buy and sold $600 worth of meat on credit prior to the harvest. He was less encouraging after the season, often refusing an Indian's request and sold only about $300 worth of meat on credit at the time. Expensive equipment could only be purchased with cash immediately after the harvest. For this reason traders are quite willing to sell expensive tools on promise of payment, preferably shortly before the coffee is ready for harvesting. One of the two major store owners in San Andrés had sold $800 worth of hard goods on credit and was still owed $500. The other major store owner, who relied completely on the income from buying and selling and had no significant amount of land or cattle, was owed $3,000 by Indians. As this particular trader did not know how to write and kept only very rudimentary records, it is impossible to calculate the total value of the goods sold to Indians on credit duri g a year and the time which had elapsed before each debt was repaid. Most other stores preferred to restrict credit sales to the minimum, and to limit them to the harvest period.

Credit sales have other advantages: in the first place the storekeeper can afford to ask a higher price for his goods than if he is selling for cash, as the Indian is in need of them and has little money in his pocket. In the second place, he can ask for the credit to be repaid either in coffee, at a price which he specifies, or by labour. In this way traders assure themselves of a clientèle of coffee sellers and of a labour force. Indians who live a retired existence far away are likely to be unfamiliar with cash and prices and are easy prey.[1]

[1] Some Indians are not familiar with the use of money and others who are find the most simple calculations difficult. Other Indians, however, handle money easily and are acquainted with market prices beyond their own locality. In the reservations of San Andrés experience with monetary economy is uneven, but there is greater sophistication with the medium of exchange than is described by Firth for Tikopia (see Firth 1959, pp. 146–52).

A trader is willing to take the risk of delayed payment in return for an unusually high profit. Money owed by an Indian was ultimately paid, traders assured me, and if they delayed too long in their payment a complaint to the municipal authorities in Inzá would either result in quick settlement of the debt or in the confiscation of an animal by the trader. It is important to note that tools and clothing are stocked almost exclusively for sale to the Indians. Whites are either traders themselves or travel to bigger towns where prices are much lower – about half the San Andrés prices – and the selection larger. Only the more important traders extend credit to Indians during the non-harvest season. This is because of the seasonal nature of their own money resources for investment in stock.

Most Indians are aware of the way in which traders manipulate credit sales in order to extract higher profits; yet they continue to make use of this method of purchase because of lack of cash and their wish to buy tools and meat to feed *minga* or hired labourers. In this way they can purchase goods long after they have consumed their meagre cash income which is so low that it is almost impossible to budget it successfully so as to cover all expenses for the year. It must be stressed that though meat is sold on credit and that on occasion other food is also sold in this way, most of the purchases on credit are of tools and equipment.

It is very difficult, if not impossible, for a Páez to borrow money. A friend may be approached for a loan of a few pesos if he is known to have cash, but it is not often that an Indian has money to lend. If he has, and lends it, he does not expect to receive interest. The same expectations underlie any requests for loans from a White settler. They are not sufficiently frequent to be considered as a business transaction, but are rather thought of as friendly help to a client or neighbour in desperate need. The Indian is more prepared to be refused a request for a money loan, than to be told to repay it with a certain rate of interest. Often there is a hidden interest in the established rate for repayment in coffee. Traders prefer loans to be paid in coffee grain, not only because interest can be charged without having overtly to state this, but also because it is easier to put pressure on the Indian to sell a few more pounds of beans at the same low rate. I found only two traders who would lend money to Indians and one of them had only four outstanding debts recorded in his book, amounting to $520, since the last harvest, six months before; a fifth debt of $30 had already been paid. There are other rare, scattered, instances of White settlers lending a few pesos, seldom as much as 20 at a time, but in general an Indian has difficulty in borrowing money when unusual expenses arise. A settler or a trader is more likely to comply when the reasons given for the need of a loan are of a personal rather than a productive nature. Lending is considered to be an expression of social cooperation between two individuals rather than as a business proposition, and is more likely to occur when it is meant to relieve misfortune than when it is used for investment.

Only those individuals who lend money as a business proposition are interested in its intended use, as the type of investment may indicate what are the chances of the borrower repaying the loan. Moneylenders are non-existent in this area, and in this way San Andrés is unlike most underdeveloped areas. The reasons are quite simple. In the first place, land cannot be mortgaged and hence the only security a lender can hope for is the coffee harvest. It is just as easy and less risky to buy the harvest while the berries are still green, but ripe enough for him to estimate the yield. The trader buys it at a lower price and in return offers the farmer an advance of money. In the second place, a man with capital can expend his trading activities, or cattle farms and obtain a higher return than by lending money at high interest. In the third place, as the Indians are short of cash and cannot pay back within a short time, profitable money-lending calls for a considerable initial investment.

The Caja Agraria, a government agency, extends loans to Indians and Whites alike for productive purposes. However, Indians are diffident about using this source. I knew of only one instance within my area when applications had been made. The representative of the Caja Agraria is located in Belalcázar, four to five hours' distance from San Andrés, and the Indians are mystified by the rules and conditions imposed on loans. The one case cited to me was that of a wealthy Indian coffee-grower who knows how to read and write and feels confident in his dealings with the White authority.

Since Indians cannot mortgage their land, as they lack individual titles, the only loans open to them at the time this research was conducted were short-term loans for a period of one year at 6 per cent interest. The guarantees required were of a personal nature, though the Caja Agraria could repossess tools, machinery and crops if repayment was not made. Credit was extended for the purpose of planting permanent or annual crops as well as to cover the improvement or maintenance of permanent crops. It could also be obtained for the purchase of machinery, tools, cattle or to make permanent improvements on the land. Theoretically a farmer could ask for $40,000, except in the case of the purchase of cattle when the ceiling was $10,000. The Caja Agraria was unlikely to extend credit to poorer and less sophisticated farmers unless the organization could supervise the farming activities involved. This is a very understandable condition, but as the organization lacked adequate personnel for such supervision, the chances that a small farmer would be granted credit were not very high. It also discouraged credit for the purchase of expensive equipment unless cooperative arrangements for the use of the machinery had already been made. It must be obvious to the reader the Caja Agraria does indeed fulfil its function of helping the small farmer (who, according to their specification, must not hold assets exceeding $120,000), but does not really help the poorer farmers or the Páez farmer.

CONSTRAINTS INHERENT IN PRODUCTION FOR CASH

The local demand for coffee is at present unlimited. Coffee buyers will continue to buy coffee, even if the price falls or profits shrink, since there are no other marketable crops and few other large-scale trading opportunities. The purchase of sugar cane for grinding and conversion into sugar will remain a minor opportunity, because of competition with the cheaper industrially produced sugar from Popayán. Furthermore, one activity does not exclude the other, as sugar cane matures after the coffee harvest, and the proceeds from the latter can be used for the former.

Coffee buyers can also use their capital in cattle-raising enterprises, and those who have been able to acquire extensive pasture-lands have curtailed their coffee buying activities. But good lands are hard to find and at present there are plenty of Whites with capital available to buy all the coffee that this valley is capable of producing. The most important point is that the Indians themselves regard the demand for coffee as unlimited and believe that the price fluctuations simply respond to the mood of the buyers in Bogotá. The first part of the statement is from the local point of view, well founded; the second is, of course, a myth. Nevertheless, it is this fact and this myth which condition their behaviour; fate affects prices and there is little the Indians can do. Furthermore, they think it is impossible to saturate the market.

Coffee prices have fluctuated considerably during the past decade as shown in Figure 1. The drop from 1957 prices is still fresh

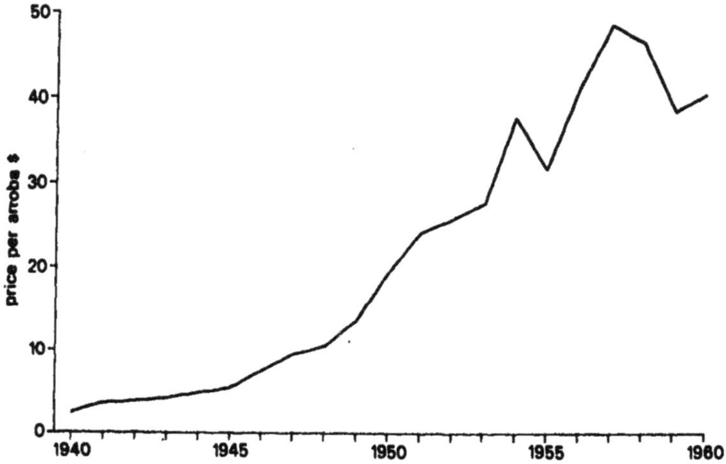

Fig. 1. Average coffee prices 1940–61[1]

in the minds of the Indian farmers and though there has been a recovery recently all Indians spoke of the unfavourable price fluctuations. The psychological effect was considerable and has made them cautious about the advisability of this cash crop. The price of wheat has risen from that which was current at the time when San Andrés gave up its wheat fields and planted coffee bushes instead. Indians talked of rehabilitating the old wheat-grinding mill and of trying again to plant this crop on the lower slopes. There is little understanding of price fluctuations and unless coffee prices are maintained on the same level or rise steadily for a few years the Páez will continue to be dubious about the advisability of coffee as a cash crop.

The 113 Indian coffee plantations produced a total of about 2,000 arrobas (50,000 lb.) for the main harvest of November-January, 1960–1, within the area studied. Eight families had a yield of 80 to 120 arrobas (2,000–3,000 lb.) and none of the remaining 105 families harvested more than 40 arrobas (1,000 lb.) each,

[1] Calderon Riveras 1960, pp. 45–6. The prices listed are the average prices given by the Federación de Cafeteros.

averaging 13 arrobas (325 lb.) each. By way of comparison,[8] 20 of the 37 settlers just outside the reservation produced 2,300 arrobas (57,500 lb.) for the same period. Some of the families harvested only 10 arrobas (250 lb.). Only eight of them were able to sell more than 120 arrobas (3,000 lb.) and the highest production was 500 arrobas (12,500 lb.). Five White settlers produced approximately 80 arrobas (2,000 lb.) and the remaining nine families ranged from 10 to 40 arrobas (250 lb. to 1,000 lb.) during the main harvest. Though the total output of the Indian coffee production is not much smaller than that of the White settlers, it is distributed amongst a much larger number of producers. Also a smaller proportion of the Indian farmers than of the White farmers can be considered large coffee producers, relative to local standards. The harvesting and planting procedures in these larger plantations are, of course, different from those obtaining in the smaller Indian coffee groves, and the problems of coffee production will accordingly be different.

The large plantations require a considerable amount of labour during the harvest month, while a plantation which does not produce much over 40 arrobas (1,000 lb.) of coffee may not need to hire outsiders if the farmer can count on the help of his wife and a son. Hence, it can be said that expansion beyond a harvest of 1,000 lb. can only be considered by those families whose income is high enough to enable them to hire labour during the harvest. In spite of the strains and stresses of the father-son relationship, some Indians with several adult sons may not have to hire labourers.

Outside labour at harvest time can be obtained, but only by advanced payment in cash. A poor Indian does not find it easy to obtain cash before harvest time. Loans are not extended unless the Indian already has a plantation large enough to provide the security of a good harvest, and even then credit is very difficult to obtain. Some of the Indian families earn cash by weeding the coffee plantations of the Whites, but July to September are the months of food shortage, of high corn prices and of little work, and the cash earned during this period is usually spent to cover immediate needs.

[8] United Nations, Food and Agricultural Organization, *Coffee in Latin America*, part 1, Colombia and El Salvador, 1958, pp. 1–104. The Survey of Colombia demonstrates that most of the coffee production is from peasant holdings. In fact, 36 per cent of the coffee plantations are 1 hectare or less, 58 per cent are between 1 and 10 hectares, and 6 per cent are more than 10 hectares in size.

Not only does a head of a household count on a small family labour force, but his time has to be divided between his own coffee grove and those of an employer. Wage labour may not be, during this season, an occupation of his own choice but he may be forced to work in order to pay off debts. Ability to stay clear of debt is important if he is to retain control over his own time and labour resources, and arrange a more efficient allocation of resources. Debts, in the case of the Páez, are not always absolutely necessary; they are often the result of purchasing on credit and inability to budget cash. This was, at least, the problem faced by one of the five families mentioned earlier who, having adequate land and labour resources for expansion found themselves working to pay off debts contracted with local traders.

The coffee harvesting season coincides with the *fiesta* cycle which starts in late November. Beans are not then dry enough for sale and money is needed. Indians do not trouble to attend a *fiesta* unless they have money for drink, or are good friends of the *fiestero*. Few would want to miss the *fiesta* of the patron saint, and therefore work as wage labourers for at least a short time prior to December. Attending a *fiesta* not only requires money, but also time. If the *fiestero* is a friend or kinsman, many days are spent at his house helping him grind cane. An Indian woman complained to me that her husband was at a *fiesta* and had not done any work for over a week. The Indians who choose to participate in the November and December *fiestas* may lose part of their harvest in so doing. Not all the Indians attend all the *fiestas*, and may attend only the morning Mass and then go home. *Fiestas* do not consistently cut down the production of the same families year after year, but affect the total yearly production of the community.

If a family decides to plant a large number of trees with the intention of hiring labourers for the harvest, sufficient land has to be set aside to plant enough manioc and plantains to feed both the family and the labourers. The more land is planted with coffee, the more land has to be planted with food. Coffee trees produce for about 20 years and perhaps more. A decision to use the land available for this cash crop means that it will not be available for any other use for a long period of time. Before the 20 years are over, very probably sons will have grown old enough to demand a plot of land for themselves. It is unlikely that a father would want to part with a section of the coffee grove he has planted himself. If a Páez has several young sons and enough land, he may try to reserve enough to allot them a piece when they are old enough so as to avoid estrangement and hoping to have them as helpers for his own coffee harvest. In order to avoid these difficulties and problems, a proper ratio of coffee and food land has to be maintained with an eye to the eventual demands for land by the sons. Furthermore, as the first coffee berries appear only after the third year and the maximum yield is reached about the seventh year, an Indian is unlikely to expand his coffee plantation after his sons reach adolescence.

The young saplings used to start a coffee grove are not selected; they are wild saplings which grow in the plantations of neighbours and are given away. Their productivity is therefore uncertain. In some cases new plantations have to be abandoned as a result of the low productivity of trees; years may have been wasted waiting for berries that will never grow. After a failure of this kind further expansion is unlikely, unless the children of the family are still quite young.

The investment of land and labour in coffee bushes brings a yearly cash reward, but the accumulation of money, particularly if it is not to be spent on *fiestas*, is disapproved by the community. Coffee has no traditional meaning and cannot be used as a substitute for any of the foods consumed by families (during a *fiesta*); planting more coffee means having less staples to lend to people in need. A large plantation demands hired labour and hence money must be saved in order to pay wages, which means that it cannot be spent during the early part of the *fiesta* cycle. Putting all one's effort into growing coffee means that a family forsakes traditional values and community obligations; bit by bit it grows apart from its Indian neighbours. Owning coffee trees is considered necessary and all Indians have some, so that the planting of larger areas would not in itself raise objection, but for the fact that the economic conditions of the enterprise entail a break with tradition. Only one of the Indian coffee producers with extensive plantations, by maintaining all his social obligations and generously dispensing drink, was still considered a good member of the Indian community. Unfortunately he accidentally killed a woman during the first month of my stay in San Andrés. He served a long jail sentence in another town and as a result I was unable to investigate the case further. Investment of cash savings in cattle accords better with traditional values and economic requirements (cattle also serve to feed guests and *minga* labourers) and gives more prestige to a family. Too great a concern in increasing one's earnings suggests a desire to emulate the Whites, which is frowned upon.

With so many limitations to expansion the reader may wonder how the eight families mentioned succeeded in planting enough bushes to enable them to compete on equal terms with the White settlers. It usually entails considerable personal sacrifice and a capacity for management of money uncommon among the Páez, but it is often also due to circumstances. An only daughter (family 23) who had left the reservation as a young girl when her father died, returned much later as a married woman with several daughters to claim her land. During the intervening years she had worked in bigger towns and had learned how to purchase, sell and bargain – in general how to calculate cash. She was successful in claiming her land, already planted with coffee bushes by her father, and by the neighbours who had taken possession of it during her absence. Her husband worked in a bigger town and sent her money which enabled her to hire labourers and plant more coffee. A loan from a government agency helped through the first years. This opportunity is open to most Indians though they are diffident about using it, as they are unable to understand the paperwork involved. In other cases, already established coffee plantations were purchased at a very low price (family 21) or exchanged for an animal, from Indians who were anxious to leave the reservation. In this way the more capable business-minded Indians were able to expand without the help of loans; nor did they have to wait for the coffee bushes to bear their first-fruits. The circumstances of these purchases were unusual, the procedure illegal and only a few families had an opportunity to profit from these transactions. The only Indian who was, at the time of my research, considering a large expansion was already a wealthy individual who hoped to obtain a government loan for the purpose.

To begin a plantation is not difficult, provided it is not very big, since a large plantation requires much time and hinders the individual from wage labour activities or from planting enough food. The task of planting can be done at almost any season and by only one person. Saplings are acquired free of charge and no other cash investment is required. The most serious initial drawbacks to starting a large plantation are the time and labour required, the shortage of land, and the fact that a young man preparing his plantation has little money or animals to hold a *minga.*

CONSTRAINTS ON FOOD PRODUCTION

Exhausted and eroded soil, coupled with primitive agricultural technique, gives poor yields. Any reasonably large increase in production requires that a much larger area be planted. Manioc tubers are quite small and sometimes almost non-existent; the stems of the sturdier varieties of plantain that can grow on the higher slopes are small, and the fruits themselves do not compare with the valley products. Furthermore, the land has be be allowed to lie fallow for about four to six years for corn but less for manioc and arracacha. Every two acres of manioc and one of corn requires six acres of available land. Often plantains are planted alongside the rows of corn so that after the harvest the land remains under production. For every three acres of manioc and two of corn, 12 acres of land are necessary for the full cycle of crop rotation. Very few farmers have so much land and often large sections are covered by huge rocks, which during the rainy season slide down the mountain, destroying the crops lying in their path. The land of other farmers consists of steep slopes which allow the rains to wash away the manioc stems and rot the tubers.

The price paid for corn and manioc locally is low in relation to the price in towns farther away. Mountain corn is lighter and not highly regarded, bringing a lower price than lowland corn, and though yields are lower it is just as troublesome to grow. Plantains and manioc are considered to be good quality and are purchased locally. But the needs of the 28 White families settled near San Andrés are quite small. Some have at least small fields of manioc and plantains, others depend mostly on purchased potatoes, as these are easier to obtain. Larger farmers can depend on the supply sold to them by their tenants. Purchases from the Indians are irregular, and therefore none of the families can estimate how much manioc and plantain they have purchased throughout the years. Measuring in terms of what was considered locally to be an adequate diet, and from observation of the household where I ate daily, the total yearly consumption of plantain and manioc among the settlers would be: 800 to 1,000 stems of plantain and 15,000 to 18,000 manioc plants; that is, no more than one hectare of each crop. This estimate does not include what might be fed to the pigs, or the amount used to feed peons. The demand, as has been seen, is not large enough to warrant production for a market, particularly as food exchanges amongst Indians are kept outside the market institution. If only 30 families doubled the amount of manioc planted, and 10 of them planted twice as many plantains they would together be able to feed all the White settlers. Production for export to other areas is unlikely. As will be seen in the next chapter, the existing market structure covers distribution between large cities where local products would have to compete with higher and cheaper valley products.

Food is associated with traditional values and compliance with certain social relations. It is to be given in exchanges to help neighbours, and is not to be offered indiscriminately for sale.

There has to be some incentive or reward to motivate expansion of food production beyond the subsistence needs of the family. Cash rewards are doubtful since the demand for food is small. A good corn and manioc harvest allows the Indian to become *fiestero* and increases his prestige within the community – food is, however, not the only expenditure. The family head also has to own cattle and have money in order to cover the other expenditures listed. There is little point in having food if, for other reasons, a *fiesta* cannot be offered.

Clearing of land for food crops can be started during March, after the last coffee berries maturing on the higher slopes have been harvested and sold. An Indian family has about six or seven weeks in which to accomplish this task before the rains make burning of the underbrush impossible. In this period a farmer with one family helper can clear about two acres of land; a longer period would be required if the land was virgin forest, which is no longer the case in the area round San Andrés. Though Indians prefer to call a *minga* when clearing land, this is not necessary unless he intends to plant a large extension. Few Indians troubled to do so (see chapter 7). The rainy season does not, however, dutifully wait for the Indian to finish preparing the land for planting. Threats of early rain force the farmer to choose between hiring labourers or reconsidering his plans for production. If he has no cash and his friends and kinsmen are busy, he has no choice; it is even doubtful whether cash would solve his plight as labourers are hard to find at this time of the year.

On two acres of land an Indian can plant enough to harvest 1–2 loads of corn, 800 manioc plants, a few pounds of beans and some plantains. If a much larger field is desired a *minga* has to be called. However, in order to invite a *minga* the family should have at least a pig, or money to purchase meat, as well as sufficient food remaining from the last harvest. Careful budgeting is necessary in order to stretch the money earned from the sale of 6–10 arrobas of coffee, which is about $240 to $400, over the necessary purchases. A pig, if it has to be purchased, costs $70 to $90. It is small wonder that, unless the poorer families already own animals, they find it very difficult to call a *minga* and plant a larger area of land. The *minga* system has the advantage of allowing the families with enough food to use the help of the poorer families or of those unable to expand their plots.

Corn, potatoes and beans used as seeds have to be purchased or saved from the previous harvest. Plantain saplings and manioc stems may also have to be purchased. The price varies a great deal; manioc stems may be given away, plantain saplings may be sold for 10 cents each, and sugar cane for about $1 a load, but the price may reach $5 a load. The cost may seem low, but it represents a considerable investment for a poor Indian. Frequently, seeds, other than potatoes and corn, are obtained from Indian friends and cash transactions thus avoided. Availability of money, or the willingness of friends to supply seeds, may determine the choice of seeds, crops and the extent of the area planted.

From the foregoing it will be obvious that the total acreage required for food is much larger than for cash crops. This is partly because of soil erosion, but also because of poor agricultural techniques. Introduction of fertilizers, etc. would not only improve the productivity of the soil, but by increasing the yield would reduce the acreage required for subsistence. Although the use of fertilizers would mean an increased labour input Indians may be able to cope with the additional work if it can be spread over the year and does not conflict with the coffee harvest. A labour input of more than three or four workers requires capital to pay wages or to buy food for the helpers. With better techniques and greater cash resources the output of food crops would easily increase as the planting season does not conflict with wage labour activities of the *fiesta* cycle, as is the case with coffee, so that the increase in demand for either *minga* labour or wage labour by Páez farmers does not raise problems in the labour market for coffee or curtail community obligations.

THE RATIONALITY OF PRODUCERS

It is methodologically impossible to test the assumption that Páez farmers behave rationally, in other words whether they combine their resources in such a way that, given their incomplete knowledge and constraints on allocations and utility of resources, they maximize their aspirations and fulfil their obligations. The information available indicates what farmers have done during one year and what they have planned for the following year. It is difficult only on the basis of this information to determine whether they had subjectively considered all opportunities and arrived at the best course of action. It could be argued that the outcome was chance development. In answer to this objection I refer the reader to Tables 26 to 33, which illustrate regularities in the solution used by farmers rather than a wide range of variation such as one would expect from chance behaviour. I have used the word 'illustrate' because I cannot pretend that a small sample of 26 families can serve as a field to test any proposition. I would add, however, that other information and further observation allows the assertion, with a certain degree of confidence, that the regularities were true for the total population of the reservation.

It could also be argued that the regularities were not the result of subjective rational evaluations but of conformity to a specified 'traditional' course of action. In answer to this criticism I would again refer the reader to the quantitative information in this chapter which indicates that farmers do not always plant the same amount year after year, or allocate their resources in exactly the same way. Furthermore, some of them consciously break certain traditional restrictions on sales in the market place and choose not to spend their assets in the celebration of *fiestas*. On the basis of the information so far presented it is difficult to ignore the existence of an area where choice is possible and necessary; the number of changes in the selection of cash crops are cases in point.

Although this book, and the research upon which it is based, were not designed to test the validity of the proposition that peasant farmers behave rationally it is important that I attempt to dispel any serious misgivings in regard to this proposition. As I have already stated in the Introduction, I use the framework of rational decision-making as a means of elucidating the factors which affect decisions as well as the relationship of factors of production to each other and to social aspirations and obligations. In order to dispel any possible misgivings I discuss and evaluate the outcomes of 26 families and hope to show as Edwards (1961) has done for Jamaican farmers and Dean (1965) for Kenya farmers, that the activities of the farmers are reasonable solutions in difficult situations. It is probable that another objection may be raised against my attempt, in which case it will fail to assure the reader that though untested the proposition of rationality is both plausible and useful. It may be said that the argument I present in this chapter constitutes a rationalization of outcome and not an explanation of such outcomes. There is no way in which I can counter the objection; but it is worthwhile to point out that such objections are valid only if levelled against any attempt to explain behaviour. If it is said to be a rationalization when I state that a given set of social and economic constraints, together with a particular set of assets available to the producer, explain the annual outcomes observed for that producer, I can answer by levelling the same criticism against those who say that the behaviour of individuals can be explained in terms of their obligations. To say that farmers produce a given amount of grain because of 'tradition' is equally a rationalization.

Both land and labour are limited but Indians succeed in allocating these two resources so as to produce sufficient food for their own consumption and yet to allow for the production of a cash crop. The cash crop chosen for production is one that is suited to the local climatic conditions, the labour requirements available and the availability of outlets for the sale of the crop. Table 25 illustrates the labour required for different crops. The maximum requirements are those for plantations where the yields are higher than average, or where the crop has to be marketed by the farmer, if the plantation is to yield the maximum profit. The average figures are based on the average coffee yield in the area and on existing practices which are more fully described in chapter 9. The maximum figure is that which an Indian could expect to receive if he sold his crop in those towns where there was a market for it; Table 26 indicates the returns to be expected within the existing organization of production and distribution.

It is clear from Table 26 that coffee cultivation yields a higher return in relation to labour than other crops and the farmer is always sure of being able to sell his harvest without assuming responsibility for marketing the crop. Coffee always brings in cash, while maize and manioc, if not sold, may have to be consumed. The labour demands of coffee production may interfere with other cash-earning activities, but not with the demands of food cultivation. Labour is needed for the cultivation of maize, manioc and wheat at the same time as for other subsistence crops and consequently expansion of these crops for sale would restrict food

Table 25. Maximum return from production for sale, per hectare

	Coffee in production	*Manioc or arracacha*	*Mountain maize*	*Plantains*	*Sugar cane unprocessed*
Labour man days	190	250	420	185	110
Capital investment ($)	70	10	42	300	100
Return ($)	1,760	1,749	1,500	2,000	370

Table 26. Expected average of crop production

	Coffee in production	*Manioc or arracacha*	*Mountain maize*	*Plantains*	*Sugar cane unprocessed*
Labour man days	100	127	120	160	110
Capital investment ($)	70	10	17	300	100
Return ($)	1,120	100	650	400	370

farming. I met only two farmers (one of them was family 22) who planted manioc for sale; both were assured of an outlet by a resident trader and whether this arrangement is likely to continue is doubtful. When land is unsuitable for the cultivation of coffee, Indians plant sugar cane under contract to a local sugar producer.

The selection of coffee as the main cash crop is, then, understandable and it should not surprise the reader that every farmer who had land where coffee produced berries had planted as many trees as possible without affecting his subsistence production. Though Indians had begun to discuss the substitution of wheat for coffee, as a result of growing dissatisfaction with price instability and reduced revenue, such a change is unlikely within the next few years. In the first place, it would be very costly to uproot the existing coffee trees and, secondly, new marketing channels would have to be established and the responsibility for cooperative processing of the grain reintroduced; both are costly and slow processes.

The combination of subsistence crops, as well as the proportion of each, was selected according to the suitability of the land, the yields, the nutritional value, the personal desirability of certain types of food, the likelihood of destruction through storage and the specific needs of individual families. Manioc requires less labour than other crops, it can be safely left in the ground until it is needed, it provides starch in the diet and the farmer need not wait long before he is able to estimate the future yield of the plant. If the yield is low he can either plant another piece of land or decide to rely more heavily on wage labour to feed the family. Maize and beans are better nutrients, but the yields are uncertain and the labour requirement is high; as a result, farmers plant maize and beans but do not rely on them as staple products.

Further expansion of coffee plantations, at present, is not possible since t e farmers with suitable land planted the maximum possible number of trees without prejudicing their future subsistence production or the future allocation of land to their growing sons.

The extension of plots planted with subsistence crops is related to the altitude, the size of the domestic group, and the number of sons who may make future demands upon the father's land. Farmers expand their production for subsistence in accordance with the family labour available to them or the assets required to hold a *minga*. No attempt is made to limit production to specific needs. Manioc and plantains are grown in abundance whenever possible, partly as a precaution against failure of other crops, but also in order to enable food to be offered to neighbours in need, or to enable a surplus to be kept as a contribution to a *fiesta*. Uncertainty and rising social aspirations encourage farmers to expand subsistence production at the expense of coffee production.

When coffee plantations reach a maximum expansion further savings are used for the purchase of tools, animals, or for the fulfilment of social obligations. The families with a higher gross income spend proportionately less on social obligations than on capital investment. Families with low cash incomes, who cannot expect to be able to buy more than a new tool, understandably spend more on social obligations. A small investment in production would probably not drastically affect their revenue, while a similar investment in gifts and *fiestas* will bring them prestige and a more secure social position within the community; by so doing, as we shall see in the next chapter, some of the uncertainties in their standard of living will be alleviated. Most Indians participate at some time in the *fiesta* cycle as can be seen from the following table, where out of the 26 families investigated, only those are listed who had participated and indicated whether they had assumed the major financial responsibility of a *fiestero* or the minor responsibilit of a helper to a *fiestero*.

Table 27. *Fiesta* participation

Family	*Fiestero* *No. of occasions*	*Helper* *No. of occasions*
3	3	1
8	—	1
9	1	—
12	—	1
13	—	2
14	1	—
16	—	2
17	1	1
18	—	1
20	1	—
21	—	1
22	1	1
24	2	—
25	—	6
26	1	—

Half the families interviewed spent in some cases half their cash income on purchases of tools such as shovels, metal pointed dibbles, most frequently machetes, and in five cases new pulping machines. Other equipment, such as coffee selectors or mesh coffee driers, are not used by the White population and are not stocked by the traders. The choice of tools available to an Indian who is unable to travel to La Plata is very small and the primitive techniques used by White farmers give them no opportunity to learn new methods and observe the operation of new tools.

Cattle raising is both possible and profitable, given the economic conditions and social limitations of cash production. It is appropriate to invest savings in cattle and to attempt to increase the herds by proper breeding. Some Indians, of course, do not have suitable land, and others have little cash for the purchase of animals. Yet there were five families whose income was high enough to have covered operational costs, limited household expenditures and cost of tools purchased and yet to have left a margin that could be, but was not, used for the purchase of cattle. In some cases the money was, instead, spent on drinking, paying heavy fines, or on long distance travel or housebuilding.

AMOUNTS PRODUCED BY SAMPLE FAMILIES

I consider in this section the productivity of the 26 families studied, in greater detail than in the previous section where I summarized in general terms the most important outcomes.

The families, which have been indicated by their code number in previous chapters, were selected because of my ability to establish a good relationship with them and thus obtain trustworthy information. Some of the Indians can be classified as 'progressive', others as 'traditional'. Among them were Indians with little knowledge of Spanish or of the use of money; neither category is proportionately represented. The quantities referred to in this section are approximations and should be treated with a certain amount of caution. All the cross-checking that was possible was carried out, and sample measurements made. Indians are not very concerned with yield measurements and it was difficult for them to answer my questions with precision. Information on maize yields were particularly difficult to gather; fresh maize was continuously picked for cooking, and that which remained to dry on the stem was considered to be the yield after the harvest. It is difficult to estimate how much was consumed fresh, or even the exact quantity harvested. Not all families harvested their maize at the same time. The bags used for carrying the maize varied in size from house to house and even within the same household. If the harvest was small and not for sale, the family would not trouble to husk it and the ears were stored in the house. The reader may wonder after so many qualifications whether the information is valid. I feel that it is, and that it will be useful in helping to evaluate the significance of the time, energy and capital investment in food and cash crops, given the differential return of each.

Table 28 lists the animals owned by each family, except for

poultry and pets. In Table 29 I list the yield of the coffee harvest of each family as well as the amount of food planted or harvested – either in weight for seed crops or by the number of plants for plantains and manioc. The acreage of food crops was calculated on the basis of observation and specific information as to the crop combinations within one plot. Special pasture lands were not kept unless an Indian owned cattle or at least three horses.

Table 28. Number of animals owned by each of 26 families

Family	*Cows*	*Bulls*	*Horses*	*Sheep*	*Pigs*
1	—	—	—	—	—
2	—	—	—	—	1
3	—	—	—	—	—
4	3	1	—	3	—
5	—	—	1	—	3
6	—	—	—	—	—
7	—	—	1	—	1
8	—	—	—	—	6
9	—	—	2	1	—
11	3	1	3	2	3
12	—	—	1	—	4
13	—	—	—	—	—
14	2	—	1	9	2
15	—	—	2	2	2
16	—	—	1	—	—
17	—	—	1	—	—
18	3	1	2	—	—
19	2	—	2	—	2
20	2	1	2	4	3
21	3	1	1	—	—
22	3	—	2	—	—
23	1	—	4	1	4
24	1	—	1	—	—
25	2	1	2	—	—
26	—	—	1	—	—
27	4	—	4	—	3

Some qualifications are necessary before any conclusions can be drawn from a comparison of column 15 with columns 5–9 indicating the amount of food required with that indicating the amount planted.

First, the 'amount of food required' – see chapter 7 – does not take into consideration unusual events or gift obligations. Family 24

Table 29. Farm production

Family (1)	Location of land (2)	1960–1 coffee harv. (3)	Food production season 1960–1: Sugar Cane harv. (4)	Manioc plants (5)	Corn harv. (6)	Plantains (7)	Potatoes harv. (8)	Beans harv. (2) (9)	Crops Planted 1961: Manioc plants (10)	Corn planted (11)	Potatoes plant. (12)	Beans planted (13)	Ht. planted 1961 (14)	Workers per family (15)	Food requirements (16)	Work for wages (17)
13	B	15 arr.	—(1) load	900 plants	30 arr.	40 trees	— arr.	— arr.	— plants	1 arr.	— arr.	1/4 arr.	1/4	1	250 manioc 150 plant. 20 corn	not
7	A	15	4	300	3	50	—	1	300	1	—	½	1/3	2	200 manioc 100 plant. 15 corn	H
24	B, C	15	—	200	20	100	—	5	—	2	—	1/4	1	3	500 manioc 150 plant. 50 corn	H
16	A, C	20	1	1,000	25	600	—	1	1,000	½	—	½	½	2	300 manioc 100 plant. 30 corn	H+
27	A	20	40	100	15	20	—	—	100	2	—	—	3/4	1	200 manioc 100 plant. 20 corn	not
6T	B	25	not	3,000	20	100	—	—	—	3	—	½	½	4	300 manioc 200 plant. 20 corn	H+
12	A	30	—	500	6	300	—	—	1,000	1	—	—	3/4	4	1,000 manioc 300 plant. 70 corn	—
25	A, C	30	3	800	10	900	—	5	1,000	2	—	1/4	1	3	500 manioc 200 plant. 30 corn	not
11	A, C	40	3	1,000	7	30	—	1	—	1	—	1/4	1/4	2	500 manioc 100 plant. 30 corn	not

Table 29. Farm Production (*continued*)

				Food production season 1960–1					Crops Planted 1961							
Family	Location of land	1960–1 coffee harv.	Sugar cane harv.	Manioc plants	Corn harv.	Plantains	Potatoes harv.	Beans harv. (2)	Manioc plants	Corn planted	Potatoes plant.	Beans planted	Ht. planted 1961	Workers per family	Food requirements	Work for wages
(1)	(2)	(3)	(4)	(5)	(6)	(7)	(8)	(9)	(10)	(11)	(12)	(13)	(14)	(15)	(16)	(17)
21	B, C	80	—	500	?	100	—	—	?	?	—	?	?	2	500 manioc 100 plant. 40 corn	not
26	B	90	1½	600	18	1,000	—	1	400	2½	—	1/4	1	2	700 manioc 400 plant. 50 corn	not
23	B	100	—	1,000	6	50	—	1	—	1	—	1/4	1/4	2	500 manioc 200 plant. 30 corn	not
2	C	3 arr.	—(1) load	200 plants	½ arr.	30 trees	— arr.	— arr.	? plants	? arr.	? arr.	? arr.	?	2	150 manioc 75 plant. 10 corn	H+
8	C	3	—	2,000	lost	50	—	—	?	?	?	?	?	2	150 manioc 75 plant. 10 corn	H+
4	C	3½	—	350	1	50	—	—	300	1	—	1/4	1/3	3	500 manioc 200 plant. 30 corn	H+
3T	A	6	—	600	4	100	—	—	500	2	—	1/4	1	2	200 manioc 100 plant. 15 corn	H+
9	C	6	not	900	3/2	—	8	1	500	1/4	7/2	1/4	1/3	1	150 manioc 75 plant. 15 corn	H+
19	C	6	1	700	8	50	—	2	500	2	—	1/4	1	2	300 manioc 200 plant. 30 corn	not

1	B	6	not	300	1/4	100	—	—	—	1/4	—	—	1/16	2	200 manioc 100 plant. 10 corn	H
20	C	8	—	200	—	20	5	10	1,000	3/2	—	1	1	2	200 manioc 100 plant. 15 corn	H
5	B, C	8	—	700	8	150	—	—	?	1	?	½	?	3	400 manioc 200 plant. 30 corn	H
15	B, C	8	—	200	—	10	—	—	—	3	—	—	1	4	400 manioc 200 plant. 30 corn	H
14	B, C	10	not	600	lost	500	—	—	?	?	?	?	?	2	450 manioc 250 plant. 35 corn	H+
22	A, C	10	7	2,500	10	250	5	—	—	3/2	5/2	1	1	4	450 manioc 250 plant. 40 corn	H+
17	B	10	not	1,500	5	350	5	1	—	1	2	½	1/3	2	150 manioc 75 plant. 10 corn	H
18	A, C	12	10	1,000 lost	7	200	3/4	2	—	1	—	1/4	1/5	2	250 manioc 100 plant. 30 corn	not

Food requirements are expressed in terms of plants and trees for manioc and plantains and in arrobas for corn. An arroba is equal to 25 lb.

Key to Table

T	indicates that the family are tenant farmers.
A, B, C	indicate differences in altitude. A refers to a valley or the lowest slopes within the reservation; B refers to slopes approximately 5,000 ft. high; C refers to the colder slopes where coffee, sugar cane and plantains do poorly.
—	the dash, when used in column no. 4, indicates that the family plants only a few canes for its own personal consumption, the amount being impossible to estimate.
beans	the quantity in arroba weight is for all different types of beans together. Wild beans are excluded.
H+	indicates that the Indian also works as a wage labourer between harvests. The H alone indicates that he works only for the main harvest.

did not have sufficient manioc because, as they explained, it did not grow well on their land near the house, and their other fields were too high up the mountain for convenience, since supplies of manioc would have to be brought home twice a week (manioc turns black and hard three to four days after being harvested). Most families would certainly have exhausted their stocks of corn before the year was out, but even if they had attempted to plant a sufficient amount to last the whole year, it would not have stored well. Families 2, 4, 9 and 19 grew only a few plantain trees as they lived at a height of about 5,000 ft. and the yield would be too small to make it profitable; family 2 was an old couple living alone who had very little land; family 4 was headed by a widower also with little land; family 19 substituted manioc for plantains. Household 1 was headed by a woman whose only help was a grown-up daughter. Family 11, whose lowland farm was suitable for plantains, reserved it for coffee and believed that if plantains were grown alongside the coffee the yield would be lower. Family 27 attempted to grow manioc, but the plot received most of the rain draining from the surrounding mountains and the manioc tubers rotted in the ground; the farmer, instead, supplemented his diet with potatoes purchased from his kin in Guambía. Family 18 had just purchased land higher up the mountain which was to be used mostly as pastureland, but where manioc would also be planted since this did not grow well in the old plot. This last family invested all its earnings in the land purchased, and there remained little money for the hire of labourers or for *mingas*. Family 15 had adequate lower lands, the only crop planted here being a big patch of coca bushes. Coca brings a good price when sold in the market but the San Andrés Indians do not plant it as a cash crop. Every family has a few bushes for its own needs, and if these are not sufficient they either purchase coca from neighbours or go without it; I was unable to discover for what purpose this family had reserved such an extensive patch, instead of planting more food.

Having made these qualifications I now compare columns 5–9 in the table with column 15. I shall attempt to explain for each crop, why the amount planted by each family was either above or below the estimate of their food needs for the year. Only after such discussion can any wider generalizations as to the nature of managerial decisions be made.

Clearing and preparing fields for planting is done by men. A long dry spell is necessary as 60–70 man days per hectare are required for the operation. In 1961 the heavy rains did not come until the middle of April, which gave sufficient time between the end of the coffee harvest and the beginning of the planting season to allow a considerable area of land to be cleared. In very few cases did the size of the new field bear any relation to what the family could clear without help, and generally it was smaller. This was usually because the family had no more suitable land, or they had enough food left from the last harvest for their needs; in some cases sickness (families 4 and 12) or miscalculations as to the approach of the rainy season accounted for the clearing of smaller fields than usual. Family 11 concentrated all its efforts on the preparation of pasture land on a recently purchased plot.

Manioc takes almost a year to reach its optimum size; it can be eaten before this, however, and can also remain for a longer period of time in the ground. Column 5 has to be evaluated, for this reason, in terms of two-year periods; it will be useful, therefore, to compare columns 5 and 15. Thirteen families produced an excess, which family 8 used to feed their six pigs, and family 19 used as a substitute for deficient plantain production. Families 16 and 18 had been helpers to *fiesteros* in 1960–1. *Mingas* required extra food production and families 6, 17, 19, 20, 22 and 25 had invited *mingas*. Family 20 had explicit plans for big *mingas* in 1961 to build a house and prepare a pasture land.

Maize does not store well and many families sold a few arrobas, chiefly to neighbours, on discovering that the maize was beginning to spoil; three families sold larger quantities in market places away from San Andrés. In general the Páez, including the 'progressive' Indians make no attempt to produce specifically for sale. The yields are too low and most of the maize planted is not of the yellow variety desired by the White purchasers. Family 16 should have planted more maize; half an arroba was insufficient for its needs. The head of the household, instead of spending time in his own fields, spent a great deal of time working on contract during February and March. In May he was assistant to a *fiestero* and also spent two weeks in jail, a time which he may have originally hoped to spend preparing a larger field than was possible in the circumstances before the planting in June.

The yield of a plantain tree varies with the altitude and the species. Family 25 insisted that they owned altogether about 900 trees and that they consumed 10 stems weekly – three times as much as other families interviewed; the household head admitted to having sold some manioc, but he insisted that he could not afford to sell any plantains; except for a few trees around the house most were planted among coffee bushes and shade trees which may explain the low yield indicated. None of the families in the sample were among those who sold plantains in the San Andrés market, or who were constant suppliers of White settlers. Family 16 did, however, have enough trees and did sell from time to time to Whites, though more frequently they sold to Indian neighbours. Families 14 and 26 must have had a surplus, yet they insisted that, apart from occasional sales to Indians, and then only as a favour, they used for consumption whatever they harvested.

In most cases a few pounds of beans were sold for a little cash to enable small necessary purchases to be made, but the total yield was so small that it could only have been intended for consumption. Beans are a relished ingredient for stews and help vary the otherwise monotonous diet. Family 20 was an unusual exception; the head of the household had planted sufficient seed to have harvested almost 250 lb. of red beans. Considering that in general the Indians dislike planting this crop because of the amount of labour involved and the high risk of losing most of the crop to birds and insects, it is curious that he could not explain why he had decided to plant so much the previous year. The price of red beans was at the time high and the local buyer had persuaded him to sell most of his crop at about the time he was ready to harvest it. This same Indian had not planted any manioc in 1960, but instead had purchased a growing manioc patch from one of his neighbours. It could be that he intended the beans as a substitute for manioc. This case also serves as an example of the unpredictable nature of some of the agricultural ventures of Páez families. The Indian in question is a young man, strong and a good worker, of whom it was often said that he preferred to work on other people's fields rather than on his own. He was not poor, however, and had good pasture land and several animals, though he lived too high up for the cultivation of coffee or plantains. When I saw him last he mentioned a plan to develop his pasture land located about four hours' walk away from San Andrés, of building a house in conjunction with his brother, and of hiring a tenant as a caretaker.

Coffee bushes are not planted on land needed for subsistence crops. Land listed in the table as category C was not suitable for coffee, and though even in this case a few bushes were planted, the amounts harvested were always very low and discouraged the Indians from increasing the few trees they grew near the house. There were four families who had suitable land but who devoted only a small part of it to this cash crop. Family 3 had a tenant-farmer status and the head of the household, highly experienced in sugar production, was required to help in the landlord's sugar producing plant; family 1 was headed by a woman with very little land; family 15, for reasons that I could never ascertain, did not cultivate most of their land, except for two small plots of coca and food; the head of family 5 argued that he could not plant more for lack of money to hire peons to help in the harvest. He could, however, have expanded so as to harvest two loads of coffee which could easily have been handled by the family. As mentioned in the previous section, a husband and wife can together harvest up to two loads of coffee. I have already discussed the difficulties encountered in saving or borrowing enough money to hire wage-labour to help with the harvest; I have also indicated that it is difficult to recruit any other form of labour during the coffee season. I shall, therefore, in discussing the table, not consider expansion of plantations beyond the harvesting capacity of each one of the families listed therein. Five families, in spite of having enough labour to be able to expand somewhat, did not do so. Family 18 reserved some of its land to plant enough sugar cane to produce raw sugar cubes for sale; families 5, 14 and 15 gave no reasons for not expanding their production.

Sugar cane not only requires low lying lands, but also rich lands which have long lain fallow; otherwise the canes are thin and dry and sugar production would not be worthwhile. Most of the families plant a few canes mixed with the other crops for the production of fermented drink. Others plant enough to enable them to sell the entire harvest to a White raw sugar producer, who sometimes provides the Indian with free seeds (families 16, 22, 25). The decision to plant or not to plant sugar cane as a cash crop depends greatly on traders who persuade and encourage Indians to enter into cooperative arrangements. However, in order to discuss this decision adequately and to understand the reason for a positive commitment, I should also need to consider the economic situation of the sugar cane producer, which would not be relevant to the main topic under discussion. Four families produced their own raw sugar either for sale or for consumption (families 11, 18, 26, and 27), but this requires a considerable investment in equipment and unless grinding is accomplished with an efficient metal press and carried out on a large scale (family 27) raw sugar production is not a profitable venture. It does not compete for labour with coffee production as the grinding is done after the coffee harvest, but it requires good low lying lands which are also useful for coffee.

CATTLE RAISING AMONG SAMPLE FAMILIES

Cattle raising has always been considered important and recent increases in price have encouraged Whites and Indians alike to

Table 30. Cash income, expenditures and capital investment among 24 families, 1960–61

		Capital investment				
Family	*Net income*	*Tools*	*Animals*	*Land improve.*	*Total*	*Other expenditures*
	$	$	$	$	$	$
8	320	25	—	—	25	25F
15	350	20	—	—	20	—
19	400	25	—	5	30	—
18	420	—	330	—	330	—
17	480	240	150	—	390	—
4	500	—	160	—	160	20F
2	500	—	—	—	—	50F
5	520	320	—	—	320	—
9	550	30	—	—	30	—
16	700	—	230	5	235	40F
22	700	—	—	40	40	5D
7	700	—	250	20	270	—
13	760	—	—	—	—	—
24	800	260	200	—	460	—
3	860	220	—	—	220	10G
25	1,000	25	—	15	40	400D
14	1,000	—	—	—	—	160D
27	1,300	300	—	200	500	? B
11	1,200	60	250	10	320	290D+60Bi
6	1,400	—	—	—	—	250D+300L
22	1,500	20	—	600[a]	620	200D+150T
26	2,200	—	—	10	10	400D+? Fi
23	2,500	200	900	160	1,260	125D+200T

Notes on opposite page

acquire and maintain adequate pasture land. Lower lands are not good for cattle because of the lack of suitable grass and sufficient soft sloping areas. Most of the families with sufficient land in category C had cattle as well as food crops. Family 16 had not bought animals, although it was no poorer than other families.

Cattle are kept for breeding purposes, or for slaughter for a large *minga* or feast; they are sold only when money is needed. Food has priority over cattle, except in the case of family 4, the head of which seemed to prefer to work for others rather than on his own land. I could not determine whether he did this from personal preference, or because his land is not very good. Nevertheless, he had received the animals in payment for his labour.

It is difficult to quantify the capital assets[4] held by each Indian, as the value of the assets depends on whether they are used for cash crop production or subsistence production and social obligations. Value varies also according to price variations and new opportunities which can reduce cost. Measurement of productive capital

[4] I am using here the definition of a capital asset in Bauer and Yamey 1957, p. 24. A capital asset is 'the accumulated stock of resources which contributes to a larger flow of goods and services through time, or which serves as a reserve sustaining a higher level of consumption at a time of more urgent demand or need than would otherwise be possible'. According to this definition land, agricultural tools, livestock, crops and money can be considered as capital assets among the Páez. Labour is excluded here.

F *fiesta* expenditures for San Juan and San Pedro, in this case.
D debts, mostly credit, that had to be paid with income from sale of coffee or labour.
G godparenthood expenditures.
B burial cost.
Bi birth expenditures.
L loss of money when visiting La Plata.
T travelling cost to towns far away.
Fi jail fines, unknown amount.

(*a*) This sum represents the cost of wire fencing and building a house for a caretaker in a pasture land very far away.

Indian 13 was sick most of the year and had not been able to plant or invest for next year. Indian 14 was very secretive and suspicious. He insisted that he owed no money and that he had none left. He seldom came to town and it was difficult to gather information about his activities. Indian 26 quarrelled with his brother and had spent, as a result, a great deal of time in jail and much money on fines. The residue from net income and investment and other expenditures had in all cases been spent on food, clothing and drink.

assets in subsistence economies or part-subsistence economies is useful only when there are strict limitations on how a resource can be used, and thus the return can be estimated. If, for example, a certain type of land is used only for cash crops the value of the land can be estimated. But land among the San Andrés Páez is used for cash crop production and food production. At the same time, some of the food is consumed by the household, or used to pay labourers or is even sold to a White settler.

In Table 30, estimates of net income are measured against productive investment and other expenditures; the *fiestas* listed are

Table 31. Tools and utensils owned and purchased by each of 21 families

Family	*Machete*		*Shovel*		*Axe*		*Dibble*		*Depulper*		*Cane mill*		*Cauldron*		*Grinder*	
	H	B	H	B	H	B	H	B	H	B	H	B	H	B	H	B
1	1	—	—	—	—	—	1	—	—	—	—	—	—	—	1	—
2	2	—	2	—	1	—	2	—	—	—	—	—	—	—	1	—
3	3	1	4	—	—	—	1	—	—	1	1	—	—	—	1	—
4	3	—	3	—	1	—	1	—	1	—	1	—	—	—	1	—
5	2	—	3	—	1	—	2	—	1	1	1	—	—	—	1	—
6	2	—	2	—	1	—	1	—	1	—	—	—	—	—	1	—
7	2	—	2	—	1	—	1	—	1	—	1	—	—	—	1	—
8	2	—	2	1	1	—	2	—	—	—	—	—	—	—	1	—
9	2	1	3	—	1	—	3	1	—	—	1	—	—	—	1	—
11	2	1	3	1	1	—	2	—	1	—	1	—	1	—	1	—
12	1	—	3	—	1	—	2	—	1	—	1	—	—	—	1	—
16	4	—	2	—	1	—	1	—	—	—	1	—	—	—	1	—
17	2	—	2	—	—	—	2	—	1	1	1	—	—	—	1	—
18	3	—	4	—	—	—	2	—	1	—	1	—	—	—	1	—
19	2	1	3	—	1	—	2	—	—	—	1	—	—	—	1	—
20	2	1	3	—	1	—	2	—	1	—	1	—	—	—	1	—
22	3	—	2	—	2	—	2	—	1	—	1	—	—	—	1	—
23	2	—	3	—	1	—	3	—	1	—	1	—	1	—	1	1
24	3	1	5	1	1	1	2	1	—	1	1	—	—	—	1	—
25	3	1	5	—	1	—	3	—	1	—	1	—	—	—	1	—
27	1	—	2	—	1	—	2	—	—	1	1	—	1	—	1	—

Tools or Utensils

H number of tools owned by the family.
B number of tools bought by the family in 1960–1.

Included are only those families investigated for whom exact information on the number of tools purchased during 1960–1 was available. Axes are owned by those families with forested land and cauldrons by those who produced raw sugar.

minor drinking events. Estimates are not precise because it was impossible to establish the exact number of days worked for wages. The table serves as an example, however, to indicate the level of productive investment. But to make the table quantitatively meaningful it would be necessary to establish the exact net income and to collect records for more than one year.

9

Distribution and Marketing of Farm Products

Every Saturday morning big markets are held in the central plazas of Inzá and Belalcázar, the capitals of the two municipalities in which the Páez reservations are located. San Andrés lies within the boundaries of the Inzá municipality and is only 10 km. away from the centre. Travelling to Inzá is not difficult on the winding, dirt road; by horse one can arrive in less than an hour, though walking requires at least two hours. Soon after daybreak most of the White settlers of San Andrés can be seen passing down the road, each followed by the pack horse which will carry back their weekly provisions of potatoes and raw sugar. To them the Inzá market is important because they can make their purchases at low prices and because they can sell any surplus of raw sugar they have produced. It is there that they meet and drink with the locally important people, with whom they can discuss business deals and political moves.[1]

For the Indians the Inzá market has not the same importance. They have no contacts with the 'big' commercial world and their contact with authority is simply in the role of citizens coming to pay a fine or present a petition. Whenever I saw an Indian friend it was usually because he had some business to conduct in the alcaldía or with the parish priest. It is not worth their while to lose a whole day's work attending the market, to save a few pennies on those few items that are cheaper than in San Andrés, unless they intend to do their annual shopping for clothing and tools.

Although Inzá is a small town (497 inhabitants), and most of the population owns land just outside the town, provision of manioc and vegetables is low. Any supply brought to the market square, particularly of manioc, is sold very quickly and at double the price

[1] For details of the network of markets and regional marketing problems, see Ortiz 1967.

in San Andrés. In spite of this only rarely do Indians bring any food for sale; they say they would be laughed at by their friends. During my stay I was able to observe only 10 instances when a San Andrés Indian brought food for sale to the Inzá market.

On Sundays another market is held in a hamlet only 6 km. from San Andrés. Few people from San Andrés attend it, and those who do are mostly from the reservation of Santa Rosa or the surrounding settlements.

San Andrés is one of the two Páez reservations that hold a weekly market. Indians from Tumbichukue and Santa Rosa come to see what the ambulant traders have brought for sale. Some have to walk for as much as three hours over very bad paths, and do so only when driven by necessity. Indians from the reservations farther away prefer to go to Silvia or Belalcázar markets where the array of goods and the lower prices make the hard one-day journey more profitable. It is interesting to note that Mosoco, a very prosperous and economically developed Páez Indian reservation, where White families have also settled in the hamlet around the church and school, has never developed a market. Mosoco is located midway on an old trading route that once connected Silvia with the department of Huila. This was once the only route that cut across Tierradentro, so that many traders travelled through, buying potatoes and selling small merchandise. Today, in order to purchase meat or a small item of clothing, a Mosoqueño has to make a trip to Silvia which lies 12 hours away by horse. Only the most basic staples are stocked in the small local stores.

Most reservations have no resident traders and the Indians there must either wait for a small ambulant trader or must travel to a bigger centre. The failure to develop at least small local food markets in this area, where sharp climatic variations make for food specialization within a very small radius, is an interesting phenomenon.

Low population density and historical developments may explain it to some extent. This area of Colombia, unlike the highlands of Peru, was never a mining area with centres big enough to absorb the agricultural output of peasants. Market places were organized in colonial towns and it was from there that traders moved out far into the rural areas. Commercial networks were thus based on the larger urban centres, expanding outwards by way of ambulant traders or rural market places, which I have characterized as outlets for urban industries and not as outlets for peasant products (Ortiz 1967). The situation remains very much as it was; partly because the pattern was established early and made competition by local craftsmen difficult, but also because the rural areas remained sparsely populated. In order to pursue this point in greater detail, historical information will be required and economic data from other Páez reservations would have to be collected. It is thus beyond the scope of this book to validate the explanation suggested. What is relevant to my argument here is that San Andrés Indians and local peasants show little interest in producing for sale at the local markets. The local peasants do not think it profitable, and the Páez Indians consider it disgraceful – a point which I elaborate later. San Andrés and Avira a are the only two reservations with a small, but regular, market place and San Andrés is one of three with permanently established trading stores.

Every Wednesday morning in one corner of the green that surrounds the old San Andrés church, the ambulant traders begin to unpack their wares. The weekly calf has already been slaughtered and the meat sales in the kiosk built for the purpose begin. By six in the morning the settlement residents stand hopefully at the edge of the paths that lead to the mountains, waiting for an Indian to bring a small supply of manioc, beans, onions, arracacha or plantains. I do not exaggerate when I say that the food brought to market is seized from the bags by anxious housewives before the Indian can release his load. Páez friends always complain to me about the aggressiveness and impatience of the White buyers, and remark that they find it unpleasant to have to sell their wares under such conditions. I must admit that after witnessing how the housewives descend upon the Indians, grabbing and bargaining at the same time, I have to sympathize with the Indians. At the same time one must admit that unless the buyer acts quickly, he loses his only chance of getting, for example, a few onions to spice the food. The amount of food brought to the market varies with the season. During the coffee harvest it is almost nil, but it increases during the months of March to July when Indians are short of cash and food is still available. By August the food supply is at its lowest and few can spare any for sale.

To give the reader an idea of the variation in the amounts of food brought to the San Andrés market I recorded the totals for the month of August when supplies were at their lowest, for the month of December when the Indians were busy with their coffee harvests, and for the month of April when they had food and time available, and were in need of cash:

August	3 stems of plantains
December	2 stems of plantains
	1 sack of spring onions
April	7 stems of plantains
	1 sack of spring onions
	15 lb. of beans
	50 ears of fresh corn
	25 lb. of dried corn
	1 bushel peaches
	24 cabbages

Depending on the amount of time and money available, the 20 to 40 Indian families linger, looking at the wares of the ambulant traders, drink with friends in any of the San Andrés stores, or leave shortly after conducting their business or completing their shopping. If a *cabildo* meeting has to be called it is reserved for this day and it gathers informally at the other end of the green, beyond the stalls of the traders. During harvest time when there is hope of good trade, one Indian woman (family 11) sets up a small stall and sells hot coffee and cooked food. Later on in the morning the White women with their wooden trays of fresh bread appear; the sale of the last bun, usually well before noon, indicates that the market is really finished, though often traders remain until lunch time.

Wednesday is the day when Indians can hope to meet a debtor, be approached by a coffee grower in need of peons, or meet a friend. It is also the day when free medicine can be obtained from the nurse without having to walk the 2½ extra kilometres to her house. The coffee buyers are all at home during market day, and during my stay a young middleman, who lives 4 km. along the path from San Andrés, also came to purchase any coffee obtained during the preceding week by the smaller buyers, as well as any brought to the market. Though Indians buy many of their tools in the market place ambulant traders come mainly to sell to White settlers. Only one Ecuadorian trader, now a small coffee grower in San Andrés, brings small merchandise especially suited to the Indians' needs, and is able on good market days to return home with $10 (Colombian pesos) in his pocket. But never did I see an Indian purchasing from another Indian; transactions between them took place in very different circumstances.

The importance of the market to the Indian population is that it offers an opportunity for social or business contacts, and also a means of purchasing from the larger and cheaper stock of ambulant traders. It has not developed into an important institution for intracommunity or intercommunity trading. I am quite certain, though I have not exact figures, that the volume of food sold to Whites other than on market days is greater than that brought to the market.

A description of the transactions on market day will not give us a complete picture of the circulation of goods in the Indian community, or of the distribution of the output of the Indian farmers. Only a small proportion of either manufactured goods or agricultural products is sold on the square. Imported foods and hardgoods are stocked by the six stores that surround the church, and the three others situated along the bridle path that leads to the main dirt road and out of Páez country.

Trading is a seasonal affair for most of the stores. Only three out of nine are able to keep a supply of goods during the low non-harvest season that amounts to more than a bag of salt and a few pounds of potatoes. It is from these traders that Indians and Whites buy their candles, kerosene and matches, and it is also from these that once a year Indians buy their new trousers, shirts or blouses.

But the traders are not middlemen in the distribution of food staples grown by the Indians. They are, however, at the same time coffee buyers and coffee exporters. There is no single chain of producers, consumers, and middlemen through which all goods produced either inside or outside the community are distributed. Food staples produced by the Indians pass directly from producer to consumer. Open competition in the market square is not the most important factor determining either the price or the amount exchanged. The factors that affect this system of direct distribution are not the same as those that affect the system of export of cash crops and the import of processed food and hardgoods. For this reason I shall discuss the two systems separately. I shall also restrict myself to analysing the outlets for the goods produced by the Indian community, since study of the activities of traders either as importers or exporters would imply a preliminary analysis of the Colombian peasant economy which is beyond the scope of this book, and therefore only the Indian sector of the coffee cash market is discussed.

I. MARKET FOR CASH CROPS[2]

Coffee is seldom, if ever, consumed by the Páez; during the harvest season a pale sugary infusion is made for special guests from the bad beans which are the only ones retained for consumption. Every pound of good dry coffee beans means cash to the Páez; it is grown for that purpose and it is sold as soon as it is dry enough, to enable meat or sugar to be purchased. In some cases the coffee is offered to a buyer before it is completely dry, even though the price will be lower, for the need for meat or the need for cash may make the sale necessary.

Coffee was introduced as a cash crop perhaps 30 years ago; I have no record of the exact date. Coffee has no traditional symbolic value; it is not included among the presents to be offered to friends, nor in traditional ritual obligations; the gift to the priest during the *fiestas* includes an assortment of every home-grown food except coffee, and in the offering made to the departed souls one can see containers full of purchased alcoholic or soft drinks, but not a single bean of coffee. On occasions when I visited an Indian friend during the harvest, if he did not have an egg, a gift of prestige, he would offer me a pound of coffee beans, knowing that I enjoyed drinking it; but if the gift was meant for another Indian other foods would be selected. The production of coffee by the Indians does not circulate wit in the community through sales, barters or gifts. It is all sold to the buyers, who in turn take the coffee to Neiva for resale. The 200 loads[3] of coffee produced during the main harvest often pass through one middleman before being sold to the biggest purchasers who transport it to Neiva. Women bread producers take their baskets of bread to the nearby houses and exchange $1 worth of bread, or a home-made Indian blouse, for a pound or more of still moist coffee beans. Some of the coffee thus purchased is roasted for local consumption, or dried, or sold to other middlemen or bigger local exporters. Discounting these small purchases carried out by probably every settler, there are 12 regular coffee

[2] 'Market' is used here to refer to a system of economic relationships and not to the market place where goods are offered for sale, unless the market-place or the San Andrés market is specifically indicated.

[3] One load is ten arrobas or 250 lb.

buyers within San Andrés and another who lives only a few kilometres away and who comes every market day expressly to buy coffee. Only six of these buyers are exporters and coffee growers as well. When to the amount purchased from the Indians is added that of their own harvests, the cost of taking the coffee to Neiva is worthwhile and does not reduce greatly the margin of profit. Furthermore, in all cases buyers have to purchase supplies for their stores, and Neiva is the wholesale centre for corn and potatoes that come directly from Bogotá, as well as for the small manufactured items that make up the stock of the San Andrés stores. These one to two day trips to Neiva thus ser e a dual purpose, and the overhead cost of the export of coffee can be reduced by absorbing it into this second enterprise. I know of only one non-resident ambulant trader who bought and exported coffee. He came to the settlement at the beginning of the harvest and remained throughout the more active buying and selling season. Big buyers from other centres do not venture into the area at all. The Indians are mostly small producers who never have much coffee ready for sale and who live too far from each other to make collection easy. Many houses cannot be approached by horse as the paths are too dangerous; while the local buyer has the advantage of being in town whenever the Indian comes with a few pounds of coffee for sale. If a buyer comes to the market he is unable to purchase more than a 100 lb. at a time unless he can offer the Indians a considerable advantage in price over local traders. In a community where the producing families can only afford to buy goods by selling a few pounds of beans, storing and waiting for better prices is difficult and rare. Only the bigger producers can afford to do this and store the coffee until at least enough has accumulated to entice the bigger buyers to visit their houses. One or more loads of coffee waiting to be purchased represent to a trader a profit of $20 (Colombian pesos) which is worthwhile. The smaller coffee producers hold no such interest for the buyers; to lose a sale from them means losing only a very small profit. The small coffee producers are not always willing to forgo the advantage of immediate reward expressed in terms of better food, tools and clothing, for a larger future reward, to be gained if coffee is stored and sold in bigger quantities. In many cases the purchases have already been made and the credit has to be repaid with the first pounds of coffee harvested.

As suggested, the price varies from trader to trader and also depends on the Indian selling the coffee. If the beans are not completely dry a lower price is quoted. It is impossible to evaluate from occasional observations an exact grading of beans in terms of dryness and quality, and the corresponding price. The wide range recorded suggests to me that the degree of wetness and the seasonal fluctuations in demand are not the only factors. The traders are quick to take advantage of the Indian who might need the money immediately, of those who owe them money for merchandise previously purchased, and of those who are not familiar with coffee prices. Buying beans that still require different amounts of sunning is not a serious drawback for the trader, as it might be in large-scale operations. An old sack or sheet of metal over the cement slab in front of his house is all that is required; each small purchase can be kept separate and can be spread to dry for a day or two until it can be mixed with his own coffee harvest; yet the price is lowered considerably.

The curves in the following graph indicate the coffee prices paid by buyers in Bogotá, Neiva, by the biggest coffee buyer in San Andrés, and by the smaller buyers residing in my area. The curves should not be taken strictly at face value as their comparability rests on the assumption that the units of weight and measure are equal in all cases – this is far from being true in San Andrés. The steelyards used locally are not always properly adjusted; weight variations can also be manipulated by readjusting the load hanging on the hook, and by balancing in a certain way the longer arm over which the counterpoint indicates the weight. If the trader is purchasing from an Indian who does not own a scale himself he will generally try to weigh it lighter than if he is purchasing from another trader or White coffee producer. If weights were standardized, prices would probably be very different from the ones I cite. Weighting procedures always produce lengthy arguments, though Indians usually resign themselves to being cheated in this way. Residents are aware that they are cheated and they discuss at length the faults of each sale, yet it is impossible for an individual without a scale to determine exactly the amount he is selling to the trader. This might partly explain why Indians do not always show enthusiasm for outside buyers offering only a slight price advantage. They can never be certain of the exactitude of his scale and they have no experience of his peculiarities. The price variations per arroba observed each month were:

October	\$30 to \$39
November	22 to 42
December	20 to 40
January	26 to 42

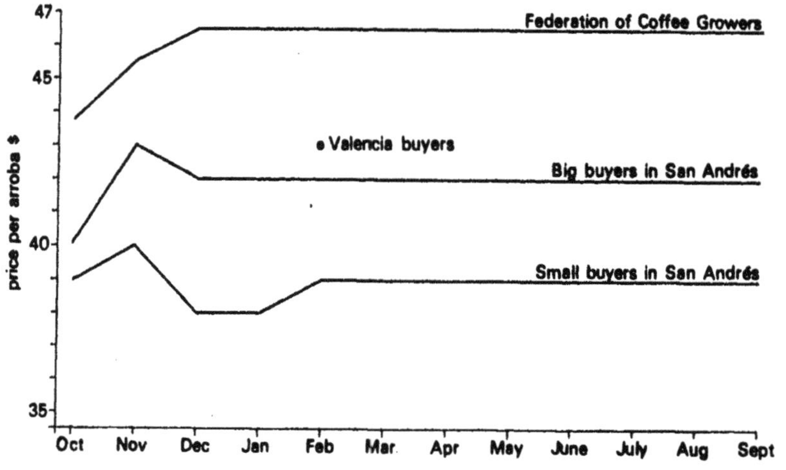

Fig. 2. Coffee prices in San Andrés, Valencia and Bogotá, 1960–61

(1) *Valencia buyers.* The Federation of Coffee Growers buys only selected beans and thus their prices are not comparable with those of San Andrés buyers; but statistics for other Bogotá buyers are not available and the Federation prices do at least reflect price fluctuations in larger centres.

Variations may be registered for the same trader, who may offer \$38 to one Indian and \$39 to another only half an hour later and for the same quality bean. A slightly higher price for his coffee is a relatively minor incentive for an Indian to sell. Distance might be a more important consideration. Harvest season is very busy; there is work to be done on the farms and time has to be spent working as a wage labourer in order to pay debts and purchase food. If an Indian has to lose time transporting coffee farther away, in order to gain a slightly higher price for a few pounds of beans, he prefers to sell to the buyer closest at hand. If one takes into account the economic value of time and the inaccuracy of the steelyards, which minimize the advantage of prices offered by the most distant traders, the gain would have to be considerably higher than it is to persuade the Indians to undertake a long journey.

As has already been mentioned, the Indian purchases on credit, either from one or at most two traders and usually just prior to the harvest season. The Indian is free to pay in cash, with coffee, or with labour. If he pays with coffee the rate of exchange is not to his immediate advantage. But by using this form of payment and offering to sell more coffee, the Indian gains the goodwill of a trader and he will be able, as a client, to approach the t ader for future credit purchases. This is particularly important to the poorer families who seldom have cash and who must exert a great deal of self-control over a long period in order to save enough money to embark on an expensive purchase. This is the reason offered by many of the Indians who expressed a preference to sell to one of the smaller San Andrés coffee buyers, though their prices are lower. In all cases they proved to be clients in the trader's own store, and they often had outstanding debts.

Thus when an Indian sells his coffee he expects either to receive cash or to cancel a cash debt or to assure himself a future credit relationship. In these three cases cash is an implicit element in the transaction. In the first case he will receive more cash and hence can buy more goods; in the second and third cases he pays a hidden interest (expressed in terms of a lower price) for the advantage of a purchase at the time he needs it. When choosing a coffee buyer the Indian must maximize the availability of cash at the critical points in his agricultural cycle, and not merely aim at maximum revenue. To earn a higher reward at harvest is not always advantageous; it means that he has to delay replacement of equipment after weeding and harvesting; it also means that he is more vulnerable to demands from family and friends for expenditures on consumer goods. Indians discuss the pros and cons of each transaction in terms that leave no doubt that they are trying to balance consumption needs and optimum timing of their purchasing potential.

The Indian producer is not the source of coffee to the middlemen. As I have already mentioned, slightly over half the local production (2,000 arrobas from Indians and 2,300 arrobas from local White producers) comes from plantations owned by local Whites. Inzá residents also contribute to the regional production, although they sell to a different set of local middlemen resident in their own township. Hence in order to understand price variations a complete analysis of the total regional market is necessary, which is beyond the scope of this book.

Prices, however, are also affected by the position of the other party in the contractual relationship. The price offered to an Indian may depend to a large extent on the economic position of the middlemen, his intentions, his requirements for immediate capital assets, plans for expansion, etc., which for lack of sufficient data cannot be discussed here. However, the final purchase price is not determined only by the economic requirements of Indian and White but also by the bargaining power of each party.

The Indian is only one party in the exchange, the middleman is the other. The Indian belongs to one community, the middleman to another; they do not share the same cultural values and social obligations. The middleman is a member of a network of traders and producers who are outsiders to the Páez economy and hence he is in a strategic bargaining position. The bargaining power of the Indian peasant is thus heavily curtailed. A trader monopolizes a sector of the available trade by tying clients through debt relationships, or by offering special goods and services which other resident traders do not offer. The Indian buyer, unless willing to travel a considerable distance, has thus to pay the price demanded. Better transportation as well as the expansion of the wholesale-retail organization which brings cheaper goods to the rural areas will release the Indian from this trading bondage to one of the resident traders. The Indian peasant, of course, is not totally powerless. He can, if he be willing to forgo any fringe benefit still owing from a previous transaction, shop elsewhere or sell his coffee to a different buyer; the threat of such action serves to warn the trader that he must satisfy some of the preferences of the Indian if he wishes to retain him as a client. The political power held by the trader-coffee buyer gives him a privileged position in any economic transaction; his threats to an Indian debtor are backed by a fine from the municipal mayor. His political contacts provide him with information not available to the Indian, who has to guess what is the price of coffee in urban centres. The trader is in a special position within the community which allows him to monopolize information and thus either to be in a position of power or to create a belief about his power, which gives him an advantage in a bargaining relationship. It is this dominance of the trader-coffee buyer which is responsible for the coalition amongst Indian peasants, which I discuss later in this chapter.

There is little competition amongst traders. They attract their clientèle either by offering special services, or by extending credit to a limited number of peasants who then have to sell the coffee to the particular trader concerned. None of them can extend credit to more than a few clients, as their own capital resources are limited, so that each store has a limited number of Indians who become their regular buyers and sellers.

2. DISTRIBUTION OF AND OUTLETS FOR FOOD PRODUCTION

Food production is more closely bound to traditional Páez economic goals than is coffee production. Manioc, plantains and corn fields are cultivated primarily to feed the family, but also to feed guests. They are offered in small quantities as presents, or in payment for services, and are exchanged with neighbours in order to maintain variety and sufficiency in their diet.

In Table 29, the areas of the food fields are indicated, and in the discussion that followed it was pointed out that certain families reserve a large section of their fields for cash crop production. Some of the other families listed produce beyond their subsistence needs. Though these surpluses are small they nevertheless represent an excess of food that finds its way out of the household either in the form of gifts and exchanges between neighbours, or as small sales for cash. I shall first describe the nature and amount of each of these transactions and in a later section shall summarize the system of distribution of food crops within and outside the community.

TYPES OF TRANSACTIONS

(1) *Gifts.* A plate of cooked food or a small bag of fresh roots or fruit to take home is given to guests or offered to an individual when a service is requested. Gifts entail an immediate or future reciprocation. Unlike other Páez reservations there is no specific offering to close kin after the corn has been harvested or an animal slaughtered. When I asked my frien s whether this practice was continued by any of the San Andrés families, they laughed and said that only their more primitive neighbours would follow such traditions. Nevertheless, small gifts are often exchanged.

An analysis of the situational factors involved in this gift-giving is impossible, as the information gathered depended on my presence. A Páez is unable to explain in any detail when a gift should be offered. Some suggested that if I wanted to initiate friendship with a family I might take them a small gift when visiting; by the same token most of the Indians who were later to become my friends brought me a gift of food at some time or another. When visiting a house fermented drink or cooked food is offered as a sign of hospitality, and if there is none available manioc tubers are frequently given on leave-taking. These exchanges vary greatly according to the available supplies of each individual; one does not always take a gift or receive a gift. Request for a service is always accompanied by a gift; and I believe this is the only strict rule followed. The amount and assortment of gifts depends on the tastes of the recipient, the amount available, and the nature of the service requested. In some cases it might consist of an invitation to share in a tasty chicken stew, in others of just a few oranges or manioc tubers.

White neighbours often become parties to these exchanges, and small sales of food to them are often considered by the Páez to be equivalent to a gift.

Though in some cases the amount of food given out annually in the forms of gifts may be considerable, the quantity varies with circumstances that are often unpredictable and for which a farmer is not able to plan. Productive plans cannot take into consideration quantitatively unmeasurable needs; the amount of food given out as gifts represents a reduction in the quota allotted for home consumption, sales or exchanges. In order to make a gift a Páez must forgo future consumption. Gifts are not an institutionalized means of distribution of surpluses, as fields are not planned with the reservation of a certain amount for presents in mind. They are considered a method of payment for occasional services.

(2) *Sales for cash.* There is a difference in attitude to the sale, for example, of several loads of potatoes and to the sale of a few ears of maize or manioc tubers. Among the families studied there were four (families 16, 17, 18 and 24) who sold considerable amounts of their maize harvest. In all cases the amount harvested exceeded one load (10 arrobas) and had to be sold, as it was already showing signs of spoiling. Two Indians (families 9 and 20) had to sell their potato harvests for the same reason. In these instances the sales were major and for cash, either to a particular party, or in the market of San Andrés, or in a town farther away. The transaction was thus similar to that of coffee, a sale for cash. The fact that some of these individuals planted more than the 25 lb. measure of maize seed,

which would have produced a harvest that could have been consumed by the family in a short period, might be significant. At the same time the excess could have been due to a miscalculation of the potential harvest or of its storability. Why the family did not find a traditional outlet for the surplus among their own neighbours is also an interesting point. The answer lies in the nature of the exchange, the limited needs of the families and the narrow range of individuals among whom traditional exchanges or sales take place. If the crop is quickly deteriorating it is reasonable to expect its sale instead of its storage, in the expectation that any demand by a friend will be for only a few pounds of the grain.

Another item sold by the arroba or 25 lb. measure is the red bean. Due to a happy turn of events beans became a profitable crop in 1961. The Indians were surprised, and some decided to take advantage of it if they could, by sorting and selling the large red beans they had harvested. This did not, however, encourage them to plant any more than the usual 6 lb. during the 1961 season. Only one Indian (family 26) had planted a considerable quantity the previous year, and sold the entire crop under the insistence of an interested White middleman, a case that has been mentioned before. He thought he might replant the same quantity in 1961. I discuss this case in the next chapter.

Big sales of manioc or plantains are extremely rare, though one Indian, a regular market seller, once paid a debt with the harvest of one section of his plantain grove. On another occasion a White manioc producer managed to buy a load of manioc from an Indian (family 22) to resell in the Inzá markets, and once a 'progressive' Indian sold a load of manioc at the Inzá market.

For the most part, however, when Indians sell food they do so in small quantities either in the market square in San Andrés, by walking down the road where they know they will be stopped by a White housewife anxious to buy, or by offering the small amount of food to a regular White client.

The total amount of food sold in the market square during 35 of the markets observed was as follows:

6 lb. of unrefined sugar
47 stems of plantain (24 of them by one Indian)
220 tubers of manioc
110 lb. of dry maize

90 cabbages (most of them by one Indian because of spoiling)
125 lb. of mixed beans
2 bushels of oranges (by the same Indian who sold the plantains)
100 ears of fresh maize
230 tubers of arracacha
8 marrows
36 cucumbers
eggs (the number is not large, but difficult to determine)
5 sacks of spring onions (most of them by one Indian)

Indians residing in neighbouring areas also brought in a few supplies:

140 lb. of potatoes
30 tubers of manioc
15 lb. of beans
20 ears of fresh maize
1 bushel of peaches
25 lb. of garlic

As the reader must realize, these supplies could not cover the food needs of the White settlers. They have to depend partly on potatoes and rice brought from other areas or on purchases they make directly from the producer.

It is interesting to note that only about 10 per cent of the resident Indians have been seen to sell food at the market place. I registered 123 sellers for the markets observed; 59 of these sellers are 18 Indians who came to the market place on several occasions. I do not know the other sellers personally and could not determine how frequently they came to sell food. The reader will gain a better idea of the amounts sold by any one Indian in Table 32 which lists the amounts sold by the families sampled. It is interesting to compare this table with that listing total sales; the reader will note that a large proportion of these sales was made by families 9 and 11.

Table 32. Families in sample who sold at market

Family 11	70 cabbages
Family 9	175 lb. potatoes; 2 lb. red beans
Family 2	10 lb. wild beans; 6 arracachas
Family 8	6 lb. sugar
Family 5	12 lb. wild beans
Family 15	17 lb. corn
Family 20	12 lb. corn; 10 arracacha plants

It is difficult to make the Indians comment on the paucity of food which appears on the market. On a few occasions close friends mentioned that they would be laughed at by their neighbours; an occasional sale would be taken as an indication that the family was so poor that they were in real need of the few coins earned, and if one traded regularly on the market it was taken as a sign of becoming a supplier to White families instead of to special friends. The market place is an institution that came with the White settlers, and it is intended to supply them with food. Considering the tensions that once existed and are still prevalent between the Whites and Indians, it is understandable that selling in the market square is regarded by all Indians as a sign of subservience to the White intruders. Indians do not buy in the market place as prices there are too high for them; if they need food they visit the field of friends or kin.

A negative attitude towards market sales on the part of the Indian community does not necessarily *explain* why the sales do occur. One could argue that if the market place were a convenient and useful outlet for exchange Indians might take advantage of it with an ensuing change in the attitude voiced by the community at large. After all this happened with cash crop agriculture which was once scorned and associated with tribute payments to their White masters.

A closer look at the local demand for products and the problems involved in transporting what is not sold at San Andrés on Wednesday to Inzá's Saturday market, leads to a better understanding of the reluctance shown by Indians. Some of the agricultural products, such as plantains and bananas, require careful packing if the sale is delayed; transport can damage the fruit and affect the ripening process. This is explicitly stated; one of the local traders who had attempted to import plantain by bus soon gave it up because he could not be sure of selling all of it on one market day and lost money when he stored the badly battered fruits. He knew how to pack them to avoid this difficulty, but he explained that transport cost would make the price he had to charge prohibitive. A direct sale to a client also ensures that the product is always sold when it is fresh, enhancing its quality and raising the price. Practical considerations are relevant, but cannot serve as the only explanation for the lack of interest shown by Indians in selling at the local market place; it only explains the difficulties of growing a large quantity of food for a limited local market and a distant urban demand.

We must ask once more why Indians prefer either to walk down the road expecting and knowing that someone will stop them and beg them to sell, or to sell to their own White client instead of bringing their products to San Andrés market square. I shall try to answer the second alternative first and suggest some of the practical considerations involved.

Although I am unable to quantify the sales to clients I am confident in suggesting that most of the food consumed by Whites is either grown in their own fields or purchased from an Indian with whom they have a client relationship. The White consumer either visits the Indian and collects the supplies or sends a message requesting delivery of food to his house, the price being higher in the latter case. The merits of certain food suppliers, their reliability, the quality of the tubers grown, and the amounts which can be purchased from each are frequently discussed by White neighbours.

The willingness of an Indian to sell depends on the closeness of his relationship with the buyer, and on whether there is mutual confidence and understanding. The Indian sells his food because he needs cash and lacks other liquid assets at the time; the buyer, on the other hand, is in need of food which is difficult to obtain, or expensive. The success of the transaction for the Indian lies in the swiftness and certitude with which he can convert his assets; for the White, the success of the trading relationship with the Indian is measured in terms of the regularity of such sales. Confidence can be gained only if the two parties understand the need of the other person, the norms that rule the transaction, and if both sides abide by these rules. The routine nature of the transaction brings security and can lower the cost of marketing the products; this routinization can be achieved through client relationships which White settlers strive to maintain with one or two Indians who live relatively near to their house, in order to facilitate delivery and to be able to arrange for sales when the Indian comes to town. Small services to the Indian help to reinforce the relationship. An Indian supplier utilizes the client's kitchen to grind maize for soups or for *arepas* (maize cakes); the host uses this opportunity to request the sale of some food from the Indian. An amusing but extreme case of a client relationship was that of an old Indian woman, Francisca, who lived far from San Andrés and walked about 6 km., stick in hand so as to ward off all potential buyers, in order to deliver her 10 or 12 ripe bananas to the house of a White client whom she highly esteemed.

This type of contract does of course limit the opportunities open to both seller and buyer and inhibits trade expansion. This is not, however, a serious problem, given the specific local conditions. I have already argued that the cost of and care required in transporting food discourages local peasants from attempting sales in distant markets; if soil productivity were higher and the cost of production lower the profit from a sale in distant markets would warrant the cost of delivery. Furthermore, local demand is small enough to be met by a few Indian families. Fifteen Indian families in the area studied supply White peasants. Frequent complaints indicate that these sales are not enough to satisfy local demand and I estimate that twice the number of suppliers might be sufficient to quell local complaints. But a demand is not a static quantity, it fluctuates with the income of local White peasants and with the availability of certain food items which they have either learned to do without or which they have not yet begun to regard as a main part of their diet as the supply is too irregular.

It is thus important to explain why only 15 families have taken advantage of the client relationship as a source of cash transactions and as a potential outlet for their food surpluses. Of the 15 families who sold to White clients eight are in my sample (families 3, 6, 9, 13, 14, 17, 18 and 22); family 16 sells food to Whites on occasion but refrains from establishing a client relationship. Of the other families in the sample families 1, 5, 7, 11, 15, 20, 23 and 24 have sold at least a small amount of food to White settlers, but the amounts cannot be indicated with any degree of accuracy. Many Indians at rst denied selling any food, and only in further discussions and when reminded of recorded information were the transactions acknowledged. Any discussion on the sale of food was always prefaced by the Indian family announcing that it grew what it needed, and that it never had to buy or sell food. These small sales are not necessarily considered small surpl ses, since the families could well have used the food themselves; in other words, they forgo home consumption in order to have money to purchase perhaps sugar or spices, and food is sold only when the need or desire for a change in the diet arises. It is interesting that those Indians who are frequently wage labourers do not offer their small food supplies for sale as often as those who work only during harvest. A more constant cash income means that variations of diet and store purchases are more frequent. Buyers of food are always easy to find.

I suggest that the fact that certain Indians have established client relationships with Whites can be attributed to personal, geographic or accidental factors which have prevented them from becoming a part of the traditional Indian exchange circle that will be described in the next section. I exclude those Indians who as tenant farmers are under very specific obligations to their landlords, and I also exclude those families who have become coffee growers *par excellence*. It is very difficult to gather and present any quantitative data that will validate this proposition. It was impossible to get information on friendship ties during the interviews and within the time that I could allow for this type of question. I was able to draw estimates from observation of occasional meetings between Indians, from casual comments, and from questions directed to obtain information on living kin. But it is difficult to calculate the exact number of friends or living kin with whom ties are maintained. However, interestingly enough, of the families listed in the sample, discounting again the tenant farmers and important coffee growers, the four families who are important food suppliers (families 9, 14, 17 and 22) have few friends and kin alive in San Andrés. Family 16 has close kin and many friends, but though the family head sells to them he also sells to Whites occasionally; he has, however, no special White client.

It is the establishment of client relationships with White families that explains why some Indian farmers expand their food plantations beyond what they may reasonably expect to consume themselves during the year, or utilize for a *fiesta*. Thirteen of the 39 Indian families who live close to the White settlers and who have sufficient land (beyond what has been planted with coffee) plant in excess of their own needs whenever their family force is greater than that required for subsistence production. The surpluses can be sold to the White settlers through already established client relationships. Only two families refrain from doing so, while three others who sell to Whites live at a great distance and often have to travel over very difficult paths.

It is difficult to determine the exact loss in cash income which sales to White clients entail, but the prices obtained from such sales are much lower than market-place prices. I have recorded manioc prices of 30 to 75 c. per plant, 20 to 40 c. for wild beans, and green plantains were sold sometimes at 5 c. for two fruits, others at 10 c. for three fruits and sometimes for 5 c. each. The price variation is partly a reflection of seasonal variation, the quality of the fruit and the fringe benefits received from the client. It is impossible to establish the price for each transaction and the cost of each fringe benefit received by the Indian; thus it is impossible to determine what the Indian forgos in order to be certain of an outlet for his surplus production and a source of cash income during the lean months of the year. The reader must not forget that though client relationships are not the best way to maximize cash incomes, the imperfections of the market are such that open sales would lead to large price fluctuations which would not necessarily be beneficial to the farmer. If uncertainty is too great, planning is difficult.

(3) *Sales and exchanges within the Indian community*. Information obtained from questioning Páez farmers would give a very erroneous idea of the volume of food sales and exchanges within the Indian community. They are frequent and varied, but any quantitative estimate is impossible owing to the sporadic and personal nature of these exchanges, and the Indians' unwillingness to admit that they are not absolutely self-sufficient. Self-sufficiency is a virtue to a Páez, and the need to purchase or beg from a neighbour is taken as a reflection of laziness or poor managing ability. At the same time agricultural misfortunes are acceptable excuses to explain the need for requesting food from a neighbour. Thus, help in the form of sales and barters is not refused between neighbours and friends; it is a matter of relieving misfortune and not a deliberately planned economic effort for the specific object of earning cash. A refusal to sell, if resources are available, means a refusal to comply with mutual obligations.

When an Indian has lost his maize harvest, or his manioc field does not produce as well as expected, he may either cut down on consumption, or buy, or exchange with another Indian, or both. Probably he will have to use less highly regarded foods as well as to cut down on consumption, since in general Indians do not produce large surpluses unless they have already committed their production to a White client.

Exchanges are in money or kind, depending on the cash resources of each party or the need for and availability of a substitute product. Chickens are often exchanged in this way against a lot of manioc or sacks of corn. The considerations taken into account in establishing the rate of exchange are many; I noticed that whenever they were discussed with me a direct cash rate was quoted. Manioc is sold at about 20c. a plant, while the lowest price recorded in a sale to a White was 50c. if delivered and 30c. if picked in the field. If an Indian buys a manioc patch in production he is charged 8c. a plant. Plantain stems are sold at about 50c. to $1.50 each instead of the $2 to $3 charged to settlers, and corn is half the price. 4 lb. of coca can be exchanged for about 8 lb. of beans (i.e. $8 and perhaps a little less) or for one chicken, which on the market would cost about $12; at the same time an Indian complained that he was asked $40 for a small turkey, which should not have sold by my calculations for more than $20. Cash prices are thus not invariably lower than in the market place. Variations in price do not respond solely to demand and availability, but to the channels of social obligation. To determine the principles that fix the rate of exchange I believe would be impossible, as I have insufficient data, but perhaps this is not of basic importance to an understanding of the traditional system of internal food distribution.

When an Indian family is faced with food shortage, supplies are not sought from any Indian neighbour, but from a friend or kinsman. A visit is made to a household where it is known that the corn harvest was good, or the manioc patch large enough, and the possibility of a transaction is discussed; at a date agreed upon the two friends meet in the field and harvest the food together. If it is a kinship relation that has not been activated through social contact, formal greetings are exchanged and an invitation for an evening together is probably extended. Kinship and friendship ties can be called upon when the need for food arises, even in those cases when the kinship tie has been passive. It is difficult for an Indian to approach anyone other than a friend or relative to purchase, and not all Indians have an equal number of friends or kin resident in San Andrés. Furthermore, kinship obligations do not override strains and possible misunderstandings between two individuals. The number of kin or neighbours with whom friendship is maintained depends to a certain degree on the personality of the individ al, on the number of close neighbours and on the internal social alignment of the area in which they live.

I have mentioned that Indian houses are sometimes located relatively close together, forming small neighbourhoods with local names and imbued with a certain regional character. Proximity facilitates visiting in the evenings but is also brings about misunderstandings in the sharing of immediate natural resources. Tensions arise and Indians are drawn apart sometimes into non-overlapping social circles, and it is difficult to make friends within a social circle towards which one has expressed animosity. In this way social alignments within the neighbourhood modify the number of individuals on whom one may depend for food exchanges.

Just as frequently one finds a single dwelling hidden between mountain crevices or isolated from others by a sharply rising cliff forcing its inhabitants to lead a more secluded life. Meetings may often be restricted to market places and as the Páez are withdrawn by nature, physical isolation might seriously limit the number of close friendships. These circles of friends are relatively constant, and though I witnessed the sudden and dramatic breakup of an old friendship, I did not notice a constant shift of affective ties. Friends and kin have to help one another, and the refusal to sell food when required is sufficient to separate two individuals. Selling to a White client is not conceived as a move away from traditional obligations of exchange. The White client is considered as a type of friend to whom one sells as a favour at a lower price than on the market, and from whom one also expects certain privileges. It is only when these sales are used as excuses not to sell to community members that resentment is expressed, or when the crops are sold in bulk in the market place or to a middleman, as in the case of the sale of manioc by family 22, already mentioned.

3. CONCLUSIONS

In the preceding pages I have analysed two different systems of distribution of goods: the market for coffee and a traditional system of sale or exchange of food products. I have indicated that each one is distinct not only in its organizational aspects, but also in the nature of the demand and the personnel that participate in the trading. Coffee is sold for cash in a free market where competition cannot be considered to be perfect as the internal-external nature of the market leads to a permanent imbalance of power. The system of food exchange is not a market as there is no sector of suppliers offering goods for exchange to a sector of consumers.

Because of its external character the coffee market defines the relationship of the Páez economy with the external world, and it does so to a greater degree than exchanges over the same community boundary in the case of the labour market. An Indian must sell his coffee harvest to White buyers if he wants to buy tools and clothing from the traders, but he may decide not to work for the White coffee growers and instead select an Indian employer.

Because of the very different natures of the two systems of food and coffee exchange, comparisons are only possible at the point where the two overlap: the household. It is in analysing the contract of sale or exchanges between households and between a household and a middleman, that the two systems may be compared. The goal of the economic action entailed is precise and direct in coffee transactions; it is more diffuse and far-reaching in the exchange or sale of food. One aims at a gain in the present or the immediate future, the other has a long-term goal of attempting to maintain the level of security.

The socio-economic contexts of the contracts also are different. In the coffee market the relationship is impersonal, while in traditional exchanges an already established tie of cooperation is necessary. In the first situation there is an imbalance of power between two well differentiated contracting parties, and in the other equilibrium is maintained. Because of the wider symbolic content of food, the implications of the contractual relationship do not end with the transference of food in the same way as they end when coffee beans are delivered. The economic position of an Indian household *vis-à-vis* other Indian households, White households, local traders, and coffee buyers, differs to the extent that existing contracts with each of these differ.

This analysis makes it easier to understand why, given the present economic conditions of unequal competition with an external system, a market for food has not developed among the San Andrés Páez. If food were to be produced not merely for family subsistence but for a cash profit, the system of intracommunity exchanges would be disrupted and the subsistence level of the Páez threatened. It is the circle of friends and kin from whom an Indian may draw food that assures each family this basic level of subsistence, and the relative certa nty that it will not have to face hunger. This is not only important in a community where outside supplies are not available, but also, as in the case of San Andrés, where economic relationships with the outside system are not always compatible with the traditional system of production, distribution and consumption. Traditional exchange obligations serve as a necessary adaptive mechanism in a case such as this, where an underprivileged Indian community has to produce food, and exchange with another community with a higher income and better trading knowledge. As long as food is kept from a market economy and reserved for home consumption, traditional exchanges, and client sales to Whites, the Indian family can better face risks and the competition of a coffee cash economy. If food production were instead destined for the market, not only would the Páez economy lose its adaptive power, but the Indian standard of living would correspondingly decrease.

The larger the number of neighbours and kin with whom friendship ties exist, the larger the supplies of food that must be planted to ensure the maintenance of the economic function of the exchange circles. The more active a family is in intracommunity sales or exchanges, the lower are its chances of ever facing hunger through loss of harvest. Increased planting is not for the purpose of increasing the total bulk of production and of converting the annual surplus into cash to be saved for years of shortage. Its object is rather to establish a precedent of cooperation with other families. Surplus in itself is not important as there is no socially approved outlet. Families with more land are not necessarily better off for the purpose of exchange than families with less land, as the sale of food is not the only way of maintaining ties of reciprocity between neighbours; services and labour exchanges are just as important. Those more numerous families with less land can offer the smaller families a source of non-cash labour to work the considerably larger farms they control.

The economic goal in food production may be described as an attempt to decrease the level of risk and diminish the possibilities of hunger. This can be achieved in two different ways: by sorting and combining available productive resources so that the cash reward will be the highest possible, or by increasing the circle of individuals involved in reciprocal exchange obligations, from whom food may be obtained through loans, lower price or barter.

The Páez economic goal may be described as the achievement of security for the individual family. This security is maintained through the traditional system of exchange. Another alternative would be to seek a greater cash income to allow the formation of savings and credit relationships in stores. This is the method adopted by 'progressive' Indians and it is in this sense that they have moved away from traditional obligations and have become more closely allied to the Colombian peasant economy. Two problems arise, however. In the first place limitation of resources and insufficient agricultural and managerial knowledge make difficult the transition to cash crop production on a large scale. In the second place the Indian farmer is not in an equal competitive position with Colombian farmers; he is paid lower wages, he receives less for his food products, and he is asked to pay double the price for hard-goods. The maintenance of a subsistence economy and the traditional circle of exchanges are necessary to lessen the chances of starvation, by safeguarding at least a minimal standard of living and by freeing the Indians from the consequences of the small risks that have to be taken in their limited production of cash crops.

The differentiation within the distributive system of coffee and food gives the impression that spheres of exchange also exist among the Páez. This would, however, be a misconception. Food can be exchanged for money; no objections are raised if food is used to establish contractual relationships which will affect the general security of the community. What concerns the Indians is not the form of the exchange, but the fact that food is withdrawn from the community and thus becomes unavailable for those who are too poor or in a critical situation and cannot afford to buy substitutes for the harvest they have lost.

It could be argued that the sale of food in the marketsquare does not necessarily lead to the withdrawal of food from the community as local residents can also purchase there. But the competitive nature of market places and the shortage of food forces the prices to a higher level than local Indians can afford. High prices for food do not, however, encourage increased productivity because with a small local population the demand would soon be satisfied and the remainder of the food would have to be sold very cheaply or consumed by the producer. Production for sale at a price that the Indian can afford would not be a worthwhile enterprise. If demand is to expand, the sale price should not be too low, so as to discourage production, nor too high so as to limit the number of possible buyers. I have said in an earlier chapter that if 30 Indian families increased their manioc production and if only 10 doubled the amount of plantains they grow, the demand of the local White would be satisfied. Thus, conversion to an economy where food is produced for the local market would have disastrous effects. In a separate publication (Ortiz 1967), I have argued that a low density of population, plus a marketing network which distributes products from industrial centres to rural areas, inhibits the distribution of goods within the rural areas and forces the peasant to compete with farmers who practise intensive agriculture in regions well suited to their crops. Peasant farmers are not likely to expand food production, when the system of distribution is unsuited to their needs and the cost far beyond their reach. Conversion of peasant farms from coffee to food production for sale is thus unthinkable. Meanwhile, restrictions on the sale of food serve to ensure a standard of living and help to meet the risk inherent in farming activities. It is a coalition, similar to that practised by players and by firms; I discuss this point further in my concluding chapter.

10

Decisions Responsible for the Allocation of Resources

In Chapter 8 I evaluated the amounts produced in relation to the factors of production available and suggested that, broadly speaking, given their technical knowledge and the opportunities available to them, Páez Indians rationally allocate the factors of production. They expand their coffee plantations as much as they possibly can without affecting production for subsistence; they retain control over their own labour during critical productive periods by avoiding credit relationships; they invest and save in the form of cattle; they diversify their enterprises in order to make better use of their labour resources and in this way also spread the risk inherent in any agricultural activity. The question remains whether these measures are the result of careful and systematic evaluation and of rational decisions, or whether they are due to chance. For example, the diversification of production and source of income may be intentional, but may also be due to lack of planning and foresight. Indians earn cash by selling their coffee, by working as wage labourers, by growing sugar cane on contract, and, less frequently, by selling food; these sales take place at different times of the year and the income so derived helps to meet unforeseen expenses and purchases on the spur of the moment. When an Indian wishes to purchase a tool or a kettle he can buy it immediately on credit, and pay for it later with labour. This form of purchasing has both advantages and disadvantages; the advantage is that acquisition can be immediate and when the peasant needs it or has the opportunity to acquire it; whilst amongst the disadvantages is that the cost is usually higher and that the Indian is then obliged to work when asked.

'Traditional' Indians find it difficult to estimate their cash requirements and to determine with numerical precision which will be the most profitable and easiest way to meet them. Money calculations are unfamiliar to most Páez and by diversifying the methods of acquiring cash, long-range planning and complex calculations are avoided. Traders were proud to tell me that Indians could be easily cheated, that they did not know how to buy and that they wasted their money in drink. As these stories are told at drinking gatherings at the same time as others about Indians having a great deal of money, a visitor would not be tempted to believe them were it not for the fact that the behaviour of the Indians does apparently reflect a very carefree attitude about money and production. For example, after having arranged to visit an Indian at a particular field I would discover, after a long and arduous climb, that he had gone up the mountain or was doing something entirely different from what he had originally said. When I complained they protested that they could never tell exactly where they were going to be. Agricultural activities are also suddenly interrupted to attend a family celebration or a *fiesta* for one or more days. Interviewing proved to be both time-consuming and arduous, since when I finally met the Indian he found it difficult to answer any question that did not refer to the present or the immediate past. In Table 29 the extent of food crops planted in 1961 is not indicated for certain families; this is not an oversight or lack of zeal on my part, but is owing to the fact that at the time when Indians were interviewed they could not tell me how much they intended to plant, though the land had already been cleared. Furthermore, some Indians were unaware of the exact quantity of food resources in their fields. Is this haphazard attitude real? How can we reconcile a statement about rationality with erratic behaviour? Looking more closely into their behaviour the reader will realize that intuitive and non-verbalized calculations are more thorough than one would predict at first sight, or upon hearing the stories of White traders. As one Indian told me, he planted manioc until he knew he had enough; he could not express the need in terms of the number of plants for the simple reason that *enough* is a relative measure, it depends not only on what he expects to need at the time he is making the decision, but also what he calculates he would have to forgo. In order to answer the question I posed at the beginning of this paragraph I shall discuss first the characteristics of the role of the manager, and then the process of decision-making. When is it that a farmer thinks of production as a problem which must be considered and decided upon? How does he decide on any one particular course of action over the others? As we have shown that we are justified in regarding the outcome of decisions as subjectively rational, we can pursue this logical model in our attempt to elucidate the intricacies of the process. In order to make the material more intelligible I shall first consider in detail the nature of the managerial role; I shall then discuss when Indians make a decision and what factors determine this decision-making point; and lastly I shall consider what elements are taken into account when a decision is made.

THE INDIAN AS MANAGER: THE NATURE OF THE MANAGERIAL ROLE

Each household is an independent productive unit. The head of the family controls the land which is registered in his name, but he controls it for only a limited span of time and subject to certain conditions. When his children grow up they have a right to a section of the paternal holding and the father-manager has to subdivide the land which he has become accustomed to consider his own. Furthermore, he is not allowed to retain land unless he uses it, or to dispose of it in any way other than by transferring it to his sons. None of these conditions applies to land which has been purchased; but as we have seen few Indians have succeeded in buying land. All these limitations, however, have not affected the involvement of the Indian with his land; perhaps this is due to the fact that his sons will benefit from his efforts. Indians do build permanent fences and express concern about any tree that they may damage unnecessarily during burning. Limitations on tenure affect some of the agricultural plans they put into practice, but not their concern for the preservation and improvement of this resource.

The head of the household administers the property he holds in the name of the family; he decides how the land will be used, how cash will be spent, and when an animal ought to be killed. Tools purchased from the household budget 'belong' to the house and are administered by him; a son living away from home cannot grind cane in the sugar mill without his father's permission. This will be granted freely if the father is not using the mill, and he will receive a share of the product not as a rent but as acknowledgment of his ownership. The machete is the only tool which is often owned personally. The harvest, and hence the seeds, also 'belong' to the house and should be administered by the head of the household.

No member of the household would dare to harvest even a small amount for sale, though no objection is raised to picking food to prepare a small snack. There are limitat ons, however, to the father's right to administer family property. His wife and his children may own animals which have been inherited or received as gifts. These animals are frequently in the care of the head of the household, but as with a privately owned machete, these animals are considered to be personal property and the manager cannot sell them without the owner's permission. Children own only small animals which are given to them as gifts in order to interest them in farming and to teach them to accept responsibility and to manage property, but women often inherit cattle, sheep, or a horse from their fathers if the latter were very wealthy or if they had no sons.

The head of the household, in the role of manager, also has a right to control the household labour resources. In practice, however, he finds it difficult to assert his demands. Ideally, a wife and dependent children must ask permission before they take it upon themselves to perform any non-routine task. But the only member of the family who most consistently minds the authority of the head of the household is the wife; at the same time it is she who will be consulted on farming projects and who is in a position to bring pressure to bear on her husband, gently but persistently and successfully. Wives have complained to me that they cannot start weaving because their husbands want them for something else, or that they have not been able to convince their husbands to take them to a *minga* or to work in a coffee plantation; but they do not challenge the husband's authority by insisting on doing what they want. The authority of the head of a household over the labour or earnings of his unmarried sons and daughters does not go unquestioned. Daughters are less likely to be able to collect a wage and retain it, but if they do so they will probably spend it on themselves. Adolescent sons find it easier to search for work elsewhere and keep most of the wages themselves. By so doing they not only withdraw labour from the family farm but retain a scarce asset: money. I have already discussed in chapter 3 how compe ition for land and the whole tenor of the father/son relationship affects the reliability and size of the family labour force available to the head of the household.

The theoretical and effective limitations to the authority of the head of the household affect his managerial efficiency. The availability of labour depends on the nature of his personal relationship with his children. They may withdraw cash and cooperation when he most needs it. Long-range planning of the use of the household labour resources is difficult for most farmers, and particularly difficult for those who either because of temperament or shortage of land do not satisfy the growing expectation of their children. If a father is authoritarian, especially if he is also poor, he will find it difficult, because of the uncertainty of labour, to plan his agricultural tasks efficiently; at the same time if he is too weak, he will not be able to direct others so that tasks are properly coordinated. The Páez are well aware of the difficult balance required of a manager. They complained bitterly and assured me that one could not trust anyone to do a job thoroughly and that it was better to do it oneself. To mention the difficulties and complaints heard does not imply that all Indians were unable to assert themselves *vis-à-vis* their labour crew or receive the respect of their children; it does imply that circumstances did not facilitate the efficient performance of the manager's role. Many even failed to keep their sons, as can be seen from the information about young deserters in chapter 2. Young married farmers found it particularly difficult to demand labour and assert themselves. This is a serious problem because it is about that time that an Indian plants his coffee and thus needs a considerable amount of help to clear the ground and plant. It was only those who had avoided competing with their brothers and who were friendly with their fathers who were able to count on a more efficient labour crew to help with the coffee planting. Many young farmers, like Manuel Santos, decided to try to plant what they could without help.

Thus a large number of tasks is performed by the manager alone. His farming techniques are learned thanks to years of close involvement with types of soil, quality of seeds, and long experience of watching crops grow. He 'feels' his way through a task; he does not need to conceptualize what he has done in order to explain it to someone else. Like an old-fashioned cook he works a piece of land until it feels good enough and, like an old-fashioned cook, he cannot quite explain what is enough and what is not. He may be a better technician than a young inexperienced agricultural expert, but he is not a good overseer because he has little experience in conceptualizing quantities, problems, and organizing his information so as to outline work plans. Furthermore, because of his direct involvement in production, a farmer does not trouble to keep records, or to measure yields; decisions are based on vague calculations of previous outcomes. Small increases in yield may pass unseen. Lack of records of time and labour spent on different tasks means that the productive potentiality of this resource is not always used efficiently. Indians do not have a precise notion of time; for example, I found it difficult to determine when their cows had last calved. Cattle remained unproductive for many years, but I could not determine exactly the number of years. Of course, cattle were considered a saving and not an investment, nevertheless, lack of quantification and recording did not bring to their attention that certain resources were underused. The fact that a manager is directly involved in production makes it less likely that he can be objectively rational, though this does not imply that his subjective evaluations are not, when seen from his point of view and given his information, rational.

Some Indians, as young men, had worked as wage labourers on big farms located near bigger towns or in the rich lowland valleys. In so doing they had become familiar with new agricultural techniques and tools. Working away from San Andrés has helped them improve their Spanish, taught them how to use money, to purchase in stores, and to bargain in market places. Other Indians acquire this knowledge after spending a few years in jails in Popayán or Silvia, two bigger towns lying beyond the mountain range. Nowadays few travel in search of work as local labour demand has developed; instead San Andrés school has become the place where at least some young Indians improve their Spanish and familiarize themselves with simple calculations. Facility in Spanish gives them greater confidence in bargaining and prompts them to travel to a town close by, where the price of tools and household equipment is much lower than locally. The local traders understand and speak some Páez, sometimes even quite fluently, but they are not honest with weight or cost calculations and a basic knowledge of arithmetic on the part of the Indian is important to protect his meagre income.

Social expectations and goal orientations are not the same among all San Andrés Indians. In chapter 8 I distinguished between two ideal types: the 'progressive' Indians who attempt to maximize their cash recources to the detriment of traditional obligations, and 'traditional' Indians who attempt to retain a closer balance between cash acquisition and subsistence agriculture. The 'progressive' Indians are interested in acquiring purchased goods and items which will increase their prestige in the eyes of the White community. Through ability, luck, and concentrated effort they have reached a level of production comparable with that of many White peasants. Possession of cattle, which can easily be converted into cash, and large coffee plantations providing a good annual income increase the purchasing power of these families and assure a basic level of security. The capital assets of 'traditional' Indians are for the most part non-liquid and the level of money income is much lower. Security is achieved by having more than enough food growing in the fields which also provides a relative independence from wage labour obligations. Food crops have another more important significance: a social function. The 'traditional' Indian families often spend more time and labour growing manioc, corn and other food crops than in cultivating cash crops. Cash is earned by working as labourers or by selling either the coffee or sugar cane harvest, and sometimes by selling food. The last method is rare because of the limited local demand, the diffidence of Páez Indians in selling on distant open markets, and the resistance to making food production a part of the cash economy.

The 'traditional' and 'progressive' Indians differ in the emphasis that each places on cash and subsistence activities, but both groups are involved in subsistence production. Unlike other peasant economies, food crop surpluses – that is beyond a family's immediate needs – are kept out of the cash market. The more 'progressive' Indians keep them to feed their labourers, and the 'traditional' Indians to give *fiestas*, to invite *mingas*, and for traditional food exchange with neighbours who might be in need.

This brief summary classification does not imply that goal orientation is an exclusively socially defined factor which affects the performance of the role of manager; on the contrary, the goal orientation is affected by what the farmer can expect and hence related to his assets. The classification is intended only to convey to the reader the differences that can be observed amongst farmers. Some farmers are 'traditional' because they are forced to lower their expectations; the factors responsible for their attitude are relatively constant so that once a traditional farmer always a traditional farmer unless the situation drastically changes, and he can accept the changes with confidence.

THE DECISION POINTS

The casual observer and interviewer may interpret the managerial decisions of the Indians as sometimes being haphazard and sometimes as careful and rational. The fact that *some* Indians may be careless with assets does not call for an economic or social explanation, but the fact that most Indians do not seem to plan certain activities has to be considered more carefully. We could perhaps dismiss the issue on cultural grounds by suggesting that they were unable to comprehend the value of the assets or that they had no aspiration to maximize them. But none of these easy solutions are open to us; for what we have to explain is why in certain situations an Indian plans carefully while in other situations he does not seem to take trouble. Why is it that sometimes he maximizes outputs while at other times he is easily satisfied?

In order to answer these questions we must first consider the timing of decisions. In the Introduction I discussed several types of decisions: decisions made ahead of time, programmed decisions in Simon's terminology (Simon 1958), and habitual behaviour or non-programmed decisions. I added that there is another type of decision: those made in the course of action.

The planting of subsistence crops and the number of days that an Indian works for wages are the result of decisions made in the course of action. An Indian continues to plant manioc until other commitments become pressing, thus forcing him to consider whether to continue planting or to stop. When he is asked to work for a White farmer he will do so for a few days in order partially to appease the demand; but then he considers whether it is worthwhile for him to work a few more days and cancel his financial or moral debt, or whether to go back to work on his own farm. He does not make up his mind before planting how much he is going to plant, nor does he make up his mind how many days he will work for the White farmer. In both cases, if he were asked, he would give a stereotype answer, which in the case of manioc would reflect his evaluation of average subsistence demands and in the case of labour the number of days which he thought would satisfy the farmer. From experience he knows that these are not the only factors that he should take into account, but they are the only factors which he can evaluate for the future. White peasants never quite understand, and probably do not *want* to understand, the reasons behind the Indian's short commitment to wage labour. One can sympathize with the coffee planter and his difficulties in organizing his daily activities when he is not certain of the number of workers he can count upon. In reaction to his frustration he blames the Indian as irresponsible and lazy, whereas he should realize that the Indian's agreement to work for a week is entirely the result of his demand for such an answer.

Decisions to purchase household goods are made at short notice and depend very much on the amount of cash in hand, or on the possibility of buying on credit. When a trader has an unwanted expensive item to sell, or if he is short of cash, he tries to sell his merchandise by offering it to one of his regular clients on credit, which can be paid in cash, coffee, or labour. When the Indian is confronted with the offer he decides whether he wants to purchase the goods or not; he considers the terms of the transaction as well as his desire for the goods. Most purchases are made as the result of on-the-spot decisions or after short deliberation; the one exception to this rule is the purchase of expensive tools, equipment, and cattle which are usually considered by the farmer during the season prior to the coffee harvest.

The amount of coffee planted is decided upon after careful consideration of other opportunities, of demands, price and other factors available. Indians discuss the subject freely and long before they are actually granted land by their fathers. More than a year may elapse before the proposition is formulated and the decision taken. A switch from one cash crop to another follows the same pattern; an example of this was the ongoing discussion about planting wheat instead of coffee which meant that the old mill would have to be put into working order.

The first and third type of decision are the more interesting ones, because it is in those instances that the pattern of economic behaviour can be dissected more clearly and where chance can be disregarded. In the case of decisions made in the course of production as well as planning decisions (that is, decisions made ahead of time), it is the individual who poses himself the problem, and who selects, indirectly at least, the opportunities he will take into account. Instead, decisions taken shortly before the action are the result of unforeseen opportunities which confront the individual. I am not here suggesting that the definition of the decision-making point in the first and third type of decision has nothing to do with the socio-economic environment; on the contrary, as I suggest in the Introduction, I intend here to show that the definition of the decision-making point depends on factors which are part of that environment and which are operative most of the time. To predict when an Indian will be confronted with a cheap or desirable good is difficult a d would require an analysis of the economic behaviour of White traders instead of the economic behaviour of Indian peasants; from the point of view of the Indian these opportunities are due to chance.

A brief list of the factors which affect both coffee and subsistence production will give the reader a clear idea of how the decision-making point is defined, how it is that sometimes the farmer thin s ahead of time, while at other times he does not. The interrelation of these factors has been discussed in previous chapters and the reader may wish to refer to chapter 8 in particular. In the next section I discuss the categories of factors which define the decision-making point.

Coffee trees produce for at least 15 years, hence the initial investments must take into account expected future needs and demands as it commits the individual to maintaining the plantation under production for a considerable number of years. Once the trees are growing only occasional replacement is necessary to maintain the same plantation under production for the lifespan of the individual. A plantation requires intensive labour input during the major harvest season and considerable labour in weeding during the remainder of the year; hence before starting a large plantation, the farmer has to estimate (and this can easily be done) the annual labour input required when, after the first three years, it begins to produce; he has to estimate also whether he will be able to procure the necessary labour. Any considerable labour input inevitably implies the contracting of wage labour so that large plantations mean a virtual conversion to a cash market economy. The demands on the land held by a farmer are many; he must plant cash crops, but he must also grow food and organize his farming activities in such a way that he can give a portion of land to his children when they grow up. Thus it can be seen that at least some of the factors which the farmer has to consider when planting coffee can be evaluated easily by a peasant; these factors are the amount of land necessary for subsistence, labour input, and the peasant's expectations about prices (not actual fluctuation of prices). Another important point which emerges is that the technical requirements of growing coffee force the farmer when starting a plantation to consider not only decisions about this cash crop, but indirectly to consider all his productive activities. He must define the amount of land he needs for planting other crops or to give to his sons; he must also decide whether he can afford to commit all his own labour during harvest time to coffee growing, or whether to work part-time as a labourer; he must also consider how the income-cycle will be affected. Most of his other activities revolve round these decisions which are taken when he is a young married man.

If an Indian wants to buy a machete he has to pay at least $30 for it; if he wants to buy a wooden sugar cane press he has to save $100; a cauldron for boiling sugar cane juice for sugar production costs a minimum of $200, while a coffee pulper may cost as much as $280. None of these items, except perhaps for machetes, are readily available in the local stores or market places; a trader will supply one if ordered but several months may elapse before it is made available. The expense of these purchases when compared with the annual cash income of the families sampled (Table 30) forces the farmer to consider them carefully as they will limit his ability to make other purchases that year. Most of the annual income is received during the coffee harvest month and credit is not extended except immediately prior to the harvest. Hence, at harvest time, the farmer has to evaluate carefully what use he intends to make of his cash assets. I have not observed any quick decisions to buy expensive items and though it is possible that occasionally an Indian acted impetuously, it is rather the exception than the rule. The price of goods varies considerably from settlement to settlement and from trader to trader; when the amount of cash required is high these variations are of great concern. Comparative shopping is carried out whenever possible and it takes both time and effort. I was always asked to get information on prices at the main urban centres long before the Indian could even consider actually purchasing the item. The prospective buyer would also inquire at the local stores as indirectly as possible so as not to commit himself to the purchase. Often the price quoted by the trader is in coffee, implying that he will order the merchandise only if the

Indian sells him his coffee. Thus the Indian has to gather information, decide on what he wants and if his decision is to purchase it locally, order the item long before he starts harvesting his coffee. It was ext emely complicated to follow the coffee transactions and purchases of my closest informant whom I visited frequently and regularly during the ha vest month. She was a very clever bargainer and had decided what she wanted to do with her harvest money; the decisions however had to be reviewed several times as her expectations were not always realized. She was always calculating what amounts of coffee she would sell to whom, in order to get the best price and be able to use the services of traders. Her week by week account of her plans reads like the study of strategies in a game of chess; she would calculate that if the labourers she had contracted came on the agreed day, weather permitting, they could harvest and dry a particular amount of coffee, which would provide her with the necessary cash to purchase some wire for fencing at the cooperative store in one of the urban centres. The day she went to La Plata the store did not have in stock the total amount required and she had to reconsider her plans and ask a trader to buy the remainder for her in exchange for some coffee (traders use this service as enticement to attract sellers, they otherwise prefer not to undertake it as it is not too profitable for them). This in turn meant that she had to reconsider her intention to sell coffee at particular outlets. This example serves to illustrate the amount of planning that takes place before an expensive purchase is made. It also demonstrates that planned decisions may have to be reversed in the course of action. It should, then, not surprise us that when experience tells the Indian that planned decisions are likely to be overruled, he will not trouble to plan. Hence the difference noted earlier about the nature of decisions: some decisions serve to organize the total organization of production, while others have an adaptive character and serve to adjust original plans to changing conditions or allow for the formulation and implementation of plans when conditions are too uncertain for long-range planning – a point I shall take up again when discussing the factors which define the decision-making point.

Planting of subsistence crops can be done sometime twice a year, though extensive fields can only be prepared during the dry season because they require burning. The land used for this purpose is not made available for other purposes except as a temporary arrangement. The labour required by these crops is high at the time when the land has to be cleared, that is the month following the coffee harvest, when the Indian is likely to have money to hold a *minga* or hire labourers. Whether the Indian is able to obtain extra help depends partly on his intention to save money for the purpose, but also depends on his success in purchasing tools and household goods at the expected price. I have already mentioned examples which describe the complications and uncertainties of these transactions; it is unrealistic to consider that an Indian can estimate his cash and labour potential for the coming planting season. If he does save money he then has to decide whether to spend it on labour or on something else. The size of the plot cleared hinges on this decision; what will be planted does not have to be decided until later. Thus the extension prepared for planting depends on the amount of cash available, as well as on conflicting demands which also require cash, on the farmer's estimate of how much he needs for subsistence, and, of course, on weather conditions.

The decision in regard to the size of the field the farmer intends to clear is made shortly before the task is organized, except when clearing is done without the help of extra labourers. Santos hoped to be a *fiestero* the forthcoming year and by very careful budgeting he was able to acquire the animals required to call a *minga* in order to clear about one hectare of land; when I left he told me he had already planted maize, beans, and that he would probably plant manioc, but he was not sure how much he would plant nor was he sure of what else he would plant – 'sugar cane, perhaps'. He was an extremely capable and competent person with a fantastic capacity for hard work; we cannot simply dismiss this example by saying that Santos valued leisure higher than work. The fact that decisions about planting are best left to the time the task has to be performed is due to the nature of the task and the prevailing economic conditions. None of the Indians who had planned and coordinated the labour required to clear a field were able to specify plans for the impending planting season. Octavio (family 13) had been considering the possibility of starting a new coffee plantation and of planting a patch of sugar cane under contract with a White trader, but he had not considered what subsistence crops he would plant and could only mention the amount of maize because it had already been planted. Paulino (family 11), when I interviewed him after he had cleared a small plot, could only say that he would plant probably a bit of everything; shortly before I left he told me that he had planted 25 lb. of maize, and this may well be his total for the year as he still had some manioc and was working very hard on clearing and maintaining good pasture land in the mountains for his recently acquired animals. He may, however, when he runs short of manioc, decide to plant another small patch during the second planting season. Machete (family 12) is a highly skilled craftsman, a good carpenter and mattress maker, but the demand for those goods is small and he has to depend on farming for cash and subsistence. When interviewed he could only say that he would have to replant manioc because he had lost all he had planted last year and that he would probably plant some maize, a response which is so stereotyped that it has little factual meaning. As it proved he planted twice the amount of manioc he had planted the previous year, and 25 lb. of maize by the time I left. Patricio (family 15) had saved $50 for a *minga* and the only decision he had made so far was to plant 75 lb. of maize, which he had already purchased. Apolinar (family 8) wanted to have a *minga* and had saved one of his pigs for that purpose, but he was not certain how much he would plant. Planting is done when the farmer can perform the task himself and as the demands made on his time are multiple, the task is not completed during a continuous span of time. It is easier to make the decision about subsistence farming when the resources are made available, that is, when the Indian can find time to work in his field or to search for seeds. The farmer starts planting after the rains have softened the ash-covered earth. If he is in good health and the weather is good he will be able to work hard. If other tasks do not demand his attention; if White farmers do not come day after day to insist that he must pay off a debt with labour; and if his family does not make other demands on him, he will be able to plant a greater quantity and finish early enough to ensure a good harvest. But if his wife is due to give birth, or if a kinsman dies, then he may eagerly decide to accept offers of wage labour so as to be able to meet immediate expenses, thus forgoing work in his own fields.

Exclusion of crops from open market exchanges means that it is not important to combine resources in order to maximize productivity of food crops but to maximize satisfaction. A small amount of food may be sold; but the marginal return is so small that even if Indians were allowed to sell freely, food crops are not likely to be planted in order to increase cash revenue. Cash enterprises are limited to coffee production, cattle- or pig-breeding, sugar production and wage labour. Thus a need for cash increases the number of demands made on the farmer's labour, not on the amount of food he produces. While a need for security makes demands on food, a 'maximum' is not the main point here, other needs being more important than large quantities of food.

FACTORS WHICH DEFINE THE DECISION-MAKING POINT

The main difference between the types of decision described earlier in this chapter is the timing of the decision in reference to the action; some are taken well in advance, others shortly before and finally, in the last case, they are taken in the process of production. This is not, however, the only difference, for we shall see that the timing itself affects the factors that are evaluated, as well as what expectations are formulated and considered. For the moment I shall consider only the timing of decisions and outline a series of parameters which precipitate or delay decision-making. I hope to have made abundantly clear to the reader that it is not chance that decisions are made at different stages in the process of production, and that they do not respond solely to individual idiosyncrasies; the fact that all decisions relating to how much and what kind of food is to be planted are made in the course of planting, while other investment decisions such as cash cropping, etc. are made well in advance, must is some way be related to the economic system.

The level of uncertainty. A farmer will evaluate a prospect when he can formulate expectations about outcomes, for which he does not necessarily need to know the probability distributions of outcomes. He will then rank the prospects as to their desirability in terms of outcomes and risks. 'An individual will defer the crystallization of any plan, waiting continually for a situation where he can feel that the number of unanswerable questions is at a minimum and is likely rather to increase on balance. Only at such a time of freedom from impending knowledge will he consent in important matters to decide and act' (Shackle 1955, pp. 111–12). For an individual to plan ahead he must be able to formulate expectations long before the action and *know* that further information is unlikely to affect his plans. This second point I shall take up later.

Though it is unlikely that knowledge is ever complete, and indeed it is unlikely that the decision-maker would be able to handle complete knowledge of the situation, nevertheless, very limited knowledge will frequently lead to unexpected results and hence to the realization that expectations cannot be formulated. Such a state of uncertainty does not necessarily paralyse the decision-maker. We owe to Shackle the realization that most decisions are made under uncertainty (see Introduction), but this is plausible insofar as the level of uncertainty does not hinder the formation of expectations. A farmer attempts to evaluate and plan rationally only when he believes that a certain range of outcomes can be expected and that certain factors are likely to be available. It would follow then that though rational decisions under uncertainty are made, the higher the uncertainty level the less likely that planned rational decisions will be made well ahead of time. A belief by the farmer about the likelihood of certain outcomes and the availability of factors will make it possible, though not necessary, to plan ahead.

Páez farmers had certain expectations about their farming activities. Manioc was expected to produce, maize seed was expected to yield a certain number of maize heads, a coffee tree was expected to yield a certain volume of kernels, but climatic variations make it impossible to predict with certainty. Furthermore, the farmer was confident that he would sell all his coffee harvest at a price which would not be much above that of the previous year, and in fact more likely to be slightly below it; he had, however, doubts whether he could sell most of his food crops; instead he expected that when exchanged or processed they would satisfy his needs and those of his family. Years of experience had told him that coffee prices fluctuate, but that there is always an available market, while food crops could not normally be sold without a loss of capital assets or prestige (which could be regarded for the purpose of computation as a social asset). The farmer also knows cash to be a necessary medium of exchange to enable him to obtain certain goods which he believes will continue to be necessary for work and to satisfy his family. If he is too uncertain whether an outcome will satisfy his needs, or, in Shackle's terminology, make him happier, he will not be able to formulate expectations. Apolinar (family 8) or Clementina (family 1) both had very meagre incomes and little land; it is doubtful whether they could decide to depend more heavily on wage earning, a problem often discussed by them and which remained unresolved. Their incomes would be too low and too uncertain to allow them to calculate what needs they could satisfy. Unable to answer this last question, Apolinar and Clementina follow the old strategy either because they prefer an unsatisfying but sure income from subsistence farming or because they are unable to evaluate the advantages of a highly liquid cash income *vis-à-vis* a less liquid part-food subsistence. Hence they remain indifferent to change.

Subsistence farming brings sufficient security in that farmers know from experience what is the likelihood of plants growing, of crops being totally destroyed, and of seeds for next harvest being produced; they also know what needs these crops will satisfy and can thus formulate expected wants and means to achieve them. Furthermore, they know that if part of the crop is lost traditional exchanges will assure them a basic standard of living. Hence, any mechanism which reduces the uncertainty of the final outcome (that is the satisfaction of the individual's needs) also helps the farmer to define a larger number of expectations and perceive the means of satisfying them. As a corollary one would expect low-income people, where needs are uncertainly satisfied, to be less willing to make the effort to win an extra small amount of cash and instead to respond by insuring themselves and/or gambling for larger prizes (see Friedman and Savage 1948). There is correlation between level of subsistence – which is better measured in terms of land-holding than of cash income – and willingness to expand production. It is the small-holder who barely attains subsistence who is more prone to gamble rather than to invest his income rationally. The only important point to be noted at present is that the higher the level of certainty as to the immediate outcome in yields or cash, or as to the future outcome of want satisfaction, the more likely it will be that ends and means will be defined in such a way by the Indian as to allow him to make rational decisions before the course of production.

Availability of factors of production. Resources can make themselves evident and confront the individual with a decision, or they may be part of the existing socio-economic environment and go unperceived by the observer, or their availability, though possible, may be highly uncertain. 'The decision-maker's information about his environment is much less than an approximation to the real environment. The term "approximation" implies that the subjective world of the decision-maker resembles the external environment closely, but lacks, perhaps, some fineness of detail. In actual fact, the perceived world is fantastically different from the "real" world' (Simon 1967b, p. 19). Land amongst the Páez is perceived as a possible asset only as part of the maturation process and in the context of the father-son relationship. The perception of its availability can be explained in terms of the social and political system of the reservation. Land is not given at a particular point in time; a young Indian becomes aware that when he reaches a certain age his status in the community will and ought to change, and that this change will become operative if he succeeds in attaining rights over part of the paternal land. His aspirations to obtain land, and the granting of land, are part and parcel of his daily relationship with his father and other members of the community. To a Páez land implies farming and so the future availability of his first and often the only plot of land that he will receive is related to his farming aspirations. I can thus say that the future availability of the resource is known to the young Indian and though there are uncertainties as to the exact time of transference and exact size of the plot, he can venture a guess and attempt to make the guess real by adjusting his relations with the father in such a way as to obtain something approximating to his wishes and expectations. The transference of land thus defines the decision-making point for the first set of productive decisions; the future owner will have to consider whether he wants to be a coffee farmer, a subsistence farmer, a cattle farmer, etc., when he comes of age. In reality land may be available to an Indian on other occasions also, though he may not perceive this opportunity either because he is not seeking it, or because he considers it unlikely that he will find land, or because he cannot make use of the land for lack of other factors of production. I have no means of ascertaining whether land was available or not; within my area of action I knew of no unclaimed land and of no Indian willing to sell. It was physically impossible for me to determine whether adequate land which could be farmed by the San Andrés Indians was available in any other place. According to information given to me there was none, but this was my informants' idea and not necessarily the reality.

Improvements to land, as well as tools and seeds which would improve the yields or the quality of the yields, require cash. This resource is available at certain times of the year either through the sale of labour during the harvest months or from the sale of coffee beans. Certainly, there are other opportunities available and an Indian may on occasion earn money, but if he follows the course of events as established by his routine of production then money and his chances for investing the money are limited. He knows that it is during the months of December to February when he will and should consider what to do with his earnings; cash during the remainder of the year is too uncertain a possibility to be taken into consideration in his plans.

Any developments which reduce the constraints on the availability of resources will also aid the farmer to plan before action. For example, if a farmer can purchase on credit or can easily obtain loans, or if he can free his own labour resources (or be free to hire labourers), then he will find it easier to formulate strategies which he can evaluate according to the desirability of their outcome. José, Antonio, Paulino, and Ercilla (families 18, 27, 11 and 23 respectively) were amongst those Indians who during the planting year of 1961 considered long-range farming enterprises, partly because they were able to avoid wage labour and partly because their cash income was higher than that of other Indians.

Once the farmer decides to plant coffee trees and once he decides to invest in tools, he commits part of his labour potential to coffee harvesting during the last month of the year, or to paying off purchases on credit, or to earning a little money for absolutely necessary productive expenses. As the White coffee growers have their plantations in the valley they mature earlier than the trees owned by Indians, so that a labour demand by a coffee grower is not likely to conflict with the harvesting in Indian plantations; but they may conflict with other agricultural commitments; this is precisely the case during the weeding season. For the Indian to plan his actions carefully when he knows that he may have to change his plans quite radically, is unlikely and irrational. Uncertainty as to the availability of resources inhibits long-range planning. It should therefore not be surprising to us that the farmer decides what he is going to do on a particular day during the course of that day, or at most on the previous day, and that he does not consider the strategy of subsistence farming.

The timing of decisions should then also relate to the point at which resources are made available or are perceived as available and to the degree of certainty as to their availability. Similar factors affect the timing of decisions in industry. Peck (1958) suggested in a case study of the aluminium industry that discontinuities in revenue or cost, hence the availability of cash assets to the firm, created decision points.

It is important to consider that so far I have dealt with decisions within the established routine of production and not with decisions which could be labelled as truly creative or truly entrepreneurial. This brings me to the third factor.

The interdependence of economic activities. Economic and social systems are so interrelated that any particular act is dependent on a number of events which may have preceded it or have co-existed with it. The existence of the market place depends on the attendance of buyers and sellers; the time spent in shopping depends on the existence of a market place; the killing of a cow depends on whether the Indian can make use of the meat which in turn depends on whether he can sell it (unlikely in San Andrés) or whether he can distribute it in a *fiesta*, etc. The disappearance of a certain event or the lower incidence of occurrence of the same event will affect the existence of others. There is a constant adjustment and readjustment that individuals have to make in order to cope with changing environment; the effect of these adjustments may be so small that they are hardly noted by the observer-analyst, or are recorded and considered as normal fluctuations, as part of the system rather than changes in the system. Changes in prices, amounts of each crop produced, variations in the number of days that a peasant is willing to work each year are considered as fluctuations which result from the normal operation of the system. What is implied in this statement is that the framework of production does not completely change and that it is within the framework that the individual adjusts his decision so as to take into account slight changes in factors of production, aspirations, etc.

For example, if there is a slight drop in coffee prices the Indian will make up the consequent loss of income by working a few days in a plantation or by cutting down on his expenditure; as long as the drop in price is small and as long as he considers it to be a temporary situation he does not re-evaluate his farming programme. A re-evaluation would be too complex and too full of uncertainties. Manuel Santos's first coffee plantation failed to produce and he was about to start another one, in spite of the fact that prices were considered to be disadvantageous by the Indians. This decision is not ill-conceived as long as coffee prices are expected to vary within a certain range. The farmer knows how to estimate his costs of production and his revenue from coffee. He has assured outlets, hence he does not need to spend much time, effort or money in marketing it. He has organized all his other activities so that conflicts of demands are minimized. An entirely new venture for Manuel Santos would be full of uncertainties and would require far-reaching readjustments.

As long as coffee remains a satisfying means of achieving an adequate amount of cash, no drastic decision will be taken. Price fluctuations did concern the Indians at the time. Many discussed the possibility of reverting to wheat farming, because they estimated that the revenue from this cash crop might be higher than the revenue from coffee. The decision is not a simple one and it is unlikely that farmers will give up coffee planting unless prices continue to fall. One of the problems involved is conflicting labour requirements; another problem is to find buyers willing to pay the current market price; another problem is that to sell wheat at a high price they must mill it, and the local stone mill is inefficient and must be rehabilitated. When I left, only a small number of Indians who had land at higher altitudes, where coffee trees did not produce berries, were seriously discussing plans to plant wheat and mill it locally.

While I was in residence in San Andrés, the price of a particular type of bean was very high and local coffee buyers became very interested in purchasing as much as they could for resale at larger centres. Indians did not consider planting larger areas of beans than usual, they merely took advantage of the opportunity by selling more than they would otherwise have done. One of the reasons is that they were not certain that, in the following years, buyers would want to pay a high price, and another reason is that bean farming is risky as the harvest can easily be lost. The uncertainty associated with this enterprise did not stimulate them to change strategies; it should not be forgotten that any drastic change in the amount of beans planted will affect the precarious balance of demand. Beans demand land which has been committed already to subsistence crops. Beans also require more labour than other crops. Domingo (family 20) was the only Indian to profit heavily from this venture. All his land was at high altitudes where only beans, maize, potatoes and wheat would grow. He purchased manioc from a close friend and earned cash by working as a labourer for this particular friend, a wealthy farmer. He decided to try planting more beans and no wheat; if the price fell he would eat more beans and less manioc, and if the price remained high he would continue to plant beans. In his very special case the new opportunity did not force him to reconsider a totally new strategy, but for most other farmers it would have done so.

Peasant farmers prefer to adjust to changing conditions rather than to change one aspect of the total strategy for fear of the consequences in other aspects of their activities. It is only when circumstances drastically change that plans may be reconsidered. An applicable, but hypothetical example, is the possible effect of a change in the system of land tenure on subsistence agriculture. If the government disbands reservations and decides to grant individual titles to land – a possibility discussed in chapter 4 – the physical as well as the socio-political unity of the community upon which traditional food exchanges and the security of the farmer rests will be threatened; the farmer may then evaluate the cost and revenue of subsistence farming against the cost and revenue of cash crop farming, and may perhaps arrive at different decisions.

How drastically any one aspect of production is likely to change depends on the degree of interdependence of economic activities. There is no society where resources are unlimited and where the pursuit of a want does not imply that other wants must be forgone. But the complexity of the interrelatedness of activities does in fact vary with the type of economic system. In an industrial society the degree of complexity is high and hence a variation of one aspect may, by the multiplication of effects, drastically affect another aspect. On the other hand, amongst the Páez, the interrelation of coffee farming and food farming is limited. I have argued that when activities are related, a small change in one may be met with a slight alteration of others, but that a drastic change will require a re-evaluation of strategies entailing a number of planning decisions.

I have also argued that the greater the complexity of the economic system the higher the chances of small changes multiplying into a large effect. It follows then that in industrial societies where the economic system is highly complex, planning decisions will prevail, while in peasant economies where the individual farmer works more directly for the satisfaction of goals and where one activity does not impinge too much on other activities, a proper balance can be maintained without frequent planning decisions. Hence, in those economies (as, for example, the Tiv or Lele) where market imperfections and uncertainties are resolved by isolating spheres of production and distribution, decisions are more likely to be made in the course of production. Difficulty in formulating expectations also discourages long-range planning.

The relative independence of productive units. In the previous section I have indicated that a decision-maker whose activities are closely interrelated will frequently have to consider all strategies. As a decision-maker he can control how he allocates *his* resources. He does not, however, control the activities or allocation of resources of other decision-makers. If other individual decision-makers are likely to affect his behaviour, his only solution is to readjust his own, so as to achieve the same level of satisfaction that was originally expected. The greater the degree of dependence on others, the greater the chances that his plans or strategies will have to be constantly revised. Persistent readjustment will discourage him from future long-range planning, except in those cases when he uses a strategy as a bare guideline for his activities. Contrariwise, if the decision-maker's activities are independent of others he will not be discouraged from making and implementing long-range plans.

There is, of course, no economic system where all producing units are equally dependent or independent of others, or where every aspect of production is equally linked to others. For example, amongst the Páez the amount of food produced is partly related to the degree of freedom from demands. At the same time, since food production is geared to consumption by the farmer and his family, they need not consider what other similar units produce. A Páez can say how much he thinks he ought to plant because it is what he expects to be able to use to satisfy dietary and social needs. But he cannot say how much he will plant, because that depends on a number of unforeseeable factors. When producing for the market, an industrial plant cannot tell how much it ought to produce, as this is a flexible amount which depends on other suppliers and the number of demanders. Coffee planting is a special case which cannot be subsumed under other goods produced for the market, because the farmers were not competing with one another for buyers and could not in any way affect the volume of production at will. Price fluctuation affected revenue but did not affect planning decisions.

The goal of productive activities. The object of subsistence activities is to satisfy the dietary and social needs of the producer and his family. Though a farmer can estimate how much he ought to plant, this estimate is only an ideal statement of what he will need. If he wishes to maximize the satisfaction of his needs he should not fix the amounts required as they are likely to change in the course of the year. Manuel Santos's wife had a child and they hoped to be able to afford a good feast to ask me to be the godmother; shame would otherwise have prevented them from approaching me with the request. Paulino's wife (family 11) did not estimate correctly the date of birth of her child and money had to be earned quickly to purchase substitutes for traditional foods. The unexpected long illness of Enriques's daughter, and her eventual death, required the attention of a healer who lived with the family for some time; the food that had been grown for household consumption was spent on feeding the healer and subsequently on those who attended the funeral; Enriques had to plant more basic staples when he became aware that he would otherwise run short of food.

Páez farmers thus sometimes act as producers, and at others as consumers. The goals in each case are quite different. For example, as a producer Venancio (family 19) may prefer to plant greater quantities of plantains, but he knows that he should have some sugar cane available to feast his friends and quell his thirst. Antonio was unlucky with his bean crop, but he nevertheless planted some every year in order to change the monotonous flavour of his stews.

The proliferation of goals and sub-goals, some related to production, others related to consumption, complicates the task of the decision-maker. He finds it difficult to integrate activities responding to different goals into one general strategy. His orientation when deciding upon the satisfaction of one goal will be different from the satisfaction of other goals. He will thus be unable to compare different aspects of his productive activities. The prevalence of one goal in the case of the industrial firm, i.e. the maximization of revenue, simplifies the compilation and comparison of information which allows the manager to programme for most of his activities. It follows that amongst the Páez proliferation of goals and sub-goals in subsistence activities inhibits the formulation of annual plans. Coffee production responds to fewer goals, and thus Indians find it easier to plan ahead in that case.

Acquisition of land was not considered in the context of farming. Farmers acknowledged the relation of land and wealth and bitterly complained about their limited resources, blaming either fate or their fathers, but they did not entirely integrate their strategy so as to gain land with their farming strategies. Often the two strategies were disparate. Apolinar (family 8) was in need of more land and felt this need acutely. But his future expectations as a farmer, and hence his present investment plans, did not hinge on the hope of receiving more land from his father. The hope, nevertheless, was very much alive, and defined the tenor of his relationship with his father and his bitterness towards him. While he argued with his father and contributed in his own way to the deterioration of the relationship, he did not keep in mind the economic cost of these quarrels. What he kept in mind was the emotional cost of the loss of his independence and self-esteem; he preferred to maintain the latter at the expense of land.

DECISION POINT AFFECTS THE SELECTION AND EVALUATION OF FACTORS CONSIDERED IN A DECISION

When making a rational decision, even though the rationality of the decision is often subjective, the individual selects from the innumerable opportunities offered by the environment, a set small enough to be able to evaluate and compare without the aid of a computer. The opportunities included in the set are those which are obvious to him, either because they are more immediate to him and his everyday activities or because they are more relevant to his main goal. In some instances the opportunities perceived are neither acceptable nor comparable, nor different enough to allow for preferential ranking. In such a case, the individual will search for other opportunities and delay action. A search does not always lead to the discovery of a more suitable set of opportunities from which selection can be made and hence either aspirations are lowered or the decision is delayed until action requires a commitment on the part of the farmer.

How an individual proceeds to select the factors he is to evaluate can only be answered by psychologists working in this particular field. Real decision situations are difficult to observe and hypotheses derived from observations do not always lend themselves to rigorous testing. There is, however, a large body of literature on the subject of perception, rating, and learning, by experimental psychologists, which should be consulted by those who wish to study the formulation and evaluation of expectations. I was unable to carry out detailed and consistent observations on this aspect of the decision process. My more general observations about decision timing allow me, however, to suggest some of the processes which affect the selection of factors. They are, however, only suggestions, and require testing. But, it is these processes which account for the fact that the outcome of decisions made in the course of action are very different from the outcomes of planned decisions.

Opportunities which demand the use of factors, the availability of which is highly questionable, or which lead to very uncertain outcomes, will be disregarded. By the same token, factors which cannot be estimated when evaluating the cost of an opportunity will not be considered. Indians never evaluated yield versus labour because they knew from experience that it was very difficult to evaluate how much time it would take to clear and plant a new piece of land. If I insisted on an answer, some either ventured a stereotyped answer or described how much time they had spent in clearing a particular field. Sandalio (family 26), one of the most enlightened local farmers, always insisted on explaining the minute difficulties of a task. Only very gross evaluations of labour input were taken into account. A Sandalio would take into consideration the fact that it is more time-consuming to plant and weed beans than manioc, but labour differences were ignored for those crops that required the same number of weedings and the same amount of care. For the same reason, a decision to accept a contract to clear land for a White farmer was not based on labour input and money return. Labour input was an unknown, difficult to estimate accurately even by experienced farmers. Hence, the decision was made on the basis of the need for cash at that particular time. Cruz (family 16) works mostly on contract rather than on a day-wage basis. He has done so for the past eight years and accepts three to four contracts a year which bring him from $40 to $200 each. He still finds it difficult to estimate correctly, and bases his final decision to accept or reject the offer on his need for cash. He considers it a gamble, and prefers this system partly because he can work alone away from the dampness of coffee plantations, and partly because he receives the money in a lump sum which makes it easier for him to budget for large expenditures or investments on animals and equipment.

Factors which impinge directly on the well-being and satisfaction of the producer are considered first. When the number of factors is too large to be evaluated *in toto*, the above-mentioned factors may be the only ones considered. When, for example, an Indian has to decide whether or not to work for a coffee planter, he does not consider what his total annual cash income is likely to be, or how to schedule his labour resources for the remainder of the year. He makes his decision on the basis of his need for cash in the immediate future, and on the basis of the labour required in his own fields at that moment. When deciding for whom to work, the Indian takes into account not only the wage offered but the quality of the food given. He is less likely to work for a considerable number of days at a plantation where he is poorly fed than at a plantation where he is better fed. The reason for this is that in evaluating what day on which to stop work the Indian begins with the most important factors and then afterwards considers the least important. The more important is his immediate need for money, the least important is the quality of the food and the personality of the planter; but while the Indian is in the coffee planter's house, these two last factors become more immediate and relevant. Decisions to stop work for a planter at the end of the third or fourth day are often explained in terms of food and comfort, with the result that Indians are unfairly considered to be irresponsible. Need for cash is considered in the initial stages.

Attention is focused on competing factors at the time of decision. An Indian working for a coffee planter will not only consider his need for cash–the goal satisfied by wage-labour–and his immediate pleasure, but also the competing need for labour on his own plantation. Cash and labour requirements are evaluated against each other and if both are equal and hence choice impossible, then the decision to stop work after a particular number of days is made, as previously suggested, on the basis of quality of food and friendliness of the planter. On the other hand, when deciding how much coffee to plant, Manuel Santos considered not the revenue to be expected in the forthcoming years, as this was too uncertain, but the cash available for a *minga* and the amount of land which would also be required for subsistence. Revenue was only considered when Indians discussed the choice of coffee versus subsistence. They knew from experience that coffee prices fluctuated too much and if subsistence depended on that income it would be too uncertain; it could not compare with the more certain yields from subsistence farming. The competing needs taken into account were, on the one hand, needs for cash and needs for food, and on the other, need for land for coffee growing and need for land for subsistence farming.

Farmers only evaluate comparable alternatives. How comparable these alternatives are depends on whether they satisfy the same or at least closely related goals. This is made more difficult for a peasant farmer as his decision is related not only to his role as a manager or producer, but also to his role as consumer, head of a household, etc. Food production directly satisfies his needs as a consumer; coffee production does so only indirectly. The cash derived from coffee is not intended to buy household staples only, but also to save, to invest in equipment and to buy luxury goods which will bolster up his social status. It is consequently difficult to compare and evaluate the two outcomes. These two sets of activities, or strategies, remain as separate spheres. Cash production is unlikely to substitute or displace food production until the cash income is high enough to make food production superfluous; this is not the case for any of the peasant farmers here considered. Purchase of animals is considered as a relatively safe way of investing savings. The farmer's goal is to safeguard himself against future misfortune. He never evaluates the return of that investment against the return in pig breeding or farming. If the cows do not calve often it does not matter; he is not losing money (in salt and pastureland), he is saving money. On the other hand, if a coffee plantation is not producing he does not invest any labour in it and would probably abandon it. But he cannot compare the value of security with the value of income. Venancio did compare the advisability of saving on cows, sheep, and cash and came to the conclusion that sheep were easily stolen, cash he might be tempted to spend, while cows were safer; if they were ill they would be sold before anyone noticed it, and if they died the meat could always be used for a *minga*.

When an Indian plants food, foremost in his mind is that he will consume what he plants, hence it is more important for him not to maximize quantities but to maximize his, and his family's tastes for particular foods. If he is deciding what to plant at a time when he has been eating nothing but manioc, he will attempt to grow a crop of potatoes or of beans, even if his land is not very suitable for it. He does not trouble to measure yields – which is difficult, given harvesting techniques – because this in itself is not the most important outcome. Evaluation of quantities and tastes are not comparable; when the second is the more relevant the first subsides in the mind of the decision-maker. The amount of beans planted responded to tastes rather than to volume or revenue. Beans are liked to give flavour to a diet, but what gives strength is maize, manioc and plantains. When farmers became aware of the high price of beans, they failed to respond to this incentive, because when planting the crop other considerations occupied their minds. It was only Domingo who took advantage of the opportunity, for reasons already mentioned. All treated the planting or the sale of beans as a gamble, inspired by buyers who offered good prices and who even took the trouble to visit the farmers in search of a sale of a few pounds of beans. Hence, the planting of beans was considered only after the farmer had insured himself by planting sufficient food and by earning enough cash. The satisfaction of his tastes was not comparable to income in cash.

I am unable to determine the empirical validity of Shackle's concept of focus gain and focus loss, or of Egerton's (1960, p. 71) extreme gain or loss. Peasants did not consider the total range of likely outcomes when evaluating them; the ranges were contracted into statements like good and bad prices, but it is not easy to determine whether the good price was a point in the scale or a section of the range. The expected coffee price for the forthcoming year was 'not very good'. This evaluation was based on the fact that in 1959 coffee prices dropped by a considerable amount and though they began to rise in 1960, they had not reached the previous high level. There was little that farmers could do to compensate for market fluctuations, as, once started, it is too expensive to uproot a coffee plantation. The price of items which farmers sold in the market place was clearly stipulated, and though they were aware that this price might be less than they hoped, the decision to spend the morning selling the goods was based on a precise and expected price. On the other hand, though a general answer about yields would be given in fixed amounts, a more precise answer about what they expected was given in terms of ranges. In reference to satisfaction, of course, the question is whether this can ever be answered in terms of points or ranges.

The above observations can be summarized as follows in terms of the three types of decision:

(*a*) Planned decisions will lead to the evaluation of the expected outcome (i.e. yield and price), the desire for the expected outcome against the required factors (i.e. land and labour), and the competing demands made on these two factors of production. Within this framework maximization will be attempted.

(*b*) Decisions in the course of action will lead to the evaluation of consumer needs for the immediate future, against present personal wishes. Factors of production are considered when they are made available or are easily accessible. Careful calculations of yields and costs are not possible because this particular strategy does not allow for the mental recording of amounts planted, the labou required, and the cost of seeds and response to different goals. Maximization is irrelevant, satisfaction and security are the main concern.

(*c*) Decisions shortly before action are either consumer's decisions or gambling decisions. In the first case satisfaction of needs and availability of cash, as well as expected future demands on cash or labour, are evaluated. In the second case Indians evaluate expected cash against required cash investment. In both cases the security of the individual was not at stake. It was the poorer families who had enough land planted with subsistence crops who gambled their small amount of cash on pig breeding or similar enterprises. Their small assets would not have been enough for them to consider a total change in the allocation of resources, and, hoping to make 'considerable' amounts of money, they did not mind risking the chance of losing a little, This is not entirely different from the gambling behaviour recorded by Friedman and Savage. When a new opportunity defines the time of the decision the set of factors evaluated is small for the simple reason that there is little time to investigate. Gambling decisions thus often lead to disastrous results.

11

Conclusion

The existence of an economic system can be postulated, if we assume that producing and consuming units behave rationally and in accordance with certain rules. The most important rule is that they consciously maximize the output of goods which satisfy their needs. Interdependence and maximizing behaviour are the factors that bring the population of producers and consumers into a series of equilibrium relationships. When there is a departure from an equilibrium position, the factors which affect the relationship will either force a return to the same equilibrium point or establish a new equilibrium point. Another very important rule is that when producers or consumers maximize they must behave rationally; they are not merely trying to produce greater quantities of goods, but to allocate assets so as to increase the marginal utility of each commodity produced or purchased. A large number of laws or hypotheses are derived from these very basic principles. Some are used as guidelines which, when followed, should help producers to maximize utility, or help governments to maximize the welfare of the population. Some of these hypotheses are attempts to adjust simple principles to the reality of the very complex and highly imperfect market situations. The concept of rationality is therefore a basic assumption in a closed logical system. It is not an assumption which, strictly speaking, can be said to be testable. Very few firms, individuals, or economists act or give advice which would maximize objective utility; they lack either the tools or the information required for such a task. It is true, however, that firms, particularly when advised by experts, are more likely to attain this goal than peasant farmers, a point cogently argued by Cohen (1967). But what can be said from observation is that for most of the time industrial firms, consumers, peasant farmers, etc., evaluate strategies and consciously maximize satisfaction. On occasion they do not;

hence a number of explanations are designed to account for deviations from the rule. Exceptions to the rule may also be the result of imperfections of the market not taken into account in the rule. All these numerous explanations are often labelled as principles. In other words, economists have created a body of laws derived logically from a set of principles, as well as a body of hypotheses and subsidiary principles which explain deviations and reconcile analytical simplicity with empirical complexity. It is a tautological system, but a very useful tautology. It does not *explain* events but it allows us to derive a set of relationships which more or less accurately describes reality and makes advice possible.

In the first part of this book, and particularly in chapter 8, I have argued that the Páez farmer can be said to behave rationally. I have not proved it and cannot do so; proof would imply that the goals had been made explicit by the farmer; that I had been able to measure factors and outcomes; and that I had been able to evaluate decisions in terms of goals, factors and outcomes. Nevertheless, the assumption can be said to conform sufficiently to reality to be warranted. In the last chapter I argued like an economist trapped in his closed system; given that people behave rationally, then certain deviations have to be explained. In order to explain them, one must take into account the decision points and their timing. Simon (1955), Egerton (1960), and later Halter and Dean (1965), have in summary fashion implied the relevance of the timing of decision points when they studied the behaviour of the firm and of American farmers: some of my suggestions must then also apply to industrial society. Whether the timing of decisions is as important in industrial societies as in easant societies has still to be established. It may well be more important in the latter for the following reasons; the economic population in any one peasant society is relatively small, each farmer is not entirely dependent on the activities of other farmers, and each producer is at the same time a consumer. In either case, a model which helps us define decision-making points will help us account for certain deviations and thus establish a bridge between the world of models and the real world.

Some issues which have dominated the literature of economic anthropology can now be viewed in their proper dynamic context. The concept of spheres is one of them. In the Páez example here discussed, goods are exchanged in such a way that two distinct but overlapping flows can be noticed: coffee and labour are exchanged for cash, and food is usually, but not always, exchanged for labour, services and other types of food. When money enters into the transaction the exchanges are with non-Indians. These money exchanges of coffee and labour are regarded as moral, but with one qualification: that in selling his labour a farmer does not endanger his status as independent farmer or his family's subsistence needs. Food, however, should be exchanged in kind or for services. It should be sold for money only in small quantities or in special circumstances; the Páez consider the exchange of large quantities of food for money as morally wrong. As we can see, no strict moral value is assigned to the transaction itself, but to the host of circumstances which are responsible for the transaction as well as to the consequences of the transaction. If a Páez sells most of his labour potential to buy luxuries, he will not be able to plant enough food for his family, to help his friends, and to fulfil his social obligations. What is condemned is not the sale of food for money, but the strategy of the farmer which includes the sale of food.

The use of the concept of spheres describes the flow of goods and hence the availability of assets to producers, consumers and entrepreneurs, but it does not explain either why certain exchanges are preferred to others, or why they are ranked morally, or why, in spite of being condemned, they do occur. In order to examine the first of these three questions we have first to consider whether preferences are ranked lineally and thus are transitive, or whether an individual is only able to state his preferences conditionally, according to a particular set of options and circumstances. It should be clear from earlier chapters that a Páez farmer can only say that he prefers more food to money after he has purchased sufficient salt and other basic items, but that if he has to choose between starvation and salt, he will prefer to do without salt. His wish to increase his cash income depends on his desire to improve his social status and his expectations of achieving it. In other words, a farmer needs and desires a number of assets and consumer goods; the preference for any particular asset or good depends on a number of factors. He is not able to make a list of items and rank each of them. He will rank preferences at a decision point and assign value only to those goods or assets which concern him at the moment. If he needs or wishes a particular good, he will not consider it morally wrong to acquire it by labour or purchase. Morality does not explain the preference ranking of the Páez, nor of the Tiv. Bohannan (1955) tells us that the Tiv are scornful of a man who is merely rich in subsistence goods, or money, yet if he converts most of them into wives or luxuries they will condemn him for shirking his social and kinship obligations. It is also said that in case of famine a father was known to sell his daughter (who would normally have been exchanged for a wife) to a foreigner in exchange for food.

This leads us to the second and third question: why are certain actions labelled morally right or morally wrong, and why do people not conform to prescribed behaviour? In chapter 9, I have discussed the imperfections of the market, how these constrain the opportunities available to the farmers, and how they increase the uncertainty of any enterprise. I have pointed out that the number of producing units is too small for all of them to benefit equally from exchanges and that the community is too isolated to produce for export. Páez have a limited amount of information and few opportunities to purchase the goods they need; shopping is an expensive and time consuming occupation. Furthermore, the White peasants and traders hold greater power and are in a better position to bargain than Indians (Ortiz 1967). Faced with such difficulties the Páez farmers do exactly what has been postulated by game theorists: they redistribute their assets amongst themselves. Some assets, however, have to be exchanged for cash in order to acquire goods produced in other places. The Páez acknowledge this need by planting a cash crop or by working for wages; when this is impossible or insufficient the farmer is expected to sell food. They also recognize that market constraints relate to food exchanges and that it is best not to produce food for sale, but to exchange it with iends in need. The fact that Indians form a distinct community and that traders are Whites, helps to reinforce and maintain this coalition. Informal social sanctions are used and are phrased as the obligations that individuals have towards the community, in order to ensure the redistribution of food, which is both uncertain and basic. Those individuals who frequently infringe the rule cannot expect to receive support and help on other occasions; in a community where starvation is always near, co-operation is a powerful sanction. An Indian who fulfils his social obligations is judged to be morally outstanding; if he does not he will be questioned. The usefulness of the coalition rests also on the acceptance that deviations must occur; the purpose is to impose constraints on exchanges so as to ensure subsistence and maximize rewards. This is why there is no objection to occasional sales and why they do occur. It is the complete strategy which is evaluated in moral terms; the wealthy farmers who do not need to be helped with food can fulfil their obligation to their community by providing expertise, knowledge, contacts, loans, etc., hence when they do sell food they are not condemned.

By analysing economic behaviour at the moment when decisions are made we can understand the reasons for the existence of spheres of exchange as well as for their overlap. Hence, it is important to determine the timing of decision first, in order to be able to proceed with an explanation of exchange systems. Some of the contradictions in Bohannan's discussion of Tiv economy disappear when the concept of spheres of exchange is not used as an explanation but as a description of the flow of goods.

M. Lipton having studied the economic situation of farmers in India warns us of the consequences of a harvest failure when no provisions are made for it:

'Arguments about optimal policies, based on false analogies with the humane, rich and risk-cushioned agricultures of the West, do not impress the subsistence farmers. A bad year or two, in an optimal policy sequence, will not prevent a Western farmer from retaining land and other assets sufficient to follow through the sequence; they will ruin an Indian farmer. His first duty to his family is to prevent such ruin; with growing population, fewer and fewer have enough land left for subsequent optimizing experiments . . . A well-off American farmer can safely prefer a 50–50 chance of $5,000 or of $10,000 to a certainty of $7,000 per year. An Indian farmer, offered a 50–50 chance of Rs X or Rs1,000 as against a certainty of Rs700 a year with which he barely feeds his family, cannot set X far below 700. *An optimizer maximises utility not profit*' (my italics) (Lipton 1968, pp. 334–5).

The greater the range of expected fluctuations and the more limited the welfare measures which cushion the farmer, the less the utility of outcome. It is thus important to bolster up the welfare measures which insure the peasant and give greater value to the utility of his assets. The separation of exchanges into two spheres, one of coffee and one of food, coupled with the exchange coalition already described, insures the peasant against heavy loss. True, this insurance tactic adds yet another constraint to an already imperfect market, but as M. Lipton warns us, we must recognize that 'imperfect factor markets in very poor countries are not relics of ignorance and conservatism, ready to collapse at the slightest incentive (or executive order). They fulfil a precise function in a tightly knit social structure' (*ibid.*, p. 337).

I hope the reader will interpret the labels of *traditional* and *progressive* which I use in this book not as indicating ignorant, conservative peasants, and an optimizing peasant, respectively, but to refer to differences in wealth of assets (not necessarily money) and hence the type of strategy used by each. Odd practices such as refraining from selling food are a disguised form of insurance, and the poorer (i.e. *traditional* farmer) has greater need for insurance than the wealthier (i.e. *progressive*) farmer. In fact, a peasant farmer who optimizes in each one of his activities is not necessarily a better manager. It is totally unrealistic to expect even a *progressive* farmer to increase his output in every sphere of his enterprise. He also needs to insure himself in relation to his assets. Each of them has a particular set of problems and will design a strategy which adequately resolves them. Ercilla (family 23) uses techniques which improve the yield and reduce the labour of processing coffee. She is conservative in her distribution of food crops and buys animals only as a means of saving. Paulino (family 11) spent a great deal of effort and time in the upkeep of his pasture land, while other activities received less attention; he is hopeful that cattle breeding will be a good solution to his problem. Antonio (family 26) has a capital-intensive sugar cane plantation and is willing to sell food if required of him and if he has any available. Cruz (family 16) a relatively poor Indian, does grow food for sale under contract to a White trader, and as he uses most of his land and labour to plant manioc and plantains, he can still sell to kin and friends.

How ready a peasant is to accept new opportunities and in how many of his activities he will choose to optimize, as well as the extent to which he makes use of well-established measures to reduce uncertainty, depends on the particular combination of his assets, his wealth in assets, and the expectations he holds. Indians with a large number of friends and kin can profitably comply with the stipulated coalition and thus reduce the threat to their subsistence (see chapter 9). Indians with few friends and kin and with a particular combination of assets prefer to expand cash production and thus solve the uncertainty of food crops; Ercilla (family 23) is a case in point. What they do depends on their experience and on their estimate of success.

A decision to invest in any enterprise which the peasant would regard as a gamble can be considered in the light of what has just been said. A gamble is any enterprise about which a peasant knows very little, where he can only estimate outcomes in terms of a particular probable loss and an expected but undefined high gain. Poorer Indians who have a considerable number of kin and friends who can help them in case of need are likely, when confronted with an opportunity, to gamble in the hope of substantially increasing their meagre cash income. Apolinar's (family 8) attempts at pig breeding on a larger scale than usual is an example of this type of gamble; the readiness of his land-poor neighbours to participate in a short-lived fibre extraction enterprise is another example. These Indians are known to be easy prey to the more reckless enterprises initiated by ambitious or ill-advised traders. Other peasant farmers, whose assets, though limited, permit them to invest in coffee, sugar cane, etc., are not tempted by the possible high gain of a gamble. They reserve their assets for safer investments. Those few Indians who have considerable wealth and feel confident about their knowledge and contacts with the outside world, do gamble in large-scale uncertain enterprises. Marco Antonio started some years ago to rear a large number of steers with a view to becoming the main supplier and butcher in the town of Inzá. When I spoke to him he considered the second venture a loss and was ready to give it up. He has enough capital to be able to adjust to adverse conditions and thus minimize his loss. Furthermore, a loss as a butcher represented only a small part of his total income, while the gain in prestige and power, as he had been able to drive one competitor off the market, was considerable. Thus, amongst Páez peasants, gambling is likely to be attractive to traditionally insured poor peasants as well as to wealthy peasants. This is the converse of what Friedman and Savage (1948) have postulated, but the elements in the argument are the same: the wish to maximize utility and lower uncertainty. Instead of making use of complex utility curves, with or without kinks (Ożga 1965, pp. 198–9), the case can be argued by determining when gambling problems are likely to be formulated and decided upon by farmers.

Poor farmers with limited land defer decisions for reasons set out in the last chapter. Instead of evaluating their assets and planning each year, they make decisions as they are confronted with routine tasks and demands. When the planting season is over and they have a little money available, they are likely to gamble it in a risky investment or spend it on consumer goods. Wealthier farmers are more likely to evaluate prospects in the future, hence they make better use of cash assets and invest them in long-range enterprises; the risk they are likely to undertake is related to their cash income. The poorer farmers are more likely to accept ventures unknown to the community and thus serve as guinea pigs for technical innovators. But their failures may be more catastrophic, and the psychological effect of these failures on the rest of the community will discourage others from following their example in the future. It is highly likely that the propensity to gamble in other peasant communities does not follow the same pattern as the Páez peasant; for example, a poor peasant may not gamble while a slightly better off peasant may be quite ready to do so. The argument which I have used to explain gambling tendencies, however, I believe applies to other cases as well.

By first defining the decision points and then determining how individuals rank their preferences, the question as to whether transitivity (i.e. that when an individual states that he prefers A to B and B to C it follows that he will prefer A to C and not the converse) has empirical reality or not may be resolved. Edwards (1967) reviews the testing by experimental psychologists and concludes that no definitive proof of transitivity or intransitivity is at present available. 'If so, the question for experimenters to answer is not whether any form of transitivity holds, but rather under what circumstances do various assumptions about transitivity hold and under what circumstances they do not' (p. 77). It is important that the conditions he refers to should not only take into account the imagination of the experimenter, but that it should also take into account the timing of decisions and the process of decision. A particular situation defines the number of possible outcomes that an individual has to rank; it is not unreasonable to suspect that a new set of outcomes which includes some but not all of the previous outcomes will be ranked differently. An empirically accurate model of rational decisions does not require transitivity of choice, as some are not likely to be compared with others.

Another problem raised in the literature is the comparability of expectations. In the Páez case the goals of the individuals as producers and consumers are so different and often even contradictory, that expectations are not always comparable. This is not a serious dilemma for them as they rarely have to confront such comparisons. Comparability of all expectations is only relevant to those models of choice behaviour which propound structures which are *invariant and perfectly exact*. Empirical situations, as can be seen in this book, are quite different.

In the Introduction, I have outlined Shackle's concept of focus gain and focus loss; because of the many decision models suggested, his concept is applicable to the case under discussion. There are, of course, a number of shortcomings in his postulates, as there are in any attempts to explain or to portray highly complex situations. Some of the criticisms have helped to refine the theory or to suggest limitations to its applicability. It is not my intention to review and evaluate these criticisms (the reader may refer to Ożga 1965; Carter, Meredith and Shackle (eds.) 1957), but to examine those aspects of his theory that can be resolved when decision points are taken into account.

Shackle has attempted to construct a descriptive model of decision, and while realizing that individuals have a limited ability to evaluate and decide, he has assumed that their method of simplification is to evaluate alternatives. This system of pairing options into sets of alternatives is commonly used in logic and to devise electronic calculators. It is a useful technique to organize our thoughts so as to be able to make logical deductions. The fact that it is a valid technique, does not, however, imply that it is the most frequently used technique. Shackle, with no empirical observations available to him, thought it useful to assume that it did describe reality. In my last chapter I pointed out that in some instances I was aware that Indians did not evaluate alternatives but a range of preferences. A similar observation made by Carter is quoted in the Introduction. Egerton (1960, p. 5) also observed a case when an individual made a decision not on the basis of alternatives (focus gain and focus loss), but on the basis of a curve. These few examples do not refute Shackle's hypothesis, but point out that in certain circumstances individuals are capable of sorting and evaluating more than two sets of outcomes or opportunities. Any further empirical research on this point would be extremely enlightening.

Shackle argues that an investor decides upon an action after evaluating the focus gain against the focus loss and that this decision is then evaluated against another set of focus gains and losses. The investor, following this procedure, selects a particular combined strategy. Shackle's quandary is that he can foresee only two analytical solutions to his decision-making model: either we choose between alternatives, or we choose amongst unlimited possibilities. In this book I argue that there is a third solution, because the real world of the individual consists of a finite number of observed opportunities which the decision-maker can evaluate. The environment itself delimits the opportunities which can be evaluated at any one moment. Thus if we introduce time and define a point in time when the decision is taken, we can predict what are the choices which are realistically open to the decision-maker. In some cases it may be that only alternatives are considered, in other cases it may be a small number of opportunities. Certain conditions may bring into focus expectations about outcomes, while other conditions may bring into focus the availability of resources or the needs which must be satisfied. What I suggest in this book is that Shackle's model can be improved if we take into account the definition of the decision point, and the conditions which at that particular moment delimit the opportunities foreseeable to the actor. Shackle's concept of time is different from that which I have stated here; he discusses time only to imply that decisions are sequential and can be changed but only insofar as the expected outcome is not realized. While he is aware that decision points are important, he relates them to expectations.

Decisions are postponed until expectations can be formulated, when the potential surprise of an outcome is determined and the choice is made. The need for action, however, may overtake the decision-maker. In such circumstances he focuses his attention on other elements which are easier to evaluate. This mechanism for coping with uncertainty high enough to permit the formulation of expectations does not hinder the efficiency of the economic system. One of the goals of the peasant economy is to satisfy the needs of the producer-consumer; decisions in the course of action serve to focus on the individual's need and to readjust productive activities so as to achieve that particular goal.

Shackle's main contribution is: that the view of the future as seen by the decision-maker determines his own choices. This view of the future is not formulated at point zero, but takes shape in the course of action.

I suggest in the introduction that a decision-making model can be used if we wish to gain an understanding of the dynamics of a social situation; there is no reason why it should be applied only to the dynamics of the allocation of resources. Every individual acts according to the decisions he makes – a point which Firth (1965) has elaborated – even though he is guided by the rules made explicit in his own society and by sanctions which may not be so explicit. There is no complete consistency of rules and rewards in any one society, nor is there complete congruency between situations assumed by the rules and reality. Thus every individual is forced to decide on the basis of expectations which he formulates; in his choice he is guided by his wish to increase his satisfaction. The concept of time has been introduced in anthropological analysis by way of recognizing that institutions go through a cycle of development and that the needs and goals are different for each stage of the cycle. This concept should be enlarged to take into account that factors inherent in the development cycle define decision points and delimit, as well, the view of the future held by the decision-maker. This second aspect of decision theory has not yet been developed. The study of choice has been approached through the study of conflict situations. The results are rewarding, but we must not forget that though conflict may push an individual to act and thus to decide, it also encourages an individual to create mechanisms to minimize conflict in his environment. Games theory has also been used to predict outcomes by determining how the behaviour of one individual will affect the behaviour of others. Like all approaches it has a number of limitations and it is most useful when individuals are clearly competing with each other and when the numbers of actors and possible coalitions is limited. Theories dealing with decisions and expectations are most helpful when individuals act relatively independently of each other, and when the situation is sufficiently unstructured to allow for choice. It is a useful approach when dealing with economic choice because we can safely assume that individuals not only maximize but also minimize, an assumption that may not be justified in some other aspect of human behaviour. This dual aspect of economic behaviour simplifies the model of choice so that it is easier to examine.

The factors outlined in this book are perhaps not the only ones which define the decision-making points. The analysis of the Páez material has led me to formulate them as elements in the model. The question remains as to what type of model is most useful in this case. One option is to retain the qualitative nature of the elements and thus allow the model to portray a wide range of relationships. Such a model will serve as a general guideline to the analyst and the planner. Another option is to narrow its scope and with a good deal of *ceteris paribus* suggest a number of neat, testable hypotheses. The disadvantage is the stricture of its applicability. The third option is to assign quantities to the elements, thus making it possible to reduce complex relationships to mathematical formulae. It is an appealing solution were it not for the fact that it is very difficult to design a technique to measure levels of uncertainty and subjective expectations.

APPENDIX I

Population Growth of San Andrés Reservation

Population of San Andrés Reservation and the Municipality of Inzá

Year	*San Andrés Reservation* *Inhabitants*	*Families*	*Inzá Municipality* *Inhabitants*
1810	194	50	—
1916	800	—	2,850
1933	•—	142	—
1938	—	—	8,717
1951	1,415	—	10,839 (2,892 Indians)
1954	—	216	—

The estimate for 1810 was calculated by a parish priest and quoted in a church manuscript.

The esti ate for 1933 was submitted by the *cabildo* authorities. The first national census gave the figure quoted for 1938.

Bernal Villa during the course of his field work carried out a careful census of the area in 1954. It is probably the most accurate of all estimates.

Other estimates were taken either from government census or from Otero (1952).

Growth of White Population around San Andrés Reservation

Origin	*Number of families*
Original settlers and descendants	25
Families from Mosoco	6
Other i migrants	6
Total	37

Source of Income of White Population

Source of Income	*Number of families*
Coffee plantations	11
Cattle raising, Cozcuro	2
Potatoes, Mosoco	1
Small farming	12[a]
Full-time traders	5
Lumber industry	1
Various	5[b]
Total	37

[a] Small farming refers to coffee groves combined with subsistence farming.
[b] 'Various' refers to small-scale trading activities, combined with other agricultural enterprises.

Baptismal figures for Inzá Parish

	Number of baptisms per year			*Number of baptisms per year*	
Year	*San Andrés Indians*	*Inzá Municipality*	*Year*	*San Andrés Indians*	*Inzá Municipality*
1920	37	283	1935	—	—
1921	22	311	1936	30	368
1922	32	324	1937	34	306
1923	20	252	1938	29	401
1924	43	292	1939	39	406
1925	26	297			
1926	41	327	1950	24	419
1927	32	352	1951	43	402
1928	56	261	1952	26	433
1929	26	338	1953	46	450
			1954	45	455
1930	24	350	1955	60	473
1931	36	377	1956	30	478
1932	31	340	1957	39	546
1933	35	352	1958	26	491
1934	27	314			

From genealogies compiled from baptismal records and from a house to house census I was able to estimate that 35·7 per cent of all children baptized die before reaching adulthood.

The death rate of the adult male population based on figures for the year of my field work was 3·78 per cent of the total male population. The male population increase per 1,000 inhabitants is 5·43. It is important to keep in mind that 60 per cent of the population are males.

Government estimates of population growth are 17·5 per 1,000 inhabitants for the municipality of Inzá and 8·6 per 1,000 for the municipality of Belalcázar.

APPENDIX II

Prices of Food, Goods and Animals in San Andrés

Item	*Price* $	*Item*	*Price* $
Foods		Coca	2.00 lb.
Beef	1.70 lb.	Plantains	5.00 stem
Pork	2.50 lb.		2.50 stem
Green bacon	2.80 lb.		1.50 stem
Blood	0.25 litre	if sold to Indians	1.50 stem
Fat	1.70 lb.		0.50 stem
Rice	1.20 lb.	Beans	1.20 lb.
Salt	0.30 lb.	Wild beans	0.40 lb.
Salt in block	0.40 lb.	if sold to Indians	0.02 lb.
Eggs	0.25 each	Fresh corn	0.05 each
Sardines	2.50 tin	if sold to Indians	0.20 each
	5.00 tin	Mountain corn	0.30 lb.
Dried fish	2.00 lb.	Oranges	0.02 each
Garlic	1.00 lb.	Cabbages	0.50 each
Noodles	0.40 pkg.	Marrows	0.70 each
Cornflour	0.40 pkg.	Cucumbers	0.07 each
Raw sugar	0.40 lb.	Apples	1.00 lb.
Raw sugar (Sept-		Avocado pears	0.05 each
Dec)	0.60 lb.	Papayas	0.25 each
Potatoes	0.45 lb.		
Corn, dried	0.50 lb.	*Tools*	
		Sugar cane press	100.00
Drinks, alcoholic		Metal press	500.00
Aguardiente	9.00 litre	Cauldron	200.00
Beer	0.70 bottle	Coffee pulper	280.00
Wine	3.50 bottle		200.00
Sugar cane fermented	0.20 litre	Machete	30.00
		Shovel	12.00
Drinks, soft	0.30 bottle	Dibble	10.00
		Wire fencing	140.00 roll
Foods sold by Indians			
Cane, sugar	0.30 cane	*Household goods*	
Arracacha	0.10 root	Hand mill	25.00
Manioc	0.60 plant	Kettle	40.00
if sold to Indians	0.20 plant	Kettle, small	10.00

Item	*Price* $	*Item*	*Price* $
Candles	0.10 each	*Animals*	
Kerosene	0.50 litre	Horse	500.00
Soap	0.25 each		250.00
Needle	0.10 each		200.00
Fish hook	0.10 each		150.00
		Cow	500.00
Clothing		Calf	400.00
Cotton	22.00 length		160.00
(material)	15.00 length	if sold to Indians	60.00
	2.00 yd.	if sold to Indians	50.00
Dressmaking	3.00	Bull	430.00
Chumbe	15.00		300.00
Poncho	60.00	Pig	80.00
	30.00	175 lb.	330.00
Indian blouse	5.00	35 lb.	60.00
Small dress	7.00	35 lb.	50.00
Shirt	8.00	50 lb.	80.00
Hat, felt	15.00	Chicken	12.00
Hat, plastic	10.00		20.00
Black shawl	30.00	Turkey	30.00
Trousers	15.00	Sheep	80.00
Wool	8.00 lb.		50.00

LIST OF WORKS CITED

Books and Articles

ARBOLEDA LLORENTE, J. M., 1948. *El Indio en la Colonia*, Ministerio de Educación Nacional, Bogotá.

AUDLEY, R. L., 1960. 'A stochastic model for individual choice behaviour', *The Psychological Review*, 67: 1–15.

BAUER, P. T. and YAMEY, B. S., 1957. *The Economics of Underdeveloped Countries*, Cambridge.

BERNAL VILLA, S., 1954a. 'Medicina y Magia entre los Paeces', *Revista Colombinia de Antropología*, 2, no. 2: 219–67.

——, 1954b. 'Economía de los Páez', *Revista Colombiana de Antropología*, 3: 291–367.

——, 1955. 'Bases para el Estudio de la Organización Social de los Páez', *Revista Colombiana de Antropología*, 4: 165–88.

BOHANNAN, P., 1955. 'Some principles of exchange and investment among the Tiv', *American Anthropologist*, 57: 60–9.

BOHANNAN, P. and DALTON, G. (eds.), 1962. *Markets in Africa*, Evanston Ill. Northwestern University Press.

CABRERA Y MORENO, G., 1942. 'Los Resguardos Indígenas en Colombia', *America Indigena*, 2, no 4: 29–33.

CALDERON RIVERAS, M., 1960. 'La Falacia del Café', *Revista de la Universidad de Caldas*, no. 6: 45–46.

CARTER, C. F., 1957. 'A revised theory of expectations', in *Uncertainty and Business Decisions* (C. F. Carter, G. P. Meredith and G. L. S. Shackle, eds.): 50–60, Liverpool.

CASTILLO I OROZCO, E. DEL, 1877. *Vocabulario Páez—Castellano*, Paris.

COHEN, P. S., 1967. 'Economic analysis and economic man: some comments on a controversy', in *Themes in Economic Anthropology* (R. Firth ed.) Tavistock.

CUERVO Y MARQUEZ, C., 1920. *Estudios Arqueológicos y Etnográficos, Prehistoria y Viajes Americanos*, ii: Editorial America, Madrid.

DEAN, E. F., 1965. *The Supply Responses of African Farmers*, Amsterdam, North Holland Publishing Co.

EDWARDS, D., 1961. *An Economic Study of Small Farming in Jamaica*, Glasgow, The University Press.

EDWARDS, W. and TVERSKY, A. 1967. *Decision Making*, London, Penguin.

EGERTON, R. A. D., 1960. *Investment Decision under Uncertainty*, Liverpool.

FALS BORDA, O., 1955. *Peasant Society in the Colombian Andes*, University of Florida Press.

——, 1957a. 'Indian Congregation of New Kingdom of Granada', *The Americas*, 13, no. 4: 131–53.

FALS BORDA O., 1957b. *El Hombre y la Tierra en Boyacá, Bases Socio-Históricas para una Reforma Agraria*, Ediciones Documentos Colombianos, Bogotá.

FIRTH, R. W., 1954. 'Social organization and social change', *Journal of the Royal Anthropological Institute*, **84**: 1–21.

——, 1959. *Social Change in Tikopia*, London.

——, 1965. *Primitive Polynesian Economy*, London.

FIRTH, R. W. and YAMEY, B. S., 1967. *Capital, Savings and Credit in Peasant Societies*, London.

FOSTER, G., 1942. *A Primitive Mexican Economy*, Monographs of the American Ethnological Society, no. 5, New York.

FRIEDMAN, M. and SAVAGE, L. J., 1948. 'The utility analysis of choice involving risk', *The Journal of Political Economy*, **56**: 279–304.

HALTER, A. N. and DEAN, G. W., 1965. 'Use of simulation in evaluating management policies under uncertainty; application to a large scale ranch', *Journal of Farm Economics*, **47**: 557–573.

HERNANDEZ DE ALBA, G., 1946. 'The Highland Tribes of Southern Colombia', *Handbook of South American Indians*, **2**, Bureau of American Ethnology, Bulletin 143: 915–60, Smithsonian Institution, Washington, D.C.

HOGBIN, I. H., 1941. *Experiments in Civilization*, London.

JARAMILLO, A., 1955. 'Costo Agrícola en el Norte de Caldas', *Economía Colombiana, año* 1, **4**, no. 10: 99–103.

JOY, L., 1967. 'One economist's view of the relationship between economics and anthropology', in *Themes in Economic Anthropology* (R. W. Firth, ed.), London.

KATONA, G., 1963. *Psychological Analysis of Economic Behaviour*, London.

KUBLER, G., 1946. 'The Quechua in the Colonial World', *Handbook of South American Indians*, **2**, Bureau of American Ethnology, Bulletin 143: 364–75, Smithsonian Institution, Washington, D.C.

LEACH, E. R., 1961. *Pul Eliya, A Village in Ceylon*, Cambridge.

LIPTON, M., 1968. 'The theory of the optimizing peasants', *Journal of Development Studies*, **4**, no. 3.

MASON, A. J., 1946. 'The languages of South American Indians', *Handbook of South American Indians*, **6**, Bureau of American Ethnology, Bulletin 143: 157–318, Smithsonian Institution, Washington, D.C.

MOSTELLER, F. and NOGEE, R., 1967. 'An experimental measurement of utility', in *Decision Making* (W. Edwards and A. Tversky, eds.), Penguin.

NACHTIGAL, H., 1955. *Tierradentro: Archäologie und Ethno raphie einer Kolumbianischen Landschaft*, Switzerland.

NASH, M., 1966. *Primitive and Peasant Economic Systems*, San Francisco.

O'CONNOR, D. J., 1957. 'Uncertainty as a philosophical problem', in *Uncertainty and Business Decisions* (C. F. Carter, G. P. Meredith and G. L. S. Shackle, eds.), Liverpool.

ORTIZ, S. R., 1967. 'Colombian rural market organization: an exploratory model', *Man*, **2**: 393–415.

OTERO, J. M., 1952. *Etnología Caucana*, Editorial Universidad del Cauca, Popayán.

OŻGA, S. A., 1965. *Expectations in Economic Theory*, London.

PECK, M. J., 1958. 'Marginal analysis and the explanation of business behaviour under uncertainty', in *Expectation, Uncertainty and Business Behaviour* (M. J. Bowman, ed.), New York.

PEREZ DE BARRADA, J., 1937. *Arqueología y Antropología Precolombinas de Tierradentro*, Ministerio de Educación Nacional, Publicaciones de la Sección de Arqueología, 1, Bogotá.

PITTIERS DE FABREGA, H., 1907. 'Ethnographic and linguistic notes on the Páez Indians of Tierradentro, Cauca, Colombia', *Memoirs of the American Anthropoligical Association*, i, Part 5, Lancaster.

REICHEL-DOLMATOFF, G. and A., 1961. *The People of Aritama*, London.

SALISBURY, R. F., 1962. *From Stone to Steel*, Melbourne.

SAYRES, W., 1957. 'Indians and non-Indians in rural Colombia', *International Institute of Differing Civilizations, Compte Rendu de la XXXme Session tenue à Lisbonne*: 457–65, Brussels.

SHACKLE, G. L. S., 1955. *Uncertainty in Economics*, Cambridge.

——, 1961. *Decision Order and Time*, Cambridge.

——, 1965. *A Scheme of Economic Theory*, Cambridge.

——, 1966. *The Nature of Economic Thought*, Cambridge.

SHEPARD, R., 1967. 'On subjectively optimum selection among multi-attribute alternatives', in *Decision Making* (W. Edward and A. Tversky, eds.), Penguin.

SIMON, H. A., 1955. 'Rational choice and the structure of the environment', *The Psychological Review*, 63: 129–38.

——, 1958. 'The role of expectation in an adaptive or behaviouristic model', in *Expectations, Uncertainty and Business Behaviour* (M. J. Bowman, ed.), New York.

——, 1967a. *Administrative Behaviour*, New York.

——, 1967b. 'Theories of decision-making in economics and behavioural science', American Economic Association and Royal Economic Society, *Surveys of Economic Theory*, 3: London.

SMELSER, N. J., 1963. *The Sociology of Economic Life*, Englewood Cliffs, Prentice Hall.

TAX, SOL, 1942. 'Ethnic relations in Guatemala', *Acta Americana*, ii, no. 4: 45.

——, 1953. *Penny Capitalism, a Guatemalan Indian Economy*, Institute of Social Anthropology, Publication no. 16, Smithsonian Institution, Washington, D.C.

URICOECHICA, E., 1877. Introduction to E. del Castillo i Orozco, *Vocabulario Páez-Castellano*, Paris.

VON NEUMANN, J. and MORGENSTERN, O., 1967. *Theory of Games and Economic Behaviour*, Princeton.

WOLF, E., 1955. 'Types of Latin American peasantry: a preliminary discussion', *American Anthropologist*, 57: 452–71.

——, 1956a. 'San José: Subcultures of a "Traditional" Coffee Municipality', in *People of Puerto Rico* (J. Steward, ed.), University of Illionois Press.

——, 1956b. 'Aspects of group relations in a more complex society: Mexico', *American Anthropologist*, 58: 1065–78.

——, 1962. 'New Lords of the Land', ch. 9, in *Sons of the Shaking Earth*, Chicago.

——, 1966. *Peasants*, New Jersey.

WOLF, E. and MINTZ, S., 1957. 'Hacienda and Plantation in Middle America and the Antilles', *Social and Economic Studies*, 6, no. 3: 380–412, Institute of Social and Economic Research, University College of the West Indies.

Manuscripts and Official Publications

ARCHIVES OF THE UNIVERSITY OF POPAYÁN, POPAYÁN

Document Sig 2892 (Col c, 1–17t).

Document Sig 2910 (Col c, 1–17t). List of tribute paying Indians of San Andrés, addressed to the Crown Officers, Popayán, 1719.

Document Sig 3825 (Col c, 1–17t). Identical document for 1740.

Document Sig 2970 (Col c, 1–17t). Report on tribute collection addressed to Crown Judicial Officers in Popayán, 1720.

Document Sig 4296 (Col C, 1–17t). Report on Indians of Province of Popayán, 1751.

Document Sig 3491 (Col C, 1–17t). List of Indians of Páez province, addressed to Crown Officers in Popayán, 1733.

COMISIÓN NACIONAL DE REHABILITACIÓN Y SERVICIO NACIONAL DE ASISTENCIA SOCIAL, Unpublished study of Tierradentro, 1959.

DEPARTAMENTO ADMINISTRATIVO NACIONAL DE ESTADÍSTICA

Censo de Población de 1938: *Cauca*. Contraloría General de la República—Sección Censos Nacionales, Imprenta Nacional, Bogotá, 1941.

Censo de Población de 1951: Cauca, Bogotá, 1954.

Anuario General de Estadística, Bogotá, 1959.

Boletín Mensual de Estadística, año IX, no. 117, Bogotá, 1960.

DEPARTAMENTO DE INVESTIGACIONES ECONÓMICAS, Caja de Crédito Ağrario 'Banano y Plátano', *Carta Agraria*, no. 25, 1959.

DIVISIÓN TÉCNICA DE SEGURIDAD, CAMPESINA, *Cauca*, Ministerio de Trabajo, Bogotá, 1957.

INVESTIGACIONES AGRÍCOLAS EN COLOMBIA, *Agricultura Tropical*, vol. XV, no. 11: 799–806, 1959.

GONZALEZ, Padre D., 1923. *Informe que el Secretario de Gobierno Rinde al Señor Gobernador* (unpublished), Archivo Departamental del Cauca, Popayán.

SECRETARÍA DE GOBIERNO, DEPARTAMENTO DEL CAUCA 'INDÍGENAS', Chapter XVIII, in *Informe que el Secretario de Gobierno Rinde al Señor Gobernador*, MS, Archivo Departamental del Cauca, Popayán, 1916.

UNITED NATIONS, FOOD AND AGRICULTURAL ORGANIZATION, 1958. *Coffee in Latin America*, Part I, Colombia and El Salvador.

INDEX

For Product Safety Concerns and Information please contact our EU
representative GPSR@taylorandfrancis.com
Taylor & Francis Verlag GmbH, Kaufingerstraße 24, 80331 München, Germany

www.ingramcontent.com/pod-product-compliance
Ingram Content Group UK Ltd.
Pitfield, Milton Keynes, MK11 3LW, UK
UKHW022111190926
475702UK00013B/1376
* 9 7 8 0 3 6 7 7 1 7 2 1 6 *